AUCTIONS

AUCTIONS

The Social Construction of Value

Charles W. Smith

University of California Press
Berkeley · Los Angeles

University of California Press
Berkeley and Los Angeles, California

First Paperback Printing 1990

This edition is reprinted by arrangement with The Free Press
A Division of Macmillan, Inc.

Library of Congress Cataloging-in-Publication Data

Smith, Charles W., 1938–
　　Auctions: the social construction of value / Charles W. Smith.
　　　p.　cm.
　　Reprint. Originally published: New York: Free Press, © 1989.
　　Includes bibliographical references and index.
　　ISBN 0-520-07201-4
　　1. Auctions—Social aspects.　2. Value—Social aspects.
　3. Auctions—Social aspects—United States.　I. Title.
　HF5476.S56　1990
　306.3—dc20　　　　　　　　　　　　　　　　90-10989
　　　　　　　　　　　　　　　　　　　　　　　　　CIP

Printed in the United States of America

09　08　07　06　05　04　03　02

10　9　8　7　6　5　4　3

The paper used in this publication is both acid-free and totally
chlorine-free (TCF). It meets the minimum requirements of
ANSI/ NISO Z39.48-1992 (R 1997) (*Permanence of Paper*). ♾

*For Abigail and Jonathan,
both precious and priceless*

Contents

Preface

THIS book is about auctions—all sorts of auctions—from the glamorous multimillion-dollar art and antique auctions of Sotheby's and Christie's and the equally glamorous and expensive thoroughbred horse auctions of Lexington and Saratoga to the rather sleazy abandoned automobile and country junk auctions. It is also about the wide range of other specialty auctions that proliferate, in which nearly everything including tobacco, fish, stocks, bonds, real estate, subsidiary literary rights, manuscripts, prints, Oriental rugs, eggs, guns, furniture, and memorabilia of all sorts are auctioned. It's about charity auctions and sealed-bid and other contract auctions.

It is also a book about people and social behavior—not the highly rational individuals interested only in maximizing their own self-interests featured in the auction models of much economic writing, but complex social actors, with combined economic, political, social, moral, and ideological interests, who participate in real auctions. It is a story about how people in their daily lives give meaning to their world by assigning specific values to specific items; it similarly shows how these people manage to allocate these items among themselves in a manner that is generally acceptable to all. It is, in short, an account of how auctions serve as social processes for establishing socially acceptable definitions of value and ownership. Greed and self-interest are clearly not strangers to most auctions, but they generally play a secondary part.

Looking back, it is difficult to determine when the idea for this study first emerged. I have had a love affair with auctions for close to twenty years. I realized only recently, however, that auctions were much more than an entertaining diversion or a peculiar form of economic exchange. The more I researched auctions, the more aware I became that they presented a formidable challenge to conventional economic theory and its associated individual-oriented methodology, which attributes reasons and preferences to specific persons without recognizing that such reasons and preferences are generated through social interactions.

The basic argument of this book is that auctions flourish in situations in which the conventional ways of establishing price and ownership are inadequate either because costs cannot be established, the item is old or used, there is something special or unusual about the item, ownership is in question, different persons assert special claims, or for some other reason. When this occurs, auctions are seen as a socially acceptable—and hence legitimate—means for establishing the value and allocation of objects. Put slightly differently, auctions serve as rites of passage for objects shrouded in ambiguity and uncertainty.

Although all auctions entail uncertainty of some sort, the source of such uncertainty varies from auction to auction. In some cases the primary cause is the aged or used state of the thing; in others, the idiosyncratic character of the item. These differences lead to differences in the particular forms auctions take—such as whether bids go up or go down, if there are minimum bids, if collaboration among buyers is permitted, if items can be removed from a sale, if goods can be returned, or if the highest bidder always wins. The possible combinations are such that each auction is in some way unique. Nevertheless, most auctions can be classified into three basic types: commodity-exchange auctions, collectible-dealer auctions, and one-of-a-kind-sale auctions. Each type entails its own communal structures, rules, and practices, which determine everything from who can participate and the form of bidding to relationships among and between buyers and sellers and the role of the auctioneer. Despite these diverse forms and practices, all auctions serve to establish socially legitimated definitions of value and provenance.

The recent growth of auctions is due in large measure to a loss of faith in many of the traditional ways of determining value. In many economic domains from publishing to real estate, once dominated by old-boy networks, an influx of new players has undermined the taken-for-granted ways of doing business. The old principles and parameters for determining both price and allocation, as well as the sense of ingroup trust—which supported private negotiations—have proved incapable of satisfying the doubts generated by more heterogeneous populations. Rather than reflecting the emergence and dominance of an impersonal marketplace, however, in each of these cases the growth of auctions reflects the continuing need for shared symbolic universes if socio-economic practices are to be possible.

Auctions are not unique in being social processes. This book—like most books—is also a social product. The people who have contributed to it are, in fact, too numerous even to name; some, moreover, were promised anonymity, though I doubt that any would feel that it was necessary. To these hundreds of persons who gave of their time and knowledge, my enduring gratitude. I feel compelled, however, to thank by name a number of people, not so much for the information and insights they provided (though they provided a good deal of both) but for being there when I needed them to open doors and point me in the right direction: Ann, Tom, and Carson Asbury, Holly Bandoroff, Gerry Fratollilo, Scott Johnson, Toinette Lippe, Delos ("Los") Luther, David Redden, Walt Robertson, Monty Roberts, Barry Weisbord, Jim Williams, and Douglas Wright.

Others deserve thanks for reading and rereading drafts, discussing ideas, and providing the intellectual and emotional support without which few books are written: Andy Beveridge, David Elkin, Tony Giddens, Joanne Miller, Dean Savage, Alan Wolfe, and, most especially, Peter Manicas, who gave more than one has the right to expect. I owe special thanks to Roz Siegel and Joyce Seltzer of The Free Press for their editorial assistance. Joyce committed herself to this project on little more than an outline, and maintained her support throughout while simultaneously demanding more from me than I often thought I could produce. For providing financial support, I am indebted to the Research Foundation of the City University of New York and the PSC-CUNY Faculty Research Grants. I am also grateful to Queens College, CUNY, for its continuing institutional support and to Wesleyan University, where I was a visiting scholar during the 1987–88 academic year.

In the end, of course, the final responsibility for any work rests with the author. The one person who could possibly be included in the final reckoning would be the author's mate if, as is often the case, he or she was forced to live with the project as intimately as the author. It is not so much the constant exposure to the ideas and questions entailed in the project as it is the emotional highs and lows of the process. My wife, Rita, was part of this process for more than seven years, not only being dragged to this auction and that or left behind while I flew off to Lexington or Newmarket, but being forced to listen and enthusiastically respond to innumerable "insights" and "flashes" and suffer along with the "dead ends" and "unresolved paradoxes." For this, among many other things, I am most indebted. In dedicating this book to our two children, I am also indirectly dedicating it to her.

Whatever else auctions are, they are normally good fun. I hope that in addition to learning how auctions work, the reader enjoys participating in their fun and infinite variety.

AUCTIONS

Chapter 1

Auctions Everywhere

A year-old colt sired by Danzig;

a rare seventeenth-century manuscript;

an abandoned 1978 Cadillac sedan;

ten tons of freshly caught haddock;

a Florida condominium;

a prize Wisconsin dairy cow;

a billion dollars' worth of government bonds;

the paperback publishing rights to a new novel;

a fairly worn antique Caucasian scatter rug;

one hundred shares of IBM stock;

ten thousand bales of tobacco;

a portrait by Rembrandt;

two hundred slightly damaged digital watches; and

a pair of Imelda Marcos's shoes.

A striking potpourri of objects that have nothing in common except that they are likely to be exchanged at auction. In fact, while auction is not the conventional form of exchange for all objects, nearly anything that can be bought and sold has, at one

1

time or another, been auctioned. We are, in short, surrounded by auctions of varying types and forms. Moreover, their numbers are increasing. Although auctions have been used at least since ancient Rome for the forced sale of goods and real estate, they have recently become the preferred method of many for pricing and exchanging such goods.[1] In 1987, Allsop & Company of London sold approximately $1 billion worth of commercial and residential real estate in three different two-day sales, while in the United States, auction sales of real estate have risen to more than $2 billion annually from less than $500,000 three years ago.[2] In nearly all of these cases, the auction format was freely selected by the seller.

Similarly, while thoroughbred yearlings (both colts and fillies) and broodmares have been sold through auctions for years, now stallion shares (part ownership) and seasons (breeding rights), traditionally sold privately, are being auctioned. (Top stallions are commonly syndicated among a number of buyers, normally forty or so. Each part owner has a share of the animal. Each share entitles the owner to a single "season," that is, breeding opportunity, with the stallion. Extra seasons often belong to the syndicate, depending on the number of mares the stallion is able to "cover" in a given year—actually, a five-month breeding season. Shares in a stallion can be and are often sold individually, as are seasons. I may own a share in a stallion, for example, but elect to sell this year's season. I may also be entitled to a bonus season, which I may elect to sell.) So, too, authors—who used to mail their manuscripts off to publishers praying to obtain a positive response—today hire agents who attempt to auction the manuscript to any of a dozen different publishers. And publishers themselves are resorting more and more to auctions to sell the subsidiary rights of books that they have signed.

The growth of art and antique auctions is reflected in the increased sales figures of Sotheby's, Christie's, Doyle's, Skinner's, and nearly every other leading antique-art auction house. Every year these firms acquire more retail buyers and collectors. Government agencies, too, rely increasingly on auctions to select contractors and assign franchises. Perhaps nowhere, however, has the growth of auction markets been more dramatic than in the various national and international bond and stock markets, from New York to Hong Kong. Today more than a hundred million shares of stocks are likely to be auctioned on the New York Stock Exchange on an average day—a dramatic increase from the ten million shares of a decade ago.[3]

Although these various auctions comprise a multibillion-dollar part of our economy, their impact is even greater than such figures would indicate because of the ripple effect that auctions have on nonauction markets. The recent auction of Van Gogh's *Irises* for over $50 million, for example, not only set the price for the *Irises* but also affected the price of all Van Gogh's paintings and all Postimpressionist paintings in general.[4] The price people pay in the Northeast for a pound of fresh fish on a given afternoon is determined by the price set at the New England Fish Exchange auction that morning. The interest paid by money market funds is largely determined by rates set in various U.S. Treasury bill and note auctions. Similar relationships affect the prices we pay for, among other things, gasoline, beef, cereal, wool clothing, and jewelry. In this indirect way, auctions affect the lives of all of us, including those who have never been to an auction.

Despite the enormous significance of auctions, we normally don't think of them as consequential. Most people, if they think about them at all, tend to see auctions as an old-fashioned form of economic behavior, peripheral to modern society. Some look on auctions as quaint if not exotic. Insofar as auctions are utilized in modern business, most people assume that they are meant to fulfill some strictly economic function. The fact that auctions are so prevalent and expanding their sphere of activity would seem to indicate that their role in modern society is much more complex.

Auctions are critical in modern societies because they are uniquely suited to solving the specific social problems that flourish in such societies. More precisely, auctions are social processes capable of defining and resolving inherently ambiguous situations, especially questions of value and price. They are equally capable of resolving questions of ownership, the allocation of goods, and proper classification, which may be only tangentially related to price; people may be uncertain as to whom an object belongs or ought to belong or how an item or items are to be categorized or graded. These uncertainties are often augmented by doubts and questions regarding who should be allowed to participate in resolving them and the means by which this should be done.

The claim that auctions are inherently social processes for resolving definitional ambiguities does not deny that auctions have an important economic component. It only asserts that this economic component must be placed within a broader social setting that includes, among other things, noneconomic interests of participants, social relationships among participants, social traditions, and norms.

While these factors serve primarily to augment the economic view of auctions, they also serve to question certain economic assumptions. It would appear, for example, that auctions are not exclusively or even primarily processes for matching the individual preferences of rational buyers and sellers, as assumed in most economic models; they are rather processes in which buyers and sellers—often acting as members of some group and with the interests of such a group in mind—attempt collectively to resolve questions of price and allocation in a way that will be acceptable to all parties. In most real auctions—in contrast to auction models—participants seldom have established preferences; they don't enter auctions knowing the specific prices they are willing to pay.[5] What broad expectations each person has regarding price tend to be shared with the other auction participants and grounded in collective opinions and views, which are themselves subject to modification by what occurs in the auction.

The uncertainties and ambiguities characteristic of auctions are due to more than disagreement among buyers and sellers as to the value of particular items. The problem isn't that the participants can't agree; it is that they individually and collectively literally don't know the precise value of certain things. Unlike the economic and psychological perspectives that view auctions as "revealing" market forces and constraints, the sociological perspective set forth here recognizes auctions as a means for generating these same forces and constraints. It argues that these meanings are inherently social in origin and character. Individuals appropriate them from the ongoing activities—the bidding, banter, and sales—of the auction itself. Where economists tend to see collective beliefs as nothing more than the sum of individual thoughts, most sociologists see them as outcomes of social processes that have their own dynamics and form. In the case of auctions, this social process explicitly entails the reproduction of new collective definitions of value.[6]

The abandonment of traditional guidelines for determining price and allocation, which results in auctions, is largely the result of shifts in the composition and mix of populations typical of modern society, which, in turn, tends to create new buyer-seller relationships. Buyers and sellers who have dealt with each other for years have a shared history that serves to establish not only a relatively high degree of mutual trust but also a common view on what things are worth. In contrast, strangers are much less likely to take each other's word as to what something costs, how much time and labor was expended, what it sold for last year, or other factors that affect the determination of value.

Other factors, including both the kinds of objects being auctioned and the types of auction participants, can also serve to accentuate such uncertainty. In the case of both objects and participants, the particular type of uncertainty generated will depend on the particular type of objects and participants. This diversity of objects and participants leads to a range of different practices suited to resolve the particular types of uncertainty present, and it explains why different auctions are governed by different types of rules and practices. It is specifically because auctions are social processes and as such must deal with a diversity of social relations, beliefs, and behaviors that they vary as much as they do. One need only observe several types of auctions to appreciate their variety.

As dawn breaks, thirty to forty men between twenty and sixty years old crowd into a room that measures approximately thirty by forty feet, inside a large warehouse-type building standing at the end of a long commercial wharf. In the front of the room there is a giant blackboard on which are listed six names with a nautical ring—*Nautilus, Captain Jack, Lightning Bay, Sandy Cove, Mermaid,* and *Sea Queen*—in a column running down the right side, followed by ten columns of numbers under headings reading Haddock, Scrod, Hake, Sm. Greys, Redfish, and other species. The *Nautilus, Captain Jack, Lightning Bay,* and other designations are the names of the fishing boats that have brought in their catches for this morning's auction. The species of fish listed are the categories by which the catches are auctioned.

There are approximately a dozen phones spread around the back and side walls of the room, and perhaps ten old desks scattered here and there. Some of the phones are in locked cages. There is a long counter in the front of the room behind which are three or four stools. Off to the side of the large room is a small one with more desks and additional phones. The men, mainly dressed in work clothes and rubber boots, walk in and out talking and joking with one another. About half are smoking, and some are drinking coffee from paper cups recently purchased from the coffee stand outside the main room or taken from the coffee pot in one of the side rooms. Numbers are written on the walls, papers are scattered about, and signs are posted here and there, giving the room an overall appearance of disarray.

At a little after six A.M., four men move behind the counter accompanied by a young woman with an alarm clock. In a conversational tone, one of the men states the name of one of the boats listed on the board followed by its catch weight of the first type of fish. "The *Nautilus*. Ten thousand pounds of haddock. All or part? The *Nautilus*. Ten thousand pounds."

This is followed by a similar announcement by one of the other men behind the counter giving the name of another ship and its catch weight for that type of fish. "*Captain Jack*. Five thousand pounds. Anyone? Five thousand on the *Captain Jack*?" Soon all of the ships have been named, with their catch sizes of haddock.

Concurrently, different men around the room have indicated an interest in the catch or part of the catch of haddock from each boat. In short, all of the particular species of fish presently being auctioned has been tentatively spoken for and allotted. No price, however, has yet been mentioned, and not everyone in the room has taken a position. Only after this preliminary allocation has been completed does one of the men behind the counter state a price per hundredweight for the catch of the species being sold from a particular ship. "One twenty for three thousand pounds of haddock on the *Lightning Bay*." This initial price tends to be a low price as compared with other recent sales. Since the price is low, another buyer—that is, someone different from the person to whom the lot was initially assigned—is likely to jump in with a higher bid for that particular allotment. Now different bidders join in upping the price for particular allotments, with bidders who have lost one allotment joining the bidding on others.

In actuality there is less switching about than might be expected, since with each increase the price on all allotments goes up, and those presently holding an allotment can maintain it merely by agreeing to accept the increase. If they agree to the increase they can keep their allotment even if someone else offers the same amount. If they hesitate or indicate they are no longer interested, their allotment will be given to someone else. Two minutes into this process, the young woman behind the counter—

who up to now has said nothing—yells out, "Three minutes!" This is followed by approximately another minute of further bidding, at which time all the catches of the particular species being auctioned are allocated to different bidders, normally at the same price.[7]

The same process is followed for each species of fish, with five minutes allotted to each type.[8] Throughout the process, the men banter with each other, first picking on one and then another among them, though there tend to be two or three preferred targets. To an outsider, many of the comments seem very hostile. At times, physical confrontations seem about to erupt. For the most part, however, it is all done good-naturedly. By seven o'clock another morning's bidding at the New England Fish Exchange is over. It is time to unload the fish and get it to market. It is also time for fish wholesalers up and down the coast to call in and find out what the wholesale prices are for the day. The members of the New England Fish Exchange have managed to check the strong competitive attitudes sufficiently to establish a consensus on price for the day, not only for each other but for fishmongers hundreds of miles away.

At about the same time that the trucks begin to pull away from the pier, another auction is taking place two hundred miles away in Manhattan. The setting here, however, is a twenty by-twenty-foot cubicle in a large office building, and the only person in the room is the subsidiary rights manager of a major trade publisher. She is about to begin an auction for the paperback rights to a book that her house is planning to publish in the next week.[9] The bidders in this case are themselves spread around the city in their own offices. From the time the manager enters her office until 11:00 A.M.—the deadline set for receiving initial bids—six bids come in from six publishing houses.

Examining the bids, the manager-auctioneer calls back the lowest bidder and informs her—it could be a "him," but women significantly outnumber men in these auctions—of the highest bid entered. The bidder then has three options: to enter a higher bid than the present high bid, to drop out of the auction, or to pass for the time being with the option of dropping out or making a higher bid later. The rights manager follows this same procedure with the other bidders, moving up from the present low bidder. This may continue for a number of rounds, until there is only one bidder left or until there are only a few who have asked for more time to consider their bids. A specific hour, normally 4:00 or 5:00 P.M., is set as the moment for entering final bids and ending the auction.

Usually the highest bid wins, but in these auctions this is not necessarily the case. The subsidiary rights manager may retain the right to take a lower bid if other factors—such as royalty rates, author's preference, or publisher's imprint—are seen as making a lower bid preferable. There may also have been a "floor" bid, which allows the publisher who established the "floor" the right to top the final bid by 10 percent and thereby obtain the paperback rights.[10] Here again we see how an auction format is used to establish a price within a community of individuals in competition with one another. In this case, the item auctioned goes to only one bidder; all participants, however, had a say in determining that price.

AT approximately the same time the publishers were calling in their first bids, another auction was getting under way in Lexington, Kentucky. In a large auditorium capable of seating nearly a thousand people, close to three hundred casually but expensively dressed individuals have found their way to their reserved seats. In the surrounding halls and lobbies, another five hundred or more similarly dressed men and women mingle and socialize. Behind the auditorium, which is called the sales pavilion, over acres of immaculately groomed grounds and in front of hundreds of freshly painted stalls, hundreds of other men and women can be found inspecting horses. Wherever they may be, nearly all carry the same paperback book with similar pens dangling from their necks.

The scene described is the Keeneland Breeding Stock Sale in November, but it could just as well be any select thoroughbred horse sale held by Keeneland or Fasig-Tipton—the two major thoroughbred auction sales organizations in North America—in Lexington or Saratoga in July, September, November, or January. In a given year there are likely to be over a hundred major thoroughbred auctions around the world, many running for a number of days. Of these approximately twenty are classified as select auctions because of the high quality of the animals sold. In the United States the most famous select auctions are sponsored by Keeneland, which is located in Lexington, Kentucky, and Fasig-Tipton, which has numerous locations but holds its select auctions in Lexington and Saratoga, New York. Other major American auctions are held in California and Florida. In Europe, the major sales are held by Goffs in France and Ireland and Tattersalls in England and Ireland. Nearly all auctions are classified as either yearling, breeding stock, two-year-old, or mixed sales.

At the beginning of a major American sale, approximately a dozen similarly dressed (blue, green, or other solid-color sport jacket, matched striped tie, and gray pants) men ranging in age from early twenties to late sixties will enter the auditorium. (At the evening sales at Saratoga, held by Fasig-Tipton, and the Match-maker Sales,[11] which are also held in the evening, they will be formally dressed.) There, an announcer and two auctioneers will take side-by-side positions on a large raised podium in the pit of the auditorium, which is surrounded by a half-oval, wood-chip covered walking ring. The others, called spotters, whose job it is to spot bids and relay them vocally to the auctioneer, will spread out in a half circle in front of the podium facing the upholstered seats. In the area behind the auditorium, where there is a large walking ring, other spotters, similarly dressed, will be taking up their positions.

Soon the melodious sound of the announcer's[12] voice is heard throughout the auditorium and back lots. "Ladies and gentlemen, would you please take your seats. The auction is scheduled to begin in a few moments." This is followed by a review of the rules contained in the beginning of the auction catalog[13]—the paperback book everyone carries—and the call to bring in the first "hip" number, which is how the horses are referred to in accordance with the numbers carried on the rear hip of each animal.[14] As the horses are brought in, the announcer describes various aspects of the horse's pedigree and any other information that may seem to enhance the animal's value.[15] This information is generally in the catalogue, and it normally takes no more than thirty seconds to review the highlights.

Once introduced, the auctioneer receives the microphone and begins his chant. "Do I hear one hundred thousand? Will you say one hundred thousand? One hundred thousand? Will you say eighty thousand? Fifty thousand? Thank you! Fifty thousand, Sixty thousand. Will you give sixty thousand? Sixty thousand, fifty thousand—" It is not uncommon for the announcer to break in if the bidding lags. Though both the auctioneer and the announcer can and do take bids from the floor, most bids are taken by one of the "spotters," located either in the auditorium or in the back areas where the horses are walked before coming into the auction ring. This process is repeated approximately every three minutes for up to twelve hours, with auctioneers, announcers, and spotters rotating and taking breaks every half hour or so. Such sales can go on for over a week, with close to two thousand horses sold at a single sale.[16]

As in the fish auctions, numerous items are sold to numerous buyers. Each horse, however, like each manuscript, is perceived as unique—as revealed by the wide range of prices paid for horses with nearly identical bloodlines. The established rituals of dress and behavior as well as the sense of tradition that pervades these auctions, however, underscores their communal character, which matches that of fish and subsidiary rights auctions. It is the rights and considerations of the community that make it necessary for these auctions to go on for twelve hours at a time, two weeks at a stretch. Only in this way can the members of the community congregate and express their collective judgments. The life cycle of a horse requires that certain decisions be made at specific times. Many people feel that they have a right to participate in these decisions, and the intensive gatherings characteristic of thoroughbred auctions are the result.

A few weeks after the November thoroughbred sales in Lexington have ended, the peculiar rhythms of an auction chant can again be heard around Lexington. The setting, however, is quite different. The chants come from five different warehouses. There are, however, no crowds, no glamour. We find instead warehouses filled with rows of tobacco through which two lines of men march. One line is headed by the warehouse owner, who yells out a price as he comes to each new stack, a four-by-four-by-three-foot cube weighing approximately seven hundred pounds, followed by an auctioneer who takes up the price and incorporates it into a chant, followed by others who are busy marking the piles as they pass.[17] Across from them another line of about eight men moves in parallel sequence with the men in this line, nodding and making vocal and physical gestures in response to the auctioneer's chant.

Although it is difficult for an outsider to understand what all the grunts and nods mean, the two lines of men seem to know. They should. For six months a year they travel together from

Florida to Virginia buying tobacco in one auction after another. By means of their grunts and nods they set the price of tobacco and determine how the tobacco is to be divided among the major tobacco houses for which they work. These communities are so tightly integrated, in fact, it is often difficult to determine when and if the buyers are actually bidding against each other. What is clear is that the price determined is a collective price.

MEANWHILE, one hundred miles north of New York City, horses of a different sort are being auctioned off in a setting and a manner very different from that common to Lexington or Saratoga. Outside Luther's Commodity Auction Barn, situated in a small, rural town, an eight-year-old mare is being walked around as Delos ("Los") Luther II exhorts those present to purchase the poor animal if they don't want her to end up at the cannery. There is no concern with frills here. Today's auction started six hours earlier with closeout items from a number of local stores. From noon to six, everything has been sold from horse liniment to rubber buckets. In most cases there were enough of each item to go around. The normal practice for selling such multiple items is to offer one item and run the bid as high as it will go; after the first item is sold, the auctioneer offers the rest at the same price to whomever wants one. Throughout the whole process, Los is apt to switch from chant to story to advice and back again, with as much humor thrown in as he can muster.

Though their style is similar, Luther's horse auctions differ considerably from his normal Tuesday auction, which features eggs, chickens, ducks, rabbits, and, in the evening, sheep and cattle. Tuesday auctions aim more at a relatively small number of professional buyers hoping to obtain merchandise for their own business. Those in attendance tend to be auction regulars who know each other and constitute a community not unlike that found at the less-select thoroughbred auctions. Los's horse auctions, however, draw a much more heterogeneous group of neighbors and strangers. This explains in part Los's use of humor and stories. For his auctions to be successful, both buyers and sellers must feel that the prices established reflect the views of the community. For this to be true, there must *be* a community of some sort. Creating this community, even if only for a few hours, is perhaps Los's major job.

In New York City, in the borough of Queens, another type

of commodity auction is being attended by a large group of regulars and an equal number of passersby. The tone and atmosphere is quite similar to Luther's Tuesday auction and generates many of the same feelings, though there is also something more reminiscent of his horse auctions. This is perhaps not surprising, given the mix of buyers. Here animals are not being auctioned but used automobiles. Like the local commodity auction, auto auctions tend to be held outdoors, though the setting is normally an open parking lot behind a garage or next to a junkyard. The sites vary depending on whether it is a police or marshal auction of impounded cars, an independent auction of cars repossessed by banks, or a wholesale auction to which only dealers are admitted. (Police auctions are run under the auspices of the police department, though they will use the services of an independent auctioneer. All the cars auctioned have been impounded for one reason or another. Marshal auctions are also run by an independent auctioneer, but the cars have been repossessed or impounded by city marshals. In these auctions the garage and towing companies that work with the marshals may also put up for sale other cars to which they have title. What are called "independent" auctions tend to be run under the auspices of an established auction firm, with the automobiles being primarily repossessed cars, though such firms will also auction cars for private individuals. Wholesale auctions also tend to be run under the auspices of an established auction firm, with buyers and sellers limited to persons with resale tax numbers.) The ethnically mixed crowd, the bullhorn and the banter, the work crews unlocking, starting, and locking cars tend to be the same. It is this mix of four to twenty distinct, ethnically homogeneous, close-knit groups of three to five dealers—groups that know each other from previous auctions—coupled with a half dozen to two dozen individual buyers that gives these auctions their particular ambience of "business as usual" and "show and tell." There is no question about the centrality of the community in these auctions; the only question is which community. The community of dealers or that which includes individual buyers who need first to be integrated into the community.

In any given week there are also likely to be over one hundred scheduled country-style art and antique auctions within a hundred miles of New York and another thousand throughout the rest of the United States. In New York City, Christie's, Sotheby's, and other art and antique houses may hold up to a dozen separate auctions. Here is where one finds everything from the old sofa, antique chair, handmade dollhouse, gilded mirror, Victorian painting, Civil War musket, and duck decoy to the first edition and old masterpiece. It is where people come to browse and examine items at formally scheduled previews before sales, where the occasional buyers try to pick out the dealers, where the dealers are looking out for the collectors, and the auctioneer is keeping his eye on all of them. It is a place where people agree to meet before going out to lunch, or to while away an afternoon instead of going to the movies. It is the home of the bidding paddle, the $2 vase and the $1 million chair.

Although there are many similarities in the types of items auctioned, Middletown's Thursday night Moose Lodge auction differs radically from Sotheby's in the normal quality of the items. Much the same can be said about the resources and knowledgeability of the participants. Compared to nearly all of the other auctions so far described, these are the public auctions that nonprofessional buyers are most apt to frequent. They tend, consequently, to be the most familiar in the public eye. More importantly, however, is the fact that the preponderance of nonprofessional buyers makes the communal character of these auctions more tenuous which in turn requires special efforts on the part of the auctioneer. This is most obviously the case in the less select auctions, in which the first job of a successful auctioneer is to create a sense of community, since a sense of community is necessary if the auction process is to be seen as legitimate. The techniques used may differ, but establishing such a sense of community and legitimacy is also a major task for Sotheby's and Christie's.

Perhaps the only type of auction in which generating and maintaining a sense of community is more important than in art and antique auctions is the charity auction—be it a summer tent auction of donated goods sponsored by the local church or grange or a black-tie Junior League auction at which everything from a trip around the world to a back massage may be sold. In some charity auctions, such as those held on the Lower East Side of New York by Orthodox Jewish synagogues that auction off religious "honors" to congregants,[18] a fairly well established community already exists. In other cases, the potential buyers are almost complete strangers to each other. In all cases, however, the auction format is seen as a means for putting social pressure on participants to give more than they might otherwise give. Community is used here not to legitimate the value of the objects auctioned so much as the amount a buyer is willing to spend. The social process, however, is the same.

THESE brief vignettes of different auction milieus and practices convey not only the variety of auctions but the extent to which they are grounded in specific social contexts, which shape the activities and outcomes of each auction. Auctions are not unique in this respect; shopping at a flea market or a department store also occurs within a social context. Auctions differ from other types of economic exchange—fixed-price and private treaty exchanges[19]—not by being more social but by being more explicitly concerned with the production and reproduction of the values, views, and routines on which any community depends. Where most other forms of economic life occur within established communities and in terms of accepted values, auctions require that such communities and values be continually reproduced.[20] It is because auctions are more manifestly concerned with generating and maintaining social relations and values that they provide us with a means for understanding the role such relationships and values play in what might appear to be purely economic transactions. As a result, auctions offer us a better opportunity than do other forms of economic exchange to examine how changes occurring within a community affect the ability of such a community to maintain itself.

The fixed-price method of exchange is the one most familiar to us. Prices are set by producers and sellers; buyers have the option either to pay the price or refrain from making the purchase. Obviously, if there are no buyers, the seller will probably be forced to make adjustments in his price. Such adjustments, however, are done independently by sellers rather than as part of the direct negotiations between them and buyers. Nevertheless, sellers in a fixed-price system are subject to a wide range of social expectations and constraints that establish not only legitimate costs (expenses for labor, transportation, investment recovery, and advertising) but also define supply, demand, and acceptable profits. Obviously there is a good deal of flexibility in prices set in this manner, but most potential buyers assume that prices so set conform to fair-marketing principles, which are, in turn, subject to review and justification by some sort of business community. Price, in short, is assumed to be governed by a set of agreed-upon communal principles that determine value.

The situation in private treaty exchanges is quite different. In these situations, buyer and seller actively negotiate the price between them. Most people recognize this system as bargaining. The seller may offer an item at one price; the buyer may counter with another, lower price, until a mutually agreed upon price is established. What is of particular interest in these situations is the fact that the prices offered and sought normally constitute a secondary part of the bargaining process. The talk isn't primarily over price per se. Whether it be between a vendor in a flea market and a tourist, or a garment manufacturer and a regular buyer, the real controversy is over the various qualities of the item for sale. Each party attempts to focus on those qualities that in terms of assumed shared criteria either increase or decrease the value of the item.

In order for such bargaining to occur, in fact, there must be some body of shared judgments similar to those that govern fixed-price exchanges. In the case of private treaty exchanges, however, there is disagreement, or at least ambiguity, regarding the applicability of these judgments to the specific objects being discussed. Price is discussed, but it is discussed in terms of specific qualities attributed to the object in question and various assumed, shared principles of evaluation.

> Look at it. It's real leather. You know what real leather is worth. Five dollars would be cheap for a plastic bag of that size. It's worth at least twenty dollars. The leather alone is worth fifteen dollars.

> That leather isn't worth any more than plastic. It's uneven and badly cured. You got them for a song. I'll probably get stuck with them, but I'll go up to ten dollars. (And so on.)

Buyers and sellers in private treaty exchanges may not exhibit the same degree of consensus regarding the value of particular items as in fixed-price systems, but they normally share certain general criteria and assumptions of evaluation, such as those related to quality of materials, workmanship, and availability. It is, however, specifically such general principles that are undermined and weakened by the social changes typical of modern society. Space-age technology challenges accepted views bearing on workmanship and materials. The breakdown of traditional groups undermines traditional forms of classification. Groups with different tastes acquire resources with which they can give financial support to their preferences. When this occurs, there may not be sufficient grounds on which negotiations can get started. Auctions have proved to be a successful mechanism for dealing with such situations.[21]

Auctions differ from both fixed-price and private treaty systems in that principles and criteria of evaluation cease to be prerequisites in establishing prices. In auctions, it is not principles of evaluation—a certain quality, scarcity, size, or other trait—that determine price, but rather price that is used to determine value. Rather than using consensual principles of what constitutes objective worth to establish price and ownership, auctions, through competitive bidding, seek to establish standards of worth through price.

While both the fixed-price and private treaty forms of pricing and exchange allow for price adjustments in response to market conditions, they lack the public competition and social interaction among buyers and sellers in which price is determined by what is offered and accepted. The term *auction* is used specifically to refer to such price-governed, public, competitive transactions. What is crucial about these situations is the dominance given to price per se: Price determines value. (This is clearly at odds with conventional economic thinking, which sees all values as determined by price. Unfortunately, the debate over the role of principles of evaluation lies at the heart of the debate between sociology and economics and cannot be resolved here, though it will remain a subtheme of the entire book.)

While price determines value in all auctions, it does so in different ways due to the fact that auctions differ in the manner in which bids are made and accepted. Why this should be so is a question we shall examine shortly. It is important first, however, to have a general idea of some of the variations.

Auction bidding can be categorized in terms of two major features: (1) the form in which bids are made, and (2) the sequence rules for bidding. More specifically, bids may be made in written, visual, or oral form. In each case, such bids may be made privately or publicly. Sequencing, in turn, tends to be governed either by a principle of bid increases or bid decreases; there are also auctions, however, where bids are made simultaneously.

Auctions that utilize written bids are commonly referred to as sealed-bid auctions or simply competitive bidding. Sequencing tends not to be a major issue since normally each bidder is allowed a single bid. While such bids need not always be submitted at the same time, they are normally opened at approximately the same time, with the highest or lowest (depending on the purpose) being accepted as the winning bid. There are a number of more complicated variations that allow for multiple written bids—some of which will be discussed later, but most sealed-bid auctions are of this simple form. (For a description of some of the more interesting types of written auctions see pp. 70–72.)

While written sealed-bid auctions are very common, the word *auction* for most suggests oral bidding, or at least spontaneous and sequential bidding, with the possibility of multiple bids from any given participant. Such bids need not actually be oral. Bidding paddles, hand signals, facial expressions, and other signs can all be used in lieu of vocal expressions. What is important is that participants have the opportunity to respond to the bidding, or lack of bidding, by others with adjustments in their own bids.

In most multiple-bid vocal auctions, the accepted sequence of bids is referred to as the ascending sequence. For a bid to be accepted it must be higher than the previous bid. Strictly speaking there is nothing to prevent a bidder from offering a bid substantially higher than the last bid, thereby preempting a number of intermediate bids. In most cases, however, this does not occur because the high bidder usually waits until the price approaches his or her own level or until the lack of other bids indicates that the item is about to be sold for less than he or she was willing to bid. This ascending-sequence form is commonly referred to as an English auction. The familiar cry of, "I have ten dollars, will you say twenty? I have twenty, now thirty . . . forty . . . I have fifty . . ." is the cry of an English auction.

In contrast to the English auction there is the Dutch auction, in which a descending sequence is used. Here the auction begins with the item offered at a high price—usually too high for there to be any bids. The price is then dropped sequentially by some established quantity until a bidder speaks out and accepts the offer. In England this was referred to as "mineing." The price would continue to drop until someone yelled out, "Mine."[22]

In the Dutch auction, the first actual bid is also often the last bid. One might question, therefore, whether there really is an active competition among bidders. There clearly is competition because, although there may be only one bid, it is made in direct response to the expectation that if it is not made some other bid will be made and the item lost. In most cases in which Dutch auctions are used, however, the reality is that there is more than one bid. This is because Dutch auctions are used most frequently when there are multiples of the items being auctioned. The Dutch flower auction is the prime example. Thousands of flowers are auctioned at the same time. The high—that is, the first—bidder is given a choice of the flowers being auctioned. He or she could take all of them but is more likely to choose those that appear to be the best. The auction will then continue, with the price falling and the other bidders vying for what is left. The next bidder will again have a choice, and so on. In such situations, there is ongoing competition among bidders even though they may be silent most of the time.

Though less common than either the English or the Dutch auctions, there is the simultaneous, or Japanese, auction.[23] In these auctions, bids are made at the same time as in the sealed-bid auctions, but they are made orally and publicly, which allows other bidders to adjust their bids in response. Such adjustments must be made very quickly since only a relatively short period is allowed for bidding. It is the job of the auctioneer to spot the highest bid and to take it. This can be quite difficult, but often the auctioneer is looking for a particular bid that he will take as soon as it is offered. Although the Japanese auction can be used to auction a single item, it is primarily used in auctioning a series of similar goods, where each sale is quickly followed by another. In this way the bidding in one sale feeds into that of the next, creating a type of sequencing across sales if not within a given sale.

These diverse methods of auctioning are not equally popular. The two most common forms found in the United States are the single-sealed-bid auction and the English auction. The sealed-bid auction is the preferred method used in the auctioning of contracts, such as government public works projects. It is also the method normally used when fiduciary instruments such as government bonds are auctioned. When it comes to most items, however, it is the English auction that dominates. But even English auctions take different forms depending upon the particular character of the items to be auctioned and the social relationships among the participants.

The value of some items is indeterminate because they are

used or old; that of others, because supply and demand are uncertain; and yet others, because of idiosyncratic factors that are highly dependent on personal tastes. Overlapping these variations are differences in the types of relationships that exist among and between buyers and sellers, which are seen to give respective participants different rights and responsibilities.

The power and utility of auctions arise from the fact that they are capable of generating rules and practices for resolving the many and varied uncertainties and ambiguities they confront in a manner acceptable to all participants. With questions of value and provenance increasing daily, and with traditional means for resolving such issues proving less and less acceptable to changing populations of buyers and sellers, reliance on auctions increases. This explains why auctions are proliferating at such a rapid rate. To explore and understand how auctions work helps us to understand not only how societies structure and order economic transactions but also how they establish economic values.

Chapter 2

For How Much and to Whom?

The Basic Questions

"What am I offered for this beautiful quilt?"

"Will someone start the bidding on this handsome young colt at one hundred thousand dollars?"

"How much for this box of tools?"

"Is there any interest in the sapphire brooch and matching earrings?"

E VEN when the auctioneer starts by asking for a specific price, there is usually an interrogative tone to his voice:

"Let's start this off at $100. $100?"

Who is willing to offer what? This is the heart of any auction. It reflects the uncertainties regarding both the value of the items in question and the identities of the persons who may be interested in acquiring them. Often the two issues are interrelated. If a noted collector is interested in a given item, it may bring a high price; if not, it may go cheaply. On the other hand, an antique Persian rug may be attractive to many buyers at five hundred dollars but of little interest to those same buyers at a thousand dollars. While in some cases there may be more interest in knowing who the eventual buyer will be than in the price per se, in most cases, it is the price that is of paramount concern.

Given that millions of items are priced and sold every day, why should it be so difficult to price some items? What makes determining their value so ambiguous that a different pricing technique is required? In nearly all cases the inability to set a price comes about because the normal criteria for establishing price are inappropriate. Price cannot be set in terms of production costs when such costs are either not known or ancient history, as in the case of antique tools; yesterday's supply and demand are of little use in knowing future supply and demand if subject to unknown natural forces, as may be the case with many agricultural commodities. Similarly, general standards are of little use when price is dependent on the subjective judgments of two or three individuals, as is often the case with rare art masterpieces or a young racehorse. In short, it is not just not knowing what a particular item is worth, but not having appropriate measures with which to determine its value.

In modern societies, most prices are set and goods exchanged in a fixed-price or fixed-posted system; prices are set unilaterally by sellers, though they will adjust price if there are no buyers. Although prices are set by sellers, such prices must conform to a wide range of evaluation criteria bearing on such things as the quality and quantity of materials, type of craftsmanship, supply and demand, and current taste. Although there are many variations and a good deal of freedom in interpreting these criteria, the popular expectation is that price will be set to reflect the cost of producing and marketing an item, plus a percentage markup for profit. It is assumed that if there is greater demand for the product than can be met currently by production, the seller may set the price higher than would otherwise be the case. Similarly, if the seller is stuck with an inventory surplus, he or she is often expected to sell the product for less. The item may even be sold below cost in order to recoup capital. In short, the price set is presumed to be a function of costs, supply, and demand.

This system works quite well providing specific values can be assumed for costs, supply, and demand.[1] If such values cannot be assumed, other procedures are required. If the problem is primarily one of determining how certain agreed-upon standards are to be applied in a specific situation, the fixed-price system is likely to be augmented, if not completely replaced, by some form of negotiation or bargaining—a private treaty system. When, however, the problem is a lack of agreement among potential buyers and sellers regarding the appropriateness of evaluation criteria, such negotiations generally prove inadequate. How much weight should be given to the three Cs of diamonds (carat, color, and clarity) when the stones are part of a two-hundred-year-old royal tiara? How does one value a famous person's love letters, or a chest of drawers that has been in the family three hundred years? There are apt to be no common grounds for negotiation. This is more likely to be the case when there are a number of interested buyers or sellers with particular concerns. When this occurs, the only alternative is often an auction.

To understand how and why inadequacies of commonly accepted criteria foster auctions, it is helpful to examine what is entailed by such criteria.

Of the various factors used in determining price, costs are normally the most easily specified. In many cases, it is possible to ascertain the actual cost of a given item. It may not be possible to produce an equivalent item for exactly the same cost, but in the case of most manufactured goods a pretty good estimate is usually available. General Motors, for example, can determine the cost of steel, labor costs, plant depreciations, and necessary profit on thousands of items. The situation becomes more difficult when the items are produced in a less standardized manner, but provided there are some commonalities in the production process from one item to another, a cost figure can be fairly accurately determined.

There are situations, however, in which this cannot be done. One of the most obvious is when the item, be it an antique tool, car, or chair, is no longer in production. In these cases, replication costs are often difficult if not impossible to determine. We might know that it took someone two days to make a given item two hundred years ago, but without the proper tools and skills, we don't know how long it would take to replicate it today, or if it could be replicated. Assuming that a perfect replication were possible, it could still be argued that the new item wouldn't be the same. Even ignoring this problem, the cost of replicating an item as it was originally, if possible, may be difficult if not impossible to estimate.

Discussing price in terms of labor costs highlights the fact that people's evaluations of value in everyday life are sensitive to the labor time and effort involved. When there is a considerable discrepancy between the labor in producing an item and that of similarly priced goods, the value of the item becomes more problematic. When an auctioneer starts to talk about the many hours that it took to weave an old rug for which only a small amount has been offered, he is well aware of the common association of value with labor invested in an item. It is one of the tangible and acceptable measures of value in everyday exchange:

> There are three hundred knots in every square inch in this rug, which means—someone figure it out for me. How many knots in a five-by-eight rug? Over five thousand square inches, which would be over one and a half million knots. If she can do five knots a minute, it would still take her over three years to make this rug, and you're offering me eight hundred dollars for three years' work?

Sometimes the issue is not the actual live labor entailed in a work such as a handmade rug, but rather the costs that were entailed in the machinery, materials, and overhead producing the items. In these cases, especially when the items being auctioned are themselves not overly impressive, the auctioneer is apt to make reference to these large capital expenses:

> I know that these old cash registers can't do what the new computerized registers can do, but it took an awful big factory to make these things, and that factory took a lot of money to build. Come on now. They're worth at least ten bucks each.

While the difficulty may lie in determining the cost of time and effort that went into making an item, it may equally be due to difficulty in establishing the quality of the effort. On an assembly line, one hour of work may be fairly equivalent to any other hour of work regardless of who is working when and where. But the time of one person's skilled labor, like that involved in carving a mantelpiece or in painting a portrait, may be valued much more highly than another's. This is definitely the case when dealing with "art" objects. Quality of effort is also often an issue when dealing with a rare, unique, or one-of-a-kind item. The skill and efforts of all breeders and all wine makers, for example, are not equal as evidenced by the very different prices paid for different bulls and different wines. What further complicates matters is that such rankings reflect differences in tastes and preferences, which themselves are apt to change over time. Drier wines come into vogue; smaller steers come into favor because they can be marketed at a younger age.

That all efforts are not equal is most vividly evidenced in the notion of artistic genius, which is accepted today as a given. We are accustomed to value a drawing by one artist a thousand times more than a drawing by another. Three hundred years ago this would have seemed quite incredible to most people. Some artists and artistic schools were considered better and entitled to more money than others, but the differences didn't warrant the price disparities that are accepted as a matter of course today. Paintings were much more likely to be priced in terms of their size, the quality of the materials used, and the reputation of the particular school or shop than according to the unique talent of the artist who painted them. Works of art were valued as products of artisans who were more or less interchangeable, not as creations of genius.[2] Differences between artists were regarded as similar to those we would presently associate with physicians. Doctor A may be seen as better than Doctor B, allowing him to charge double what Doctor A is able to charge. It would strike most of us as bizarre, however, to hear that while Doctor A and most other doctors were paid $15,000 for a heart bypass, Doctor B regularly charged $100,000 to remove a gall bladder because of his flare with the scalpel and the artistic way he stitched.

The notion that all efforts are not equal is not a new idea. Labor that has benefited from special training or education is commonly perceived as having increased value due to the training that has gone into it. Genius, however, is a completely different issue and introduces less quantifiable variations in perceived value, unrelated to those dependent on training. It is essentially this "genius" element and associated uncertainty that make fine art objects so suitable for auctions.

Other factors, like age and use, complicate matters further. Each can elevate or depress a price. In the case of many used items, such as automobiles, we might know what it cost new but be uncertain as to how much of the original value has been already "used." The ambiguity isn't over the original cost of the item but its value at this moment. While normally a used object is worth less than a new object, sometimes past use actually adds to an object's value by contributing some positive element. A graphic example of this reverse impact of use on value is the premium paid for used blue jeans a few years ago. Teenagers were willing to pay more for them used than new because they had already been repeatedly worn and washed, which not only saved them the labor and discomfort of doing it themselves but freed them from the stigma of having to wear new jeans. For similar reasons people sometimes will pay more for a housebroken dog or a saddle-trained horse.

Then, too, people are often willing to pay more for a used object because of the added luster associated with a particular user. The practice of paying a premium for used American jeans was even more pronounced in Europe, especially Eastern Europe, where their value was increased because they had been worn by American teenagers and hence had been part of the American teen experience. Similarly, the increased value assigned to a pen used by Abraham Lincoln is due to its association with Abraham Lincoln rather than to any benefits derived from its use. Perhaps the most extreme example of illustrious past ownership conferring value is the recent auction of the "psychedelic" Rolls-Royce owned by John Lennon. It was estimated to sell for $150,000 to $200,000, which was five times the price that similar standard Rolls-Royce automobiles had brought at auction. It was actually sold for $2,500,000. Here the association with John Lennon and the Beatles, as well as its idiosyncratic paintwork, served not merely to increase the price of the object dramatically but to transform it. The psychedelic-painted Rolls-Royce became a cultural icon. The only thing analogous to this in the art world would be when a painting goes from being a beautiful picture to a work by a famous artist and then becomes a priceless masterpiece in its own right, such as the Mona Lisa.

Another factor that can introduce an element of ambiguity into cost calculations is differences in quality produced by uncontrollable forces such as those due to weather. Too much or too little rain or sun can dramatically affect the quality of crops regardless of the time and efforts expended. Such forces of nature play a significant role in the determination of the price of nearly all commodities, be they fish, cattle, or grain, and generate either higher or lower income for producers. As two farmers putting in the same hours, having the same expertise, and making the same investment in supplies may produce very different crops due to differences in rainfall within a few hundred miles, so two fishing boats can ship out of Boston Harbor on the same day and work the fishing banks equally hard for the same number

of days and come back into port with very different catches. Much
the same thing can be said for cattle ranchers, flower growers,
and tobacco farmers. As the captain of a fishing boat said one
chilly morning on the Boston docks,

> Who can say what fish is worth. It's not like we have any control
> over what we bring in. I've had trips when everything went
> right. All we had to do was drop the nets and the nicest-looking
> fish you ever saw jumped in. Other times we go out, work our
> butts off, and still come back with stuff we used to give away.

There is nothing that unusual about similar efforts leading
to different results. In most cases, we attempt to resolve such
inequalities by setting prices in terms of average results obtained
over time. This means that sometimes we get a little more for
our efforts and sometimes a little less, but in the long run things
even themselves out. The differences associated with agricultural-
type labor, however, tend to be both sufficiently significant and
erratic that averaging seems inappropriate. Often it is not the
case of one worker producing a slightly better crop but a case of
qualitatively distinct products. Be it the grade of tobacco, the
species of fish, or the size and quality of the fruit, chance and
external factors rather than productive skill can be responsible
for major qualitative differences in production.

Genius, use, and luck. Three factors that in some cases, such
as those just described, must be accounted for in the everyday
determinations of inherent value and legitimate price and whose
erratic nature makes it difficult to apply general pricing guidelines.
The more significant each is, the more practical the auction process.

Still other factors can undermine the process of establishing
value. The most common of these are supply and demand. Setting
price according to supply and demand is a fairly familiar notion.
It is, in fact, the crux of the auction paradigm favored by most
economists. According to neoclassical microeconomic theory, price
is determined by the intersection of supply and demand curves,
the latter reflecting the sum of individual preferences. When supply and demand curves are known, price can be calculated. When,
for whatever reason, they are not known, however, we face a
problem of uncertainty.

Like costs, certainty of supply and demand varies with the
situation.[3] Highly perishable goods, for example, exhibit consider-

able uncertainty for reasons similar to those linked to the quality of such items. A sudden freeze can not only damage a Florida orange crop but utterly destroy it. Bad luck may result not only in poor-quality fish but no fish at all. Long-term trends may be fairly consistent, but short-term fluctuations can nevertheless have dramatic impact on prices. Moreover, it is often difficult, if not impossible, to extrapolate present or future market conditions based on past conditions.

While this is most commonly the case with perishable goods, similar shifts in supply and demand can cause rapid shifts in prices for nonperishable items such as bonds and collectibles. In these cases, it is often dramatic shifts in price that generate sudden changes in supply and demand which in turn cause further shifts in price. An increase in interest rates may induce many companies to postpone proposed bond sales, which results in an undersupply, which forces interest rates down. A temporary dearth of Victorian furniture may lead to higher-than-normal prices, causing dealers and collectors to sell pieces they had no intention of selling, with the result that a surplus of such items is created, driving prices down.

The problem of determining price according to supply and demand can become more complex when multiple markets for the items exist, especially when the different markets operate at different times. Most agricultural commodities are both auctioned and later resold through secondary markets. Many racehorses auctioned as yearlings are later resold, either through another auction or privately as two-year-old horses in training and sometimes later as broodmares or stallions. Similarly, most bonds and new stocks are resold after their initial offering. Changes in price in one such market can effect supply and demand in a related market.

Adding to these complexities is the problem of determining *what* the item is: How is it to be classified? This problem commonly arises when dealing with "natural" products, where each item is likely to be slightly different from others of its "type" and where types themselves may overlap. The fact that there is a strong demand for California oranges doesn't necessarily mean that there is a strong demand for Florida oranges. On the other hand, a strong demand for California oranges may carry over to and be alleviated by Florida grapefruits. A demand for red snapper may or may not carry over into a demand for haddock, though they may be tied together on the production side. Similarly, the fact that there is strong demand for AA New Jersey ten-year bonds paying 9 percent may not indicate that identical bonds from Vermont will meet with similar demand. The broader and more interchangeable the categories, the more stable the patterns of supply and demand, since substitutions are possible. The more singular the item, the greater the possibility of erratic shifts in supply and demand and, hence, price. In the case of very rare and one-of-a-kind objects, there may, in fact, be no market in terms of which the notions of supply and demand make any sense.[4]

Moreover, certain categories can change and be changed, especially when a market is highly dependent on a group of experts or dealers. Lean beef, which has historically been graded as inferior because it has little marbling (fat), may soon be significantly upgraded for just that reason. Light tobaccos move in and out of fashion in much the same way, with demand and price changing accordingly. Furthermore, previously interchangeable items may cease to be interchangeable. Dealers may no longer accept brown eggs in place of white; or suddenly "near-perfect" Oriental rugs may become interchangeable—for a specific price adjustment—with "perfect" rugs. The value of items subject to such redefinition is clearly unstable, which makes them appropriate objects to be auctioned.

The affinity between items of uncertain worth and auctions can be seen in many situations. Consider, for example, tobacco auctions. Of the various commodity auctions held regularly, the most familiar is probably the tobacco auction—made famous in the then American Tobacco Company's Lucky Strike radio ads in the 1940s, which featured the auctioneer's chant followed by the final call "Sold American!"[5] Although the auctioning of tobacco is related to many of the various factors discussed above, most of the bidding at such auctions is perfunctory. The reason is that there normally exists a fairly firm consensus among bidders as to the value of each grade. In fact, in most cases, the warehouse owner, who normally functions as the lead man—the person who sets the opening price for each bale of tobacco and then turns the auction proper over to the auctioneer, who follows him down the row of tobacco bales—"knows," based on continuing negotiations with the companies preceding the sale, the price the companies are willing to pay for each grade of tobacco. Such auctions, consequently, serve primarily as allocation processes.

There are, however, exceptions to this rule. These occur when there is what is known as a "bad" bale of tobacco, which is actually a mixed bale containing different grades of tobacco. In such situations, bidding is no longer mechanical since, though the bidders know what the different grades of tobacco are worth, they don't know what this particular bale is worth. That price needs to be arrived at communally, through an authentic auction process.

Something quite similar occurs in the publishing business. For a number of years it has been common for publishers to auction off the paperback rights of books to paperback houses. However, not all paperback rights are auctioned off. Some—most commonly those of known, established authors—are negotiated with a single paperback house. Often there is a clause in a contract that gives the paperback publishers of the author's last book a first option on the new one. More important, however, is the fact that if an author has an established track record, both the hardcover house and the paperback house have enough information to allow them to set a price without an auction. New authors, on the other hand, who are unknown fiscal quantities, whose "grade" has not yet been established, are more frequently auctioned.

The tendency to use auctions when criteria for determining price are weak is revealed in yet another situation, the thoroughbred racehorse business. For as long as anyone remembers, it has been the practice to sell yearling horses through auction. Sizable numbers of broodmares, horses-in-training, and weanlings—foals under a year old that have been weaned—have also been sold through auction. Stallion shares (part ownership) and seasons (breeding rights), however, have traditionally been exchanged through private treaty, under the auspices and control of a management syndicate. Given that much is known about each stallion, the absence of an auction is understandable. There is not only a public record of the racing performance of each stallion, but similar records of all progeny as well as a record of the money received for horses previously bred and sold. The number of mares that a stallion can cover in a given year is also known.

Recently, however, there have been changes that have dramatically unsettled the stallion market. The influx of new owners and new money has upset the traditional balance of supply and demand. They have introduced a further degree of uncertainty insofar as they are often unwilling to follow the guidelines established by the syndicate managers. Some have also complained that as newcomers they were not treated as fairly as those who had been in the business for years. As a result of these developments, auction sales of stallion shares and seasons have increased substantially in recent years.

In summary, the sine qua non of most auctions is the failure of normal pricing criteria, where such criteria bear on the "inherent" value of the item; supply and demand; or grading and acceptable substitutions, technically known as fungibility. Uncertainties regarding inherent value, in turn, may be due primarily to differences in the quality of labor; the effect of aging or use on the item; the part played by fortune in determining the final results of the effort; or simple ignorance as to the efforts entailed. Doubts regarding supply or demand may be seen to arise from the variability of natural causes; changes in categorization; or manipulation of markets. Substitutions and grade distinctions, finally, may be indeterminate as the result of changes in public tastes, the opinions of specific experts, or changing markets.[6]

Although each of these factors may play a role in any particular type of auction, their relative importance varies. The major auction types, namely, art/one of a kind, collectible, and commodity, can be distinguished from each other specifically in terms of the relative importance of each of these uncertainties. What is more, the particular cluster of these uncertainties gives distinctive tones to these different types of auctions.

In art/one-of-a-kind auctions, for example, value uncertainty is primarily due to questions bearing on the inherent "artistic-distinctive" value of the piece and is tied up with the notions of artistic genius and uniqueness. Given the very singular nature of such genius, the issues of fungibility and grading—whether the work is a good or a bad Picasso or an exceptional or average first edition—is often a matter of individual taste or expert opinion. If the buyer has sufficient resources, his or her opinion can establish the price. Furthermore, the singular nature of such items often makes questions of supply and demand somewhat irrelevant. On the other hand, this also makes such markets more vulnerable to manipulation since what supply exists may be more easily controlled.

There is generally a good deal of uncertainty regarding the inherent value of most collectibles such as memorabilia, stamps, antique automobiles, old tools, or apothecary jars. The question in these cases, however, tends to center on the effects of age and use. In these cases, supply and demand is of crucial importance and highly susceptible to changes in categorization, which are, in turn, controlled in large measure by the present consensus of recognized experts. In these situations, the collective opinion of experts tends to take priority over individual tastes because the number of items is too large for an individual's personal preferences to support the price of all such items. In fact, in order for an item to be considered a collectible there must be a sufficient number of them to allow for some system of categorization. While the uniqueness of a work of art usually enhances its value, such uniqueness can work against collectibles, as a collector of antique clocks commented in response to the offer of an unusually designed and quite beautiful old mantel clock: "I wouldn't bid on it and most of my friends won't either unless they have a known buyer for it. It really is a one-of-a-kind piece, and there is no way to compare it to anything else."

Collectors of these items prefer to defer to some form of collective judgment. There is still plenty of room for ambiguity, but the ambiguity is related to interpreting use—that is, aging and condition—which is not as subjective as artistic taste. A forty-year-old car in bad condition may be regarded as a piece of junk, whereas the same car in perfect condition may be worth more than it was originally. Key decisions of value revolve around questions of grading and fungibility. These decisions, in turn, may influence supply and demand. It is equally true, however, that supply and demand may impact on judgments of grading and substitutions. If the supply of a given collectible suddenly increases, it is not uncommon for new distinctions to emerge that will create a rarer and hence more valuable subcategory. An oversupply of diamond gemstones some years ago led to the downgrading of many stones that had very slight flaws—previously ignored—in order to maintain the price of "perfect" stones. Similarly, if supply drops to very low levels, items that previously were not highly regarded, because of condition or some other factor, may subsequently be judged acceptable, as occurred some years ago in the quilt market.

Supply and demand in these situations may be open to degrees of manipulation, but given that the number of items is normally quite high and that such classification systems are based on a consensus, such markets are normally difficult to manipulate. An exception arises, however, if a few collectors manage to corner a particular market. Under such circumstances, manipulation not only becomes possible but quite probable.[7] The same is true if, as in the case with diamonds, the market is controlled by a few major dealers.

In many commodity auctions, the uncertainty about inherent value tends to be due to the role fortune plays in the production process. The question is not the value of different efforts, the effect of aging, or uncertain grading, all of which tend to be widely accepted. Ambiguity is rather due to the way fortune—in the guise of mother nature—serves to bring forth different-quality goods from similar ingredients. In other cases, such as oil and various minerals, it is often political fortune that plays the dominant role.

Natural and political fortune play an even greater role in determining supply and demand and, indirectly, grading and fungibility. Many commodity categories reflect neither the tastes of those with major resources nor the opinion of experts, but distinctions generated in the complex of secondary markets into which the auctioned items flow. Commodities in high supply are often subdivided into distinctive grades of different value, while different commodities in low supply are often lumped together. In recent years, the scarcity of many valued fish species has resulted in the upgrading of many others. Fish that once were thrown back are now sold as table fish. Similar modifications are often brought about in regard to other commodities by political changes.

A multimillionaire may be able to transform the works of an unknown artist into priceless works of genius by continually bidding for his or her paintings. A network of dealers and collectors may succeed in redefining how old a rug must be in order to be labeled a "semiantique" Oriental rug. Nature, however, is the dominant force in determining the supply and hence the price of haddock, tobacco, and peaches; admittedly, the various agricultural producers can and do affect such supplies by promoting alternative products and hence changing demand. Oil and minerals recently appear to depend primarily on which political policy is in vogue.

Although inherent value, supply and demand, and grading judgments play a role in nearly all auctions, judgments regarding inherent value tend to be more important in art and one-of-a-kind auctions; classification and equivalency judgments, in collectible auctions; and perceptions of supply and demand, in commodity auctions. This can be graphically depicted as follows:

Types of Auctions by Types of Uncertainty

Type of Uncertainty	Auction Type		
	ART/ONE OF A KIND	COLLECTIBLES	COMMODITIES
Inherent Value	*Genius/Unique**	Age and Use Condition	Comparative Quality
Fungibility and Grading	Personal Tastes/Opinion	*Expert Opinion/ Classification*	Natural Types
Supply and Demand	Manipulation	Dependent upon Classification	*Nature and Existing Markets*

* Key factors italicized.

Uncertainties relating to inherent value, fungibility and grading, and supply and demand are related to the item itself. Other uncertainties that play a role in muddling the process of evaluation, however, are linked to the motivations of the participants. Three of major importance relate to desires for personal aggrandizement, professional publicity or anonymity, and market control. Each is as much a consequence of auctions as it is a causal factor in supporting auctions. Like the uncertainties related to the item itself, each tends to be primarily associated with a particular auction type.

The desire for personal aggrandizement at an auction is often closely related to strongly held personal tastes. It tends to become a significant factor when dealing with idiosyncratic objects, especially expensive idiosyncratic objects. The very fact that these items are unique encourages individuals to define and evaluate them in their own way. There is nothing to stop someone from paying thousands of dollars for a copy of last week's *The New Yorker*, but given the number of copies available for considerably less, such an act would not cast a favorable glow on the buyer. On the other hand, if someone elects to spend a million dollars for a one-of-a-kind antique wooden armchair, he or she may gain prestige simply by virtue of being willing to support that judgment in such an expensive manner. For the price to reach such heights, there obviously must be at least one other person who also feels the chair is worth a great deal. It is the comparative uniqueness of the object, however, which insures that the buyer won't be made to look foolish by a sale of a similar chair for much less.

Nevertheless, there are significant differences between buying for personal taste or personal aggrandizement. In the case of personal taste, it is the item itself that is central, and the primary source of ambiguity. Uncertainties regarding the item's value are based on uncertainties about the qualities of the item, be it a painting or a thoroughbred yearling. The auction format is an attempt to provide a means for dealing with this uncertainty. In cases of personal aggrandizement, or what have been called "tournament[s] of values,"[8] what tends to be most important is the social context within which the auction occurs. The motivation for a bid is often stimulated by competition with others. Rather than resolving such competitions, auctions become the context for promoting them.

Anyone who has attended more than a few auctions has observed at least one such episode. The item being auctioned need not be very expensive. The individuals involved may be comparative strangers or they may know each other well. But their egos play a major role, linking a positive self-image or identity with successful bidding. It may be two major dealers bidding against each other for a famous painting where each is as much, if not more, concerned with beating the other and asserting dominance in the field than with acquiring the particular painting. It may just as easily be two women fighting over a relatively inexpensive, fairly common cookie jar at a country auction.

This desire to exhibit or experience self-aggrandizement through an apparently economic venture is not unique to auctions. It is common in gambling, where the essential element is a degree of uncertainty that leaves space for fantasies of personal influence and capacity—the power to control luck or the roll of the dice. In gambling, this uncertainty is provided by chance. In auctions, the ambiguity is inherent in the items themselves and the actions of the other bidders.

It could be argued that what appears to be a psychological motivation, personal aggrandizement, may actually be economically motivated. Rather than merely acting on a need to assert him- or herself, a buyer may actually benefit financially from paying what initially appears to be an inflated price. An individual who overpays for personal reasons may succeed, especially if he or she has great resources and the items being auctioned are limited in number, in both driving the market up and restricting the market in such a way as to actually end up making a profit on his or her purchases. Of course, the individual may also develop a reputation as such a crazy bidder that other buyers will be unwilling to compete. As a result he or she may be able to buy many other things comparatively cheaply, even coming to believe that he or she is an auction genius. If successful, others may adopt a similar view, though more often than not, persons who continually use auctions as a means for such self-aggrandizement end up losing money, not making it. What is important in the present context, however, isn't whether such buyers make or lose money, or even if they drive prices up or down, but rather the added uncertainty their actions bring to an auction.

While the auction format not only allows, but often encourages, such behavior, it also can and does often serve to restrain such actions. The simplest way it does this is by bankrupting such individuals so they can no longer play the game. Auction practices also allow for less extreme corrective measures. Persons who attract attention by overbidding in an apparently irrational manner are generally counseled by other regular buyers, auctioneers, and even sellers to bid more restrainedly. The other buyers clearly have an interest in restraining such persons, but sellers and auctioneers also prefer that such expansive bidders not self-destruct. They would much rather convert them into long-term, if slightly less extravagant, buyers than have them driven away through their own overexuberance. The major techniques used to inhibit such "suicidal" behavior include everything from friendly advice to ridiculing gossip. Given the overlapping financial and social networks to which most big spenders belong or aspire, most individuals are subject to controls that extend beyond the auction itself. A thoroughbred owner who overbids may find that bankers are less willing to lend him or her money in an unrelated venture; an Oriental rug dealer may find that other dealers are less willing to exchange inventory; a wholesale fish dealer may be forced out of certain markets.[9] In short, ego trips are tolerated provided they are kept within limits.

Other social factors obscuring the evaluative process are the desire for professional publicity and market control for personal gain. They are similar to instances of personal aggrandizement in that the prices bid are influenced by factors not directly related to the value of the items per se and are dependent on opportunities created by the social character of auctions. The public character of auctions gives them a visibility that few fixed-price or private treaty transactions can obtain. A dealer who buys a painting from a private collector for a million dollars may find his or her name and the transaction mentioned briefly in the newspaper the following week. If the same painting is bought at an auction, however, the dealer can generally be sure that not only will his or her name be prominently displayed in the paper but there will be a background story on the gallery and its owner. The same publicity is likely to occur if the item is a million-dollar chair, horse, diamond ring, or stamp or a five-thousand-dollar bottle of wine, antique tool, poster, or fishing fly.

Free publicity can have significant economic benefits that offset losses attendant on overpaying for a particular item. Provided such purchases do not occur too often at too high a cost, they can attract customers and enhance the reputation of the buyer. The restaurateur who bid many thousands of dollars for a magnum of wine that he personally believed was probably no good calculated that the free publicity he and his restaurant would receive would pay for the bottle three times over. Much the same could be said for another restaurateur who often followed a similar path in bidding for prize beef cattle. Not only did such publicity seem to support the claim that his restaurant served only the finest steaks but it helped keep his suppliers on their toes. Similarly, an art dealer known as a specialist in abstract paintings bid one hundred thousand dollars over the resale price he had negotiated with a private buyer for an Impressionist painting because he sought to establish himself as a major Impressionist dealer as well.

Though such publicity is normally reserved for buyers, a seller may also use the auction to generate publicity. More than one breeder of thoroughbred and standardbred race horses has indicated that while horses could often be sold for as much privately as at auction, auctions provide important advertisements for participating stables. Collectors have been known to auction off odd pieces now and then for very similar reasons. These practices, however, differ from the publicity-seeking action of buyers insofar as they seldom serve to affect prices in any unusual manner. An exception might be a dealer or collector who for publicity purposes elects to liquidate a sizable collection at lower-than-normal prices.

In most cases, however, both the costs and rewards of publicity-seeking actions on the part of sellers fall outside the auction proper. A dealer or breeder heavily advertises an upcoming auction sale not so much in the expectation of obtaining higher prices at the auction as in that of obtaining other business through the visibility afforded by the auction.

Ironically, whereas some individuals use auctions to attract attention, others prefer the greater anonymity that auctions allow because buyers and sellers can act through the auctioneer or auction firm. Like publicity, anonymity may entail economic benefits unrelated to the price paid for a particular item. Perhaps the most obvious of these are tax benefits that might result from a hard-to-document transaction. Here, as with the publicity benefits that might accrue to sellers, such benefits have little or no effect on auction prices themselves. For others, however, especially persons known to be very wealthy or major collectors-owners of particular types of items, the anonymity of auctions allows them to accumulate or disburse holdings without informing others in a way that may affect prices. If it is known that a collector is liquidating a collection, prices may become depressed. Similarly, if it is known that Sheikh Maktoum of Dubai or D. Wayne Lukas is interested in a particular horse, the seller may enter the bidding to increase the price artificially. As with publicity-seeking sellers and tax dodgers, anonymity in these situations is not a source of price instability.

Anonymity may serve other purposes. There are collectors and dealers with reputations for possessing items of dubious provenance and authenticity. Their association with a particular piece may have a negative effect on its evaluation. Obviously, if a piece is well known, the seller's identity will matter less. There are sellers, however, who have such dubious reputations that it is in their interests to conceal their identities when their properties are put up for auction. The more reputable houses will not knowingly take stolen or misappropriated goods, but as a fairly recent case involving religious books smuggled out of Nazi Germany reveals, these issues are not always easy to determine. Here anonymity is likely to increase prices, but not in the erratic manner associated with bidders seeking personal aggrandizement or publicity.

The price ramifications of auction practices aimed at establishing market control are most like those of personal aggrandizement insofar as they entail a rather heavy-handed use of inflated bids, but most like those of publicity seekers insofar as they are governed by economic objectives. In these situations, a bidder may be willing to suffer short-term losses on specific transactions in order to obtain longer-term gains as do the publicity seekers. They differ, however, insofar as the benefits to be derived are directly related to the price paid at auction. The purpose of the inflated bid is not to acquire prestige but to increase the price of similar items previously purchased for a lower price. Such practices can and do confuse the evaluative process.

Although many items lend themselves to such manipulation, the method works best when the other goods are traded through a nonauction market linked to the auction markets. A dealer with a large inventory of early Victorian prints and an established clientele may find it economically profitable to run up the price of such prints that come to auction. It is also helpful for the auction market to be relatively small, though it has also been tried with large-volume commodities continually traded through both retail and wholesale markets with a comparatively small reserve, that is, a minimum price below which the item will not be sold. Three commodities that fit this description and that have been subject to such attempts in recent years are diamonds, silver, and oil. In each of these cases, as in many commodity situations, universal prices may be set in auctions through which only a very small percentage of a total commodity moves. Given the size of these markets, it requires vast resources to attempt such manipulations, and even then, things may not work out because of various protective regulations. Nevertheless, the ratio of auction to nonauction sales has made inflated auction bids profitable, at least in the short term, in secondary markets, and explains why market machinations of this sort occur primarily in commodity and other high-multiple auctions linked to secondary markets.

The use of personal aggrandizement, by contrast, is primarily limited to auctions of idiosyncratic items that are not subject to resale and whose price cannot be compared with those of similar items. Successful public relations efforts depend neither on the number of like items available nor the probability of future resale, but on the existence of a recognized professional group operating within and for a larger population. The key variable in these cases tends to be ongoing businesses dependent on a public and a professional network engaged in defining some market. Most collectible-dealer auctions exist within such a context. It doesn't matter whether the items are antiques, stamps, coins, or Oriental rugs. There exists a network of professionals who not only have the resources to control most auctions but also operate their own businesses, which benefit from any publicity they receive.

Of crucial importance in understanding the social dynamics of auctions is the fact that these personal motivations—aggrandizement, publicity, and control—generally serve to muddle the evaluation process by introducing secondary factors that can and do effect the price of the items auctioned. Ironically, rather than reflecting item-related uncertainties that the auction format serves to resolve, they are participant-related uncertainties that are generated, or at least made possible, by the auction itself.

Both groups of uncertainties, however, impact on the way the items in question are evaluated. They help determine what the item is worth and how much someone is willing to pay. Price, however, represents only one way to define an item. Objects may possess a significance quite distinct from, if related to, their economic worth. Provenance and ownership of items—past, present, and future—are often equally important defining characteristics as price. Like price, provenance and ownership may be difficult to determine, making certain items particularly suitable for auction.

Traditionally, people have assumed that auctions serve to resolve the questions of price and ownership simultaneously. Ownership is determined by who is willing to pay the highest price, while the price is determined by the highest bidder. In actuality, however, things are not this simple. Both provenance and the issue of future ownership may raise questions that—though they may affect the price—are quite distinct from those related to proper price. Current debates over the acceptability of various national treasures, be they Egyptian tomb ornaments or British paintings, being bought by foreigners are a case in point. They may also generate uncertainties that are not only unrelated to price but not resolvable through price determination alone. Disagreements between tobacco warehouse owners and company buyers over the number of bales to go to each can lead to such a situation. It is the allocating power of auctions, their capacity to assign items to one bidder rather than another, based on which of two similar bids the auctioneer saw first, which is significant here rather than their pricing capacity.

The importance of provenance and ownership underscores

the fact that objects are seldom if ever confronted in isolation. They are rather perceived as embedded in a complex social reality.[10] Central to this context is not only the history of ownership and origins of the items in question but the relationships between the people with an interest in the items. In this respect, items commonly auctioned are no different from items commonly exchanged through either a fixed-price or a private treaty system. Where they differ, as with the determination of economic values, is in the greater degree of uncertainty relating to ownership, manner of acquisition, or the character of owners.

In some cases, such uncertainties generate uncertainties of value. A Picasso offered for sale by a person of questionable character may be stolen or even a forgery. An antique chest with an unknown past may have undergone repairs that, if known, would dramatically change the piece's value. A truckload of fruit labeled California may actually be from Mexico and worth less. In each of these situations, the risk of misrepresentation and hence incorrect evaluation may vary from minimal to very great. Auctions provide a means for attempting to judge the degree of risk.

The provenance of an item may affect the price bid at auction even when it has no direct bearing on the item's perceived value. The issue may be more one of entitlement than worth. One of the best examples of this can be found in one of the earliest auctions, the booty auctions of ancient Rome. Returning soldiers would stand outside the gates of Rome and auction off their shares of the spoils of war. While most of the items offered for sale were everyday objects such as pots, clothing, and weapons of "known" value—similar goods were sold within the city for fairly stable prices—because of the way the goods had been acquired, there was considerable uncertainty regarding what the soldiers were entitled to. They had neither made nor bought the items. Even their right to the goods could be questioned. The auction process provided a mechanism for solving these questions by providing the public forum in which an acceptable price could not only be determined but the right of new ownership could be witnessed. Similar attitudes often color modern liquidation and foreclosure auctions. It is often as if those present at the auction were saying,

The tractor may be worth $10,000 but given the way it was obtained [foreclosed], we will pay no more than $7,000. In ac-

knowledgment of your acceptance of this fact, we will legitimate
your right to dispose of it. For conforming to our standards,
we also accept the buyer's right to it.

While price and provenance are perceived as separate issues
in the instances just discussed, they are clearly interrelated. Although price may not control the allocative process, it is used as
a supportive mechanism. Friends and neighbors, at a comparatively closed estate auction of a person they all knew, agree that
a particular item really should go to a particular close relative.
The bidding is orchestrated in such a way that others drop out
of the bidding as the intended recipient becomes more hesitant.
This may occur at a price significantly below the fair market price
for the item. There are times, however, when price is of practically
no help in resolving such allocative tasks. The two situations in
which this is most often the case are when the resources of buyers
are for all practical purposes unlimited or when prices are predetermined.

Situations in which there are multiple bidders with unlimited
resources who want the same item are situations about which
most auctioneers dream. There are times, however, when a free-
for-all between such bidders may prove counterproductive insofar
as it generates irrational prices that can have a negative effect
on a larger industry or lead to disruptive, hostile interpersonal
relationships. Such circumstances may arise at charity auctions
where the resources of the participants overshadow the value of
the goods being auctioned. They can also arise at a Keeneland
Select Yearling Sale or a Sotheby's Impressionist sale, with scores
of multimillionaires present to whom the difference of one, two,
or even five or ten million dollars may be of little importance.
Such situations could arise if there were a number of different
buyers on their own ego trips at the same time. The situations
being described here, however, are characterized not so much
by a desire for personal aggrandizement as by conflicting senses
of entitlement, coupled with a disparity between the value of
the items and the resources of the bidders, which makes reliance
on price as the sole determining criterion impractical.

A very similar situation can arise if a number of buyers feel
entitled to a given item whose price has, for all practical purposes,
been predetermined. This can occur when there exists a common
secondary market to which all bidders must eventually sell, or

there may simply be an established consensus among dealers so that at one price there is significantly greater demand than supply, whereas at a slightly higher price, supply would be much greater than demand. At a used jewelry auction, for example, it is quite common to observe half a dozen dealers indicate a willingness to buy a particular piece of jewelry at one bid, but not one who is willing to make a higher bid. Here it is a case of the dealers "knowing" what the wholesale values of the particular stones are. This is very common in wholesale auctions that are tied to retail secondary markets.

In such situations auctions are more a means of allocating than of pricing goods. The issue is who will be "allowed" to purchase the item, or, as may also be the case, who is expected to absorb the item. Uncertainty in these cases bears on the respective rights and responsibilities of the players more than on the value of the items. Auctions prove to be most adept at resolving these problems through the public give-and-take that is at the heart of every auction. The participants negotiate a consensus regarding these rights and responsibilities much as in other cases they negotiate a consensus on price. In some cases, much of such negotiation occurs outside of the auction proper and is confirmed formally in the auction. This is common with tobacco.

As noted earlier, tobacco auctions seldom set the price for tobacco. The price, or minimally a narrow price range, is set by the major tobacco companies, which in turn "inform" the various tobacco warehouse–auction firms what different grades of tobacco will be bringing this year.[11] There is little, in fact, which is not predetermined, from the number of bales that can be sold by any warehouse on a given day to the number of buyers. The number of piles, made up of approximately half a dozen bales, is determined by law, while each tobacco company is allowed one buyer. The tobacco companies employ a number of buyers, but each buyer is individually assigned to one of approximately five sets of buyers. These various sets of buyers travel with different auctioneers from Florida north during the tobacco auction season. A different set is assigned to a particular warehouse each day, with perhaps five sets working simultaneously.

With the exception of bidding over a mixed or bad bale, these conditions create a situation in which all buyers make basically the same bids. It is the auctioneer's prerogative to select from among these bids. This decision, in turn, is governed by the warehouse owner who also has personal relationships with the tobacco companies. Warehouse owners and tobacco companies do each other favors in providing different types of information. The warehouse can tell a company what the harvest looks like and what stock is on hand, and the company can tell the warehouse owner what supplies are low and what the price is apt to be. The warehouse owner also has special relationships with certain farmers.

In a given sale the warehouse owner will attempt to "balance the books" by ensuring that, in accordance with earlier agreements, certain percentages go to different companies and particular farmers get specific prices for their allotments. The warehouseman has to treat all farmers pretty much the same, but he still has some room to juggle a penny here and there for a particular set of bales for a major seller or one whom he owes a favor. It is not uncommon, therefore, for the warehouse owner to inform the auctioneer exactly what percentages are to go to Reynolds, what to American, and what to the other tobacco companies. The owner can control the price for individual farmers by setting the price on each bale. The price is sufficiently determined, in fact, so that the warehouse owner will step in and buy any tobacco that drops a few pennies below the set price. He may then turn around and ship it to the company which had promised him a certain support level. In doing so, he may have to absorb a penny or so loss on some bales to protect his position with a particular farmer.

Although an individual buyer can change things dramatically by offering a penny more a bale than the others are willing to bid, the percentages and prices are normally set before the auction, based on the rights that have been established through the preauction negotiations. The warehouseman and auctioneer are able to maintain such an allocation because the buyers' bids tend to be the same. This allows the auctioneer to allocate the piles in accordance with the warehouse owner's instructions. But it can be difficult to do if one buyer bids higher, since by the rules of the game he gets not only that pile but the next one if all bids are again the same. Since there is a gentleman's agreement that all will pay basically the same, such a bid increase generally occurs only if a buyer feels compelled to go for a larger proportion of a particular sale than what has been prearranged. The big question then becomes, How much more does he want?

The tradition of the auction works toward maintaining well-established allocations. If a buyer attempts to get only a little more than his share, he will generally be allowed to buy it. He'll be given a few extra piles for the extra penny. If he seeks more, however, the warehouseman is likely to up his asking price in order to ensure the prearranged allocation. If the asking price rises, it is then up to the buyers to go along or relinquish their shares. The latter is difficult to do, since they will have to increase their shares elsewhere, and that normally means paying more than the predetermined price. A company getting squeezed in one sale may then be forced to increase its bids in the next sale, thereby denying another company the percentage it expected from that warehouse, and so on. This process admittedly entails changing the price of tobacco, but the real issue being decided is who is getting what. This decision, in turn, is commonly decided more by established rights than by auction bids. While other bidders are likely to be tolerant of a buyer seeking slightly more than his share in a given auction, especially if he has been denied his expected share somewhere else, a buyer who attempts to change normal allotments in a significant manner will confront an organized response that will make such a test expensive.

Perceived allocative rights and responsibilities may generate a reverse situation. If buyers reduce their bids in an effort to cut back on their shares, the warehouseman may find it difficult to disburse the tobacco and maintain the prices promised to farmers. Here he may attempt simply to allocate the tobacco at the predetermined price. If he can't, he may buy the tobacco himself, which will usually serve to get the bid back to where it was meant to be. By buying the tobacco himself, the warehouseman lowers the supply and creates a situation in which, in order to obtain their expected quotas, the buyers are forced to increase their bids. The warehouseman may even ship the tobacco he bought to the companies with which he had "negotiated" preauction prices and charge them what he paid for the tobacco. Here again the issue tends to be more one of the rights and responsibilities of the different auction participants to specific quantities of tobacco than one of price.

TOBACCO auctions are not the only auctions in which allocation tends to be more important than price, and rights and responsibilities of participants more important than their financial resources. It is more often than not the case in most commodity auctions.

This does not mean that price is irrelevant. In fish auctions, for example, the buyers are not sufficiently organized to set prices, as in tobacco. On the other hand, competition and cooperation are so intertwined that whatever price is set that day becomes the price for all.[12] Moreover, in nearly all cases, whatever the price, buyers will be able to resell the fish. What is of central importance is that each buyer is able to acquire a sufficient quantity of fish to satisfy his regular customers. The allocative rights and responsibilities of each buyer are tied to his relative position in the industry. The major wholesalers are entitled to a larger share of fish when supplies are low; on the other hand, they are also expected to absorb fish when there is a surplus. It is this pattern of allocation rather than price that is central.

Sometimes the rights of buyers are equal, there is consensus over price, and there is a scarcity. In these situations the auctioneer may allocate goods in a random manner, converting the auction into a sort of quasi lottery. He may scan the bidders in a fairly systematic way, taking bids at specific intervals. Part of the brilliance of auctions, especially commodity auctions, is that they can function in this way but project an image of rationality and spontaneity that a lottery cannot. At the same time, they can avoid the appearance of arbitrariness that would result if allocation were left to certain assigned "wise men," or appraisers. The auctioneer doesn't have to explain why he gave the bid to one bidder rather than another. He can simply say he saw one bid first. Provided that he does not favor particular buyers, continues to act as if he is taking first bids at a given price, and maintains a demeanor of control, he is not likely to be questioned. Similar skills are necessary for the successful management of any auction.

The extent to which fish auctions turn on allocation rather than price is reflected in the types of comments one hears and deals one observes. Before the fish auctioneers even mention the opening price for a given species, they make a preliminary allocation of the catches of that species from the various boats unloading that day. This is usually accompanied by a good deal of chatter between auctioneer and buyers. Only when this is done is a price introduced, and then, though it is formally announced as the price of the catch or part of the catch of a single boat, everyone knows that the price also applies to all the other catches. As prices move up, it is not unusual for buyers who have been moved out of the bidding to look around the room to determine who is still in. If they see someone of lower status, they are likely to bid on that allotment. If there is no one they want to challenge, they are likely to search for a buyer who may be willing to share the lot they are bidding on. At the same time, a buyer who was willing to take 3,000 pounds of large cod at $1.10 may want to unload 1,000 of his 3,000 pounds when the price hits $1.25. The same objectives are sought by switching bids from larger to smaller allotments or vice versa. Most telling, however, is the reaction of the group when, in the middle of the bidding, one buyer makes a move for a much larger share of the overall catch.

A large catch of a particular species from a single boat will normally be broken up into smaller lots during the initial allocation. In offering such a catch, the auctioneer would normally announce "40,000 haddock, *Captain Joe*. All or part?" If a buyer indicated an interest in 20,000 pounds, the auctioneer might then add "I've got 20,000 left on *Captain Joe*. Does anyone want all or part?" Once allocated in this way into perhaps 20,000, 8,000, 5,000, 5,000, and 2,000 pound lots, the catch would normally continue to be sold in these parts, though the 20,000 lot may be broken up into two 10,000 lots as the price goes up. With each new bid in which a specific allotment would change hands, those with previous bids on other allotments will either nod agreement and maintain their lot or drop out and wait for someone else to take their old lot. If, however, a buyer calls for the entire catch at the asked-for bid, he will have priority over the others who will find themselves without an allotment.

Such a move is normally met with cries of foul play. "Hey, what's going on here?" "Whose bid is that? He can't do that." "Who's screwing around?" This may be followed by cries of, "Watch your language!" The culprit may then curse back or attempt to put down the others. Sometimes the whole process is just a bluffing game with the big bidder settling for a smaller allotment. Sometimes, however, he won't. The real competitive element in these auctions is this contest over allocation. What is at stake here is normally much more than the particular catch. It is the relative positions of the buyers. In most cases, such exchanges result in the maintenance of preexisting shares of the market.

In both the tobacco and fish examples given above, the reason that price plays a secondary role in comparison to allocation is that in both cases price is severely constrained by secondary markets, which set limits on price expectations. That is, there exists another market—the retail market—which is governed by quite specific price expectations. Given these limits and relatively similar costs in bringing the product from the auction floor to these secondary markets, the buyers are really not in position to outbid each other. If they go too high, they are likely to lose money because they can only buy so much and then the competition will undersell them.[13] If they bid too low, they will probably have too little for resale. This is the case whenever products must be moved directly into a secondary market, whether they are agricultural commodities, oil leases, precious metals, jewelry, or bonds.

There are instances, not subject to such financial constraints, in which assumed rights and responsibilities of auction participants yet dominate—namely, situations subject to patterns of interpersonal deference. In many instances such patterns reflect the belief or knowledge that a particular bidder is more committed and wants the item more. At other times, however, there is deference for the position or power of the opposing bidder rather than his financial clout. Bidders may drop out of an auction far below their limit on spotting, or even suspecting, an opposing bidder whom they hold in particular regard as the following two examples reveal:

> Two young men had elected to bid up to one hundred thousand dollars on a horse at a standardbred yearling auction at the Meadowlands. They owned a few horses between them, and they were eager to buy a particular filly. Shortly into the bidding, with one of the pair quite active and the price at fifty-five thousand dollars, he was elbowed by the other, who whispered something into his ear. He then stopped bidding. Shortly afterwards, the bidding ended with the horse having been sold for eighty thousand dollars. They had dropped out because a particularly well-regarded trainer who had been of some help to them years earlier was bidding against them. It was not a case of matching his bankroll. Nor was it fear of confrontation. Their horses had already run against each other on more than one occasion. It was out of deference to a respected member of their trade with whom they had had a special relationship that they elected not to bid against him for that particular horse.

> During an auction of rare books at Sotheby's, a well dressed middle-aged woman in the first row entered the bidding with

a bid of $16,000 just when it looked as if it was about to end
with a bid of $15,000. Within two bids there were no other
bids in the room, but a very aggressive telephone bidder remained. With the bid jumping rapidly by thousand-dollar increments, the woman leaned forward in her chair and, addressing
her remarks to the auction house employee on the phone, and
indirectly to the auctioneer himself, said: "Oh, I hope I am
not bidding against the university. I wouldn't want to do that.
Is it the university?"[14]

The auctioneer informed her that he could not say who
the telephone bidder was, but added with a smile that he was
sure that wherever the book ended up, it would have a good
home. The woman hesitated for a moment and made another
bid, which was quickly topped by the phone bidder. Again she
inquired as to the identity of the phone bidder. When the auctioneer said he could not tell her, she responded: "It must be
the university. I can't bid against the university."

The book was knocked down to the telephone bidder for
substantially less than the woman would ordinarily have been
willing to pay.

While the auctioneer would have preferred the woman to
stay in the bidding, he accepted her decision with grace, as all
professional auctioneers would have done. Since their earnings
tend to be directly related to the price at which items are sold,
auctioneers want to sell everything for as much as possible. They
know, however, that auctions entail much more than getting the
highest price or even determining ownership of goods. They also
establish the social identities of such goods. In fact, auctions commonly constitute rites of passage for the items that pass through
them, in which a new social identity is established for the item.
Such identities entail not only price but ownership and often
category-grading status.

The rites-of-passage nature of auctions helps shed light on
both the history of auctions and their recent dramatic increase.

Roman auctions of war booty are among the earliest recorded
instances of auctions. Earlier yet, however, is Herodotus's report
of wife auctions—auctions in which young women were sold to
the highest bidder as future mates, or if unwanted, taken with
the least dowry offered. What is fascinating about these two ancient
auctions is that in both cases a significant change in social identity
was entailed. In the case of war booty auctions, objects of questionable provenance were transformed from alien into native objects.
In wife auctions, social status and social relationships were dramati-

cally altered; a stranger might become a brother-in-law, while a daughter became the property and responsibility of someone else. It was specifically the need publicly to legitimate these changes in identity that made it preferable to hold such auctions rather than arrange marriages privately.

Though mates have not been formally auctioned for some time, the practice of negotiating dowries and bride-prices often constitutes a form of auction. In more modern marriages, this auction quality has disappeared, as has the associated exchange of significant moneys, but insofar as social identities are transformed, the public retains certain participatory rights, as evidenced by the familiar phrase "and if anyone knows reasons why this marriage should not proceed, let them speak now or forever hold their peace." The fact that auctions lend themselves to the process of acquiring mates, however, carries over to the charity bachelor auctions that have sprung up around the country, in which bachelors are auctioned off for an evening on the town with the proceeds going to charity.

Considerations similar to those operative in wife auctions explain the historical practice of exchanging slaves through auctions. The central concern was not establishing a fair price or even proper allocation, but establishing publicly their new social identity as slaves; in the resale of slaves, it was the change of ownership that had to be established publicly. This explains, in part, why slaves continued to be publicly auctioned even when such public exhibitions served to generate opposition to the institution of slavery. Slavery entailed specific social identities that could only be established publicly. If the process of establishing such an identity also entailed negotiating a price, the only practical solution was likely to be an auction.

In ancient times, most goods, in contrast to war booty and human beings, were not auctioned because they could be priced and allocated in accordance with established traditional criteria. That a greater range of goods is auctioned today and the number of auctions is increasing are due to the fact that traditional criteria no longer work as well. This, in turn, is due to disillusionment and lack of faith with traditional principles and criteria that characterize modern societies. New, improved forms of communication and transportation bring people who previously had little if anything to do with each other into contact. Old ways of doing business often prove inexpedient or unacceptable to the new players and expanded markets.

From real estate to publishing, horse-racing, art and antiques, and collectibles auctions, an influx of new people and new money has upset the old ways of doing business. Ambiguities that previously didn't exist have arisen, and professionals are no longer certain of the worth of products or how they should be allocated. Expanded markets, new groups of buyers and sellers—all have undermined the old practices and the old boy networks. Nowhere is this more apparent than at one of the major real estate auctions sponsored by Allsop in London, where Hasidic Jews wearing their traditional black hats and coats stand between pin-stripe-suited Englishmen from the City and Pakistani businessmen in traditional Karakule headgear. All are equally at ease bidding and using their portable telephones, but they speak very different languages. Some would claim that the Arab, Japanese, South American, English, French, Irish and ethnically mixed American assembly that constitutes a select thoroughbred or fine art auction nowadays is more than a match for these Allsop auctions.

Although these new players serve to break down the old communal walls and associated criteria that previously enabled goods to be priced and exchanged through some mix of fixed-price and private treaty, they definitely do not make such communities of interest irrelevant. Through the auction they represent the emergence of a new community. Indeed, the basic task confronting any auction is establishing a consensus on socially acceptable definitions and identities for otherwise ambiguous objects. Such a consensus requires a social context. Without such a context, there can be no auction.

Chapter 3

Creating and Maintaining Auction Communities

W HEN people participate in auctions they act not only as individuals intent on pursuing individual self-interests but, consciously or unconsciously, as part of a community. These auction communities have their own goals, the most important of which is achieving a consensus regarding the values and allocation of the goods bought and sold. The pursuit of this goal requires the production and reproduction of these very same communities. That is, the processes of determining the price and allocating objects are linked to other processes that serve to define and maintain the communities within which these processes occur. These latter practices include determining who can participate in the auction, managing the interpersonal relationships of participants, and regulating auction behavior. As most auctions require a community of some sort for their very existence, so the auction commonly serves as a means for maintaining such communities.

One of the best ways to understand a given auction is to determine its particular communal structure and the way it is reproduced and transformed. What groups exist? Who is linked to whom? How transitory are these relationships? What are the agreements, if any, among the different groups? When are such ties and agreements likely to become visible? What practices are used to support these relationships and agreements? And, finally for each question, why?

Auctions are not unique among pricing and exchange pro-

51

cesses in entailing such social structures; both fixed-price and private treaty transactional systems require them. In fact, they tend to be more embedded in established social routines than auctions; they tend to be more integrated with the established practices of everyday social life. Everyone knows—even if only tacitly—what is expected and the roles of the various participants. In most department stores, we can tell who are the customers and who are the salespeople, what is a dressing room and what a storage room, and what we are to do if we want to buy a particular item. This taken-for-granted awareness, however, serves to make the social aspects of these forms of transactions less problematic and consequently less salient. What gives auctions their intense social tone is the extent to which this communal character is being continually reproduced and modified. Auctions are special not because they are more social but rather because they are more actively focused on their social status.

The more problematic communal condition of auctions is due, in large measure, to the undercurrent of uncertainties and ambiguities that characterizes them. Unlike fixed-price situations, there do not exist clearly defined sets of shared expectations that serve to bind the participants together, even if they are unaware of them. In auctions, the participants often not only do not know what to expect of others but what to expect of themselves. Perhaps most important, they are uncertain of how the goods are to be valued and allocated. In auctions, uncertainty is the norm.

It is the sharing of uncertainties and ambiguities, however, rather than their mere existence that generates auctions. There must be certain commonly experienced or minimally linked objectives that foster a common concern in resolving the uncertainties surrounding the goods. If not, there is no reason for the communal effort of resolution which results in an auction.

It is the need continually to monitor and manage communal relationships and beliefs that distinguishes auctions from fixed-price systems and private treaty systems. In short, auctions exhibit a communal interest in their own fluctuating communal status rather than an established communal structure. Where both the management and customers of an established department store such as Macy's tend to endow the store with its own independent identity, a knowledgeable auctioneer looks on an auction as an unfolding process. Tom Caldwell, the head auctioneer at Keeneland, describes the Keeneland auction as a large family with generations passing on and new generations being born.

In fixed-price exchanges we are enmeshed within particular communities.[1] If one makes a purchase, for example, from an established sales outlet, specific rules govern the transaction. Things must be properly represented; there are certain rights of return or exchange; and goods normally come with some sort of guarantee or warranty. Accompanying these accepted rights and practices, which vary from community to community, there usually exists a wide range of less formal rules that govern transactions.

If, for example, a customer purchases a microwave oven from a local dealer and two days later sees the same oven for considerably less at another store, the local shopkeeper would probably be willing to make an adjustment in price if the customer firmly requested it. There is an implicit assumption on the parts both of the shopkeeper and customer that the price has been set in accordance with certain communal standards and that, as such, there exists a social bond, an agreement on fair price, between the parties that transcends the specific transaction. They are united by the normative order; that is, by the norms of the buyer-seller relationship inherent in the fixed-price economic system.

Despite the prevalence and importance of these social rules of a fair and competitive price and the implicit communities associated with them, we are generally unaware of both, accepting them as givens not subject to review or change.[2] There are, of course, differences in ritual and etiquette, depending upon the type of goods being offered. One can enter a very expensive boutique, for example, look at and try on a number of garments, but elect not to make a purchase because all the clothes one really likes are too expensive while those within one's price range are not sufficiently attractive. It would not normally be acceptable behavior, however, to enter an equally expensive restaurant, look over the menu and then leave because the items one wants are too expensive while those that were affordable did not titillate the palate. For this reason, many restaurants place menus in the window, so new customers can read the prices before they enter—thus maintaining restaurant etiquette. In nearly all fixed-price situations, we are constrained by a complex of such rules, which we accept without much thought or concern.

THE situation in private treaty transactions is quite different. In the course of most private treaty negotiations, we are generally highly conscious of the problematic nature of the rules and relationships of the transaction, as anyone who has negotiated the purchase of an automobile knows. We generally recognize that not only the price but also the rules are subject to modification. Determining exactly how and when a particular exchange will occur, in fact, is often as central to such negotiations as determining the price. It may even be necessary to negotiate what will actually be exchanged. In the case of an automobile purchase, it is not just the price of the automobile that is negotiated but what will actually be sold (that is, what make with what accessories), when it will be delivered, how it will be financed, and, last but not least, whether there will be a sale at all.

Each participant tends to have his or her own predetermined set of expectations, which he or she attempts to promote by structuring the negotiations in a certain way. If sufficiently shrewd, a prospective buyer will often bring his or her own supporters and attempt to pick the right time of day and even, if possible, the right weather. In the case of a used automobile, this may mean bringing a companion to complain about the color and upholstery, and a mechanic to express reservations about the engine, fairly late on a rainy Saturday afternoon when the salesman is tired and wants to go home, the boss would like to make an extra sale for the week, few other customers are around, and the cars are streaked with rain.

In a fixed-price exchange both the item for sale and the price are set. As such, they (or rather their determination) do not play a significant role in structuring the relationship between buyer and seller. The relationship, in fact, tends to be quite independent of the transaction itself, except insofar as it confirms previously established identities and expectations. This is not the case with private treaty transactions, where the relationship between the two parties tends to be tenuous and unstable. A neighbor entering into friendly negotiations over the sale of a secondhand lawnmower or bicycle may end a relationship as the result of a breakdown in negotiations. Similarly, another neighbor may find that such negotiations have generated a new relationship. The point is that such transitions have the potential to affect the relationship between buyer and seller.

Although private treaty transactions can and do mold the social relationships of the participants to a much greater degree than do fixed-price transactions, they tend to be most common on the edge of established communities. Admittedly, an encompassing social context must exist for there to be any type of negotiation, but here the parties are often in transient and temporary roles, such as that of a tourist at a flea market in a foreign city. Whatever the case, the actual transactions and the associated social modifications tend to have little if any impact on the encompassing social structures. The normal routines of the flea-market vendor and the tourist are unaffected by what transpires. The transaction may serve to transform the "social distance" between participants, but whatever realignment of relationships may occur nearly always occurs as an unexpected by-product of the transaction rather than an intended and necessary component of the process. Whatever decisions are made tend to have little repercussion on larger normative orders. This is true not only of the tourist at the foreign flea market but of the relationship between buyer and seller in a private sale of a used automobile, and buyer and seller in house transactions.

In the case of a house sale, for example, buyer and seller are likely to have had no previous relationship with each other nor are they likely to maintain a relationship once the transaction is completed. They are likely to be aware of specific expectations that apply to the roles in which they find themselves, such as the need to provide copies of various documents, bank references, names of lawyers, and courtesies related to house inspections, but they are unlikely to have any sense of permanent responsibility toward the temporary roles in which they find themselves. They are interested in appropriately applying the various rules and meanings normally applied to house buying and selling, but they have little vested interest in the rules per se—as would, for example, a realtor who lives by such rules daily. Though both buyer and seller are likely to share certain communal expectations and values that pertain to the transaction, neither these expectations nor the interpersonal relationships associated with the transaction are likely to have any long-term social consequences for buyer or seller.

The limited social character of private treaty transactions is reflected in the fact that they are limited not only to the participants but to the specific exchange. In a fixed-price exchange, a transaction tends to have a publicly recognized status. It is normally not only possible to return goods later but to do so even if the actual salesperson is not present. With most private treaty transactions, once they have been completed they are over. It is very difficult to return an item and expect to renegotiate a transaction based on new information or changing circumstances.

Thus, most fixed-price exchanges are subject to the normative order of an established community, but they seldom modify the expectations or the patterns of established buyer-seller relationships within these communities.[3] Private treaty transactions, in contrast, have the potential to affect significantly both the social relationships and governing definitions of the specific situation, as in the purchase of a house. But these relationships and definitions are likely to be seen as temporary and therefore peripheral to the community or communities involved.

What is peculiar about auctions is that the rules and practices bearing on the transactions are generally seen as having broad significance for the community, and open to manipulation and management. One of the primary tasks of any auction, in fact, is to manage the malleable process of defining the situation, the social relationships, and the pervasive sense of community in a way that is significant to the community as a whole. Such management may entail increasing the sense of community by decreasing the sense of social distance among the participants, as when auctioneers address participants individually, tell jokes and personal stories, and introduce their assistants in familiar terms; it may also entail decreasing the sense of community by increasing social distance among participants, as when bidders are referred to by number, and absentee and phone bids are accepted. In both cases, the need to manage social distance is generally tied to tensions generated by the conflicting cooperative and competitive interests of the participants. This requires that the relationships among the participants be orchestrated simultaneously with the orchestration of the selling price. To a great extent the appropriate script is built into each type of auction, but there is always the need for a skilled auctioneer to direct the production. The primary objective in all cases is creating and maintaining a sense of community capable of generating a socially accepted definition of the situation—that is, a community capable of pricing and allocating the items.

Neither in fixed-price nor private treaty systems is there ambiguity regarding a shared normative order. In fixed-price systems there are shared standards of value, price, ownership, and reciprocity and an implicit sense of an encompassing community of merchants and customers that leaves little room for ambiguity; whereas in private treaty situations, there are differences of opinion and perspective that result in little sense of an encompassing community or of a relevant shared normative order. It is specifically ambiguity regarding a shared and pertinent normative order, which characterizes auctions and which consequently makes the establishment of "community" problematic.

Auctions are both different from and similar to fixed-price systems and private treaty systems in other ways. They are clearly like private treaty systems insofar as price is "negotiable." Moreover, in auctions as in private treaty transactions, social relationships are quite explicitly subject to change. Auctions tend to be much more like fixed-price systems of transaction than private treaty transactions, however, when it comes to assumptions regarding the completion of the transaction. In auctions as in fixed-price systems, it is normally assumed not only that there will be a transaction but that it will be a public one.

Fixed-price systems are public in that all buyers normally assume that they have a right to the same item at the same fixed price. If you hear that a friend just bought an item at a particular department store for a given price, you assume that you could buy the same item for the same price. This is not the case in private treaty transactions. The fact that a friend bought a given item at a flea market for a particular price this morning does not guarantee that you will be able to do so this afternoon, or that you will even be able to find the item or the person who sold it.

Despite their similarity to private treaty transactions when it comes to the indeterminacy of price, auctions exhibit a public character similar to that of fixed-price transactions. Auction transactions are not limited to one buyer and one seller, which is the norm in private treaty transactions; in auctions, by definition, there are always other potential buyers, and sometimes other sellers, who have the right to participate in the negotiation process. Buyers and sellers often tend to take the role of the other in auctions, making their roles more complex than similar roles in private treaty and fixed-price systems. This is due to the peculiar competitive-cooperative tensions among participants in an auction. (This contingent quality of auction communities gives rise to the impression that such communities do not exist.) It is, in fact, often not clear on an auction floor who is cooperating and who is in competition with whom. Relationships are apt to be very fluid, with participants literally and figuratively switching roles throughout the auction. Professional identities of varying sorts—antique clock dealer, fish wholesaler, horse trainer, or stamp collector—often take precedent over an individual's momentary status as buyer or seller of a particular item.

Not surprisingly, the particular social structure of any auction is related to the types of items being auctioned. Different types of items entail different types of uncertainties, each favoring different types of social structures for their resolution. More specifically, art and one-of-a-kind items tend to be auctioned in "sale" auctions, collectibles in "dealer" auctions, and commodities in "exchange" auctions. Although these types merge into each other, they capture many of the distinctions that characterize the ways in which buyers and sellers are interrelated.

Commodity-exchange auctions are the most closed in terms of participants. In most cases, by definition you must belong to a particular exchange if you want to bid in the auction. This is true not only for major bond and stock auctions, but most fish, cattle, and other types of commodities auctions.[4] There is normally an initiation fee of some sort and an annual membership fee. In many cases it is also necessary that you be approved by the board of the particular exchange.

Restrictions tend to be somewhat less severe on the sellers in such "exchange" auctions. They often only need have exchange rights of one sort or another. More often than not, however, sellers are themselves "regulars." In most commodity situations there are many more sellers bringing their goods to market then there are buyers. The buyers tend to be at the auction day in and day out, whereas the sellers come when they have produce to sell. Not surprisingly, the buyers tend to control these types of auctions. The rules are their rules, the auctioneer is their auctioneer, and more often than not, the physical plant is their plant.

It is not just membership and rules, however, which hold the participants together. They see each other almost every day. They know each other's families. In the case of most agricultural and marine commodities, membership in a particular exchange may be multigenerational. On a typical morning at the New England Fish Exchange, for example, one will hear members asking each other about relatives: "Where's your dad? I haven't seen him. Is he down in Florida?" "Your wife still have the flu?" Others can be heard discussing past or planned vacations. There will also be a fair amount of ribbing and joking, which assumes shared knowledge of individual preferences and prejudices bearing on sports, politics, and past behaviors.

When the auction proper begins, most of the more personal small talk ends though the ribbing and joking, especially ribbing and joking which relates to the auction itself, is likely to continue. A number of the buyers seem to be more interested in the telephone conversations they are having with partners and bosses at their own places of business. From comments made by buyers and auctioneers, however, it becomes clear that these men not only know about each other's families and vacation plans, but also a good deal about their businesses and the fish in which each is likely to be interested. Specific people are questioned about specific lots, and specific people are pressured to take specific lots.

Although prices do vary from day to day, price itself seldom seems to generate much excitement. The buyers are all professionals and no one is either going to steal an allotment or overpay. In fact, as indicated earlier, the various lots of each species will be sold for either the exact same price or prices very close to each other.[5] The issue is rather who will get what. It is here that the competitive-cooperative tensions are most revealed, with buyers forming continually fluctuating alliances to ensure that no single buyer gets too much of a given species at too good a price.

As one might expect, this constant seesawing between buyers creates a fair degree of tension. Some of these tensions are worked out through humor. Some of it, however, is expressed in more hostile form. This, in turn, generates a continuing though intermittent series of comments intended to keep matters under control. Depending on how heated the particular auction, one can expect to hear anywhere between twice and a dozen times each morning, "Hey, watch your language, there's a lady present." The prohibition against swearing is, in fact, covered by one of the dozen rules posted on the wall on blue ditto sheets. (These rules cover such things as auction times, rights of withdrawal of fish, and proper behavior within the auction.)

While the number of formal rules governing the New England Fish Exchange are few in number, the informal rules are quite numerous. Day-to-day operations are embedded in a fairly complex ritual covering everything from the size of increments asked for and accepted and the types of pooling that go on to the amount of time allowed for each sale. Given the type of games played among the various buyers, it is not surprising that the issue of time has created the most difficulties. This has proved to be a bigger problem for the Boston exchange, which sells each species separately, and has led to the introduction of a clock. Initially, five minutes were allowed per species, but this has recently been reduced to four. New Bedford still uses a twenty-two-minute clock for everything.

In the New Bedford Exchange, which is both the largest auction and, primarily because of labor problems and some violence during the last few years, the most closed, catches are sold by boat under very tight time constraints. An entire auction of over three hundred thousand pounds of fish from a dozen boats will normally be sold in less than a half hour. The fact that catches are sold by boat, however, under a fairly complex system of bidding, often makes it difficult to know the true price for any given species. More specifically, in New Bedford the buyer with the total highest bid for the total catch of a particular boat gets the entire boat. This allows a buyer to bid up a particular species above its market price in order to have the highest total bid. In order to get a large catch of yellowtails, a buyer may bid high for the small catch of cod on the same boat. He is increasing his total bid in an attempt to acquire the yellowtails, but formally he has increased his bid on the cod, not the yellowtails. As a result, New Bedford's quoted prices often appear quite irrational. Cod on one boat sells for a dollar a pound while it sells for two dollars a pound on another. The extra dollar on the second boat, however, was really for the yellowtail.[6] As a result, Boston prices tend to be quoted as the daily price even though considerably more fish are sold through New Bedford.[7]

While the intimacy of the New England Fish Exchange is characteristic of commodity-exchange auctions constituted by a set of regular buyers, it is perhaps more intense than the intimacy of most exchange auctions, given its relatively small size, the highly exclusive character of membership, and the fact that most members have belonged to the exchange for years. In addition, the auctioneers are employees of the exchange and closely tied to the exchange, although they are actually paid by the fishermen. Exchange auctions vary in all of these respects. In some auctions, all buyers must formally belong to the exchange (most fish exchanges), whereas in other cases (most live cattle and small-scale livestock auctions), a formal exchange may not exist. Some exchanges are limited to a few dozen members, whereas others may have hundreds. Others, including most stock and futures exchanges, not only have numerous members but allow nonmembers to trade for themselves through the members. In some cases the auctioneer works for the exchange though sellers actually pay for the service (fish), at other times he is an independent entrepreneur, and in some cases he may be more closely tied to the sellers (tobacco). Some fishermen, ranchers, and farmers regularly attend the auctions of their goods and may even participate in the process by bidding or scratching (withdrawing) their goods, while others hardly ever attend.

What gives these auctions their distinctive character, however, is the core community of regular professional buyers who continually monitor each other to ensure that no one has access to some private supply, is making separate deals, is paying too much, or is receiving kickbacks of some sort. It is these buyers who either formally or informally constitute the "exchange" that is at the center of most commodity auctions and that gives them a strong sense of community awareness and interaction.

Nowhere is the sense of professional togetherness stronger than in tobacco auctions. During the tobacco auction season, which normally runs from July till the end of the year, buyers and auctioneers literally live together. Moreover, the same auctioneers generally work the same warehouses in each community—in each town there are likely to be a half-dozen auctioneers working simultaneously in a half-dozen different warehouses—and each warehouseman, also referred to as the lead man, in a given town will also own a warehouse in a number of other communities. As a consequence, while the auction of a particular warehouse may only run a few weeks a year, the participants tend to have much more extended relationships with each other. They know each other very well. It is also quite common for special relationships between specific tobacco companies and specific warehousemen to exist, based on the ongoing exchange of information and allocation preferences discussed earlier. Most of these special relationships are common knowledge among the regulars.

In most commodity auctions, when people discuss the market they are often not discussing the auction but rather the secondary market for which the items being auctioned are destined.[8] Most commodity auctions cover just the first of a series of transactions through which the goods will be sold. In fish and flower auctions, for example, discussion about the market normally refers to post-auction transactions between wholesalers and retailers. The latter transactions are commonly some combination of fixed-price and private treaty transactions. It is specifically these secondary markets that generate the collective constraints characteristic of commodity auctions, by setting the outside limits for which the goods being auctioned can be resold. Within these limits some fluctuation doesn't matter provided everyone else is paying the same thing. This explains why it is nearly always the case that commodities that are sold in numerous multiple units, such as specific grades of fish, cattle, oil, and even bonds, are sold on a given day for a single price. It is not the invisible hand of the market at work, but the quite manifest power of a collectivity imposing its will on its members. Each individual does not come to the same conclusion based on self-interest, but rather the shared conclusion is determined collectively.[9] This is not to suggest that individual buyers cannot affect the outcome of an auction in a given situation, but only to note that they do so by influencing the *collective* judgment. What one individual does is normally of little consequence unless such actions affect how others perceive the situation and alter their behaviors.

Given the apparent power of the buyers in such auctions, one may question why sellers agree to participate. The answer is that in many cases the sellers have little choice and, in others, the auction is better than the private treaty or fixed-price alternatives. When it comes to commodities, especially those that are perishable and require processing, the individual producer is generally at a bargaining disadvantage as compared to the commercial buyer. Under these conditions, the producers must either take the offer that is made or leave with empty hands. The auction format, though generally intended as a means for buyers to keep a check on each other, benefits producers or sellers by ensuring that a buyer is not allowed to "steal" a particular crop. The simplest way this is done is by the other buyers bidding the price up. Buyers, however, have other powers over each other, since their relationships are not limited to the auction. They commonly have business relationships that entail the informal sharing and exchange of both information and material goods. If a particular buyer refuses to cooperate in the auction, he or she is likely to discover that the other wholesalers or processors—depending on the type of auction—won't cooperate in ways essential for him or her to stay in business.

The auction format often benefits producers additionally by giving them a "champion," namely the auctioneer. Given that auctioneers are usually paid a percentage of the sales price, they have a vested interest in selling at as high a price as possible. The auctioneer also has more power than an individual producer by having access to the produce of numerous sellers and being in a position to affect the ways this produce is allocated. On the other hand, the auctioneer's success depends on the ability to convince producers to dispose of their goods through his auction rather than some other way. To some extent, this can be done by developing a reputation as an auctioneer who can't be pushed around by buyers. More often than not, however, producers realize that the buyers generally control the price.[10] Hence, what they look for in an auctioneer are the types of courtesies that we look for in our local merchants. As one tobacco warehouseman said:

> They [the farmers] come in here with a $50,000 crop, but if I don't give them the free bottle of whiskey or moonshine they get all upset. And I have to remember what they want—whiskey or moonshine. You have to go out of your way to let them know that you care about them and that they're special.

Obviously, the corporate CEO bringing a major bond offering to market differs in many respects from the captain of the fishing boat coming into port with 85,000 pounds of fish. Similarly, the "uniforms" worn by the fish buyers, the cattle buyers, the bond buyers, and flower buyers differ, as do the languages, information sheets, and rituals of each group. While the specifics vary, however, the general patterns are remarkably similar. In nearly all cases, value uncertainty is grounded in external variables—which tend to effect supply and demand—over which neither buyers nor sellers have much control. While buyers generally have a good deal of freedom to pay what they want—they are normally in a position to get the price they need on resale—they cannot afford to deviate much from other buyers. It is, consequently, the competition among the buyers themselves that is critical and that the exchange format is meant to control. In short, for both buyer and seller, the commodity-exchange auctions offer an opportunity to minimize significant loses, even if it entails forfeiting the possibility of major gains; it serves to reduce the risk element for all.[11] It offers each the necessary goods—for example, fish for the buyers, money to fish again for the seller—to continue in business if not to strike it rich.

Although most commodity-exchange auctions entail the type of competition among buyers just described, there are times when buyers seem quite oblivious to each other. One clear case of this would seem to be the stock market—which is technically a double auction; that is, it accommodates both multiple bids and offers simultaneously, where participants are on the whole unaware of each other. Here, however, we have a case where the exception seems to prove the rule.

That most stock market participants are indifferent to their fellow participants is closely tied to the fact that they experience value uncertainty as unrelated to the activities of other buyers and sellers. Because the stock market is ongoing, there is relatively little ambiguity regarding the value of a particular stock at any given moment. There may be a good deal of uncertainty regarding its future value, but given the liquidity of most stocks, its value— by which we mean here what it would sell for—in the immediate future is likely to be very close to what it is at present. Past prices normally set—within certain limits—future prices. As a result, participants tend to be less concerned with what other buyers or sellers may be doing at any particular moment. (This process is examined in detail in chapter 7.)

This lack of uncertainty gives the stock market more the tone of a fixed-price market than an auction at any given moment. Buyers and sellers "know" within a few pennies what they can buy or sell a particular stock for at that moment. In a "real auction," you don't know what you will have to pay or what you will get until the auction is over. This lack of uncertainty also serves to minimize the importance of community since there is no need for the community to resolve the uncertainty. In most auctions buyers are interested in seeing who is present and who is active; in the stock market, it is generally enough to know what is the present price of the stock in which you are interested. Admittedly, Wall Street professionals can be considered, and often consider themselves, to constitute a community of some sort; they also take an interest in what other professionals are buying and selling. But they constitute more a professional-occupational community with various shared interests than a self-regulating normative community. Stock market professionals tend to see themselves as operating on their own, unconstrained by the opinions of others to a much greater degree than the participants in other types of auctions.[12] In fact, it is not accidental that it is called the stock market rather than the stock auction.

In point of fact, many buys and sells on the stock exchange do not even take an auction form. Rather than making a bid or an offer at a given price, many stock market orders are "market" orders, which means that the price is determined by the last price, modified by the specialist responding to supply and demand at that moment. Most market purchases and sales are not based on matching bids at a price with offers at a price, but rather merely matching "market bids" and "market offers." In these cases, the sequence in which orders come in coupled with the size of the orders determines the priority of buys and sells, not price per se.

The communal character of commodity-exchange auctions is closely related to the need participants have to position themselves properly vis-à-vis the secondary markets such as retail stores in which the items bought at auction will be resold. In most collectible and art/one-of-a-kind auctions, however, there may not be any immediate resale. The items auctioned may be directly "put to use" in order to produce a profit rather than being resold for profit, or they may be purchased for personal reasons. Two good examples of such auctions are racehorse auctions and auctions of subsidiary rights to a literary work. In both cases the objective is to use the item purchased to make a profit, whether it be winning races, acquiring a potential stallion, selling millions of paperback copies of the original book, or making a successful movie. Works of art and many collectibles are examples of items bought primarily for personal appreciation, even though their investment potential may be a significant secondary consideration.

The fact that an established secondary market does not exist for these goods obviously changes the relationships between and among buyers and sellers. Buyers don't feel constrained to agree on a price and to obligate each other to it. Rather, there is likely to be only one successful buyer for a given item, with each competing buyer attempting to maximize his or her own interests. Yet even these auctions are pervaded by a sense of community; it serves not to ensure that all accept a common price as in commodity-exchange auctions but rather to ensure that everyone has the same opportunity to compete for the item. The community in collectible and art/one-of-a-kind auctions uses the auction process to open up the transaction to all those who want to participate, whereas in commodity-exchange auctions, the goal is to ensure a degree of conformity from all the buyers.

The need to assure equal access to the item being auctioned is most important in auctions in which there is likely to be only one item of a particular kind. There is no way to divide up items in a manner that will ensure that the risks and rewards are evenly distributed. Since this is impossible, the next best thing is to ensure that all members of the community have an equal chance to purchase each item. The stronger the sense of community, the stronger the sense of individual entitlement. Such feelings clearly characterize the thoroughbred and publishing communities.

Both subsidiary rights and racehorse auctions are similar to commodity auctions in that there is considerable uncertainty regarding the value of the items in question. The range of values covered by the uncertainty, however, tends to be greater than in commodity auctions, creating situations in which the potential for large profits and losses is extremely high. They differ in that there is normally only one of each kind of item offered. Yet many may feel entitled to ownership by virtue of the fact that they perceive the horse or the rights as being offered to a particular community and themselves as members of that community. Their sense of entitlement grows out of their sense of membership in the particular community. Given that there is just one item to be sold, and that there is no way of predetermining a "fair" price, everyone is likely to feel unfairly treated if the item is sold privately. It is the combination of uncertainty and of the communal right to bid that favors the auction format for such goods.

The sense of entitlement—the right to bid on an item—is characteristic of many, if not most, auctions. In auctions with a smaller sense of communal coherence and constraint, it relates primarily to achieving a fair price. It also clearly reflects a sense of privilege based on membership in the group, be it a formal group such as the New Bedford Fish Exchange or a less formal association of dealers and collectors. This sense of entitlement is often sufficiently strong to make auctioneers refuse very attractive preauction bids for items. As a senior Sotheby's director commented:

> If I sold a major lot to a private buyer before an auction, especially
> an advertised auction, I would make too many enemies. If I

get a particular good offer on an item here or there, I can normally get away with it, but not anything major. I once received an entirety bid—a single bid for everything—on a large estate. It was a very attractive bid. I had to turn it down. On the other hand, I have on occasion personally told potential consignors to take such offers when they have been made directly to them rather than put their things up for auction. If they do it, it is one thing. If I did it, even though legally I could, I would be in trouble with my regular buyers.

Similar sentiments have been expressed by auctioneers of almost every thing from used machinery to rabbits. All participants in an auction depend on a basic adherence to practices and courtesies which are collectively upheld.

It is important to note that in all of the cases so far noted, the auction communities are part of larger enterprises within which most of the auction participants have other parts to play. This is clearly the case with exchange auctions and the one-of-a-kind auctions discussed, in which auction participants are commonly related in a number of projects unrelated to the auction, such as sharing trainers, warehouse space, customers, and suppliers. In all cases, there tends to be a high degree of social interaction quite separate from that associated with the actual auction. In some cases, especially those dealing with collectibles, there are usually a number of in-group publications and a great deal of quite specific, shared community knowledge that helps give a member a strong feeling of belonging to a distinct community. There is seldom any question of whether an individual belongs or not, for language, knowledge, and interests will reveal his or her participation in the community.[13]

At a thoroughbred horse auction, especially a select yearling auction, one is immediately struck by the style of dress of the participants. Although there are a number of exceptions, the standard Lexington attire for men is khaki pants; a solid-color, preferably blue, sport or polo shirt; and loafers. Most women dress equivalently in blouse and skirt or pants. Such dress is neither accidental nor due to external factors. It is quite self-conscious. If asked, participants will tell a visitor how to dress. Even people only tangentially related to the auctions know the dress code, as revealed by a recent bank advertisement in a Lexington newspaper. The ad featured a young man in khaki pants, blue polo shirt, and loafers standing by some stables with the caption: "The first thing an equine Banker learns is how to dress for success."[14]

Group identity is also preserved in the way all the participants carry their catalogs and wear the special pen around the neck or stuck into a shirt pocket. The catalogs themselves further attest to the community character of the auction. Filled with different kinds of codes and types, they are unintelligible to anyone who is not a regular.[15] They assume the participants' special knowledge of the bloodlines and family trees of the horses for sale, a knowledge shared by all involved and providing a firm basis for their community.

It might appear that specialized knowledge is essential if one hopes to make a rational bid on any of the horses for sale. In point of fact, however, it is often of tangential practical use since the knowledge required tends to become so specialized, as the ability to tell the difference between individual animals with exactly the same bloodlines, that it is relatively rare. Even for those possessing such knowledge, buying a yearling racehorse is an immense gamble. For most, consequently, their knowledge is not instrumental in helping them to select a winning horse; it may even lead them to overpay for a horse with bad knees because it has good bloodlines. Knowledge is rather expressive and serves to link them to the community.

Though thoroughbred horse auctions probably embody and project a sense of community as much, if not more, than most types of auctions, they clearly are not unique. If they differ in any major way from most other auctions, it is that they combine the openness of access associated with art and antique auctions with the closed communal character of most exchange auctions. Like most art, antique, collectibles, and country auctions, horse auctions do not require that you be a member of an official exchange. On the other hand, it is necessary that you have established credit; at the select auctions, it is also necessary to reserve seats ahead of time. Only regular buyers, or persons highly recommended by a regular, are given such reserved seats. The likelihood of someone completely unknown to the "fraternity" just dropping by and being willing or able to spend a hundred thousand dollars or even thirty thousand dollars on a horse is slight at best.[16]

The ability to participate in other select auctions, whether the items be paintings, antique furniture, or rare collectibles of one sort or another, is often highly restricted due to the necessary resources required. As a result, most of these auctions are similarly characterized by strong and visible in-groups even though they are formally open to all. Given, however, that most art, antique, and collectible auctions allow major bidders both to leave bids and to bid by phone, the sense of community tends to be less than is found in most horse auctions. At horse auctions, the buyers are in the immediate area, and the sellers themselves constitute a more structured and coherent community.

Though the less-expensive art, antique, collectible, and country auctions tend to be more open, even they are seldom random collections of individuals. In nearly all cases, there can be found a subset of core members made up primarily of dealers and collectors who know each other and each other's tastes. They may not dress quite as uniformly as horse people, but they speak their own in-group language. They also frequently attend the same round of auctions. In fact, most of the regulars maintain a standing paddle number at each auction house, even maintaining the same number at different houses. As important as are the uniformities of jargon, dress and practice, the single most important factor which accounts for their sense of community is their shared view of the worth and value of the goods they pursue. This shared view, which is constantly evolving, is grounded and reinforced not only in the auctions, but in the various periodicals which service the different auction markets and which the regulars all read.[17] These publications not only advertise upcoming sales and review past ones but also provide background stories on collectors, dealers, and specific types of items from duck decoys to quilts.

The fact that these communities are embedded in larger, less organized groups creates its own communal tensions. Where the primary objective of closed exchanges is to insure that no one gets too far out of line with the rest of the group, and the primary objective in one-of-a-kind auctions is to insure a fair chance for all, the primary objective of the dealers and collectors is often to differentiate themselves from the nonprofessional auction participants. This entails maintaining their own special relationships among themselves and mutually reinforcing their joint status as experts.

To begin with, professionals try to ensure that they are recognized by the auctioneer as professionals. Using the same paddle week in and week out is one way of doing this. In a crowded room, the auctioneer may not always be able to see the face of who is bidding, but he or she will know the number. The professionals will work just as hard to go unrecognized by the amateurs present.[18] To achieve this end, the professional needs, expects, and normally gets the cooperation of the other professionals present, who have similar needs. Such cooperation often amounts to little more than being publicly indifferent to each other, which insures that nonprofessional buyers will not spot them as dealers and thereby attempt to buy what they bid on.

Other actions that dealers can and do take tend to be more disturbing to both sellers and auctioneers; professional buyers may enter into collusive practices of their own, known as "pools" and "rings." In such cases, in order to buy a particular item at the lowest possible price, a group of professional buyers agree not to bid against each other. They rather select one of their members to bid against any nonpool-members and then hold their own private auction later. These private auctions are called knockout auctions. They can, however, take different forms depending on the character of the group.

The round-robin knockout is the most common of these private dealer auctions. Oral bids are made in sequence, with each new bidder required to enter a higher bid if he wants to remain in the competition. This bidding pattern continues with bidding going around and around until someone wins. The difference between the price paid for the object in the first auction by the representative of the ring and the final price received in the knockout auction is then divided up among the pool members. A rug that was bought by the ring for $1,200 and sold in the round-robin auction for $2,000 would net a difference of $800. If there were five dealers in the pool, each would get $160. The rug would therefore cost the dealer who bought it in the round-robin auction $1,840 ($2,000 minus his share of $160) and the other ring members would make a profit of $160.

In the more complicated "English knockout," each member of the ring is allowed to make a single bid that is submitted in writing without the others seeing it. All the bids are then opened and the highest bid wins; the way the difference between the price paid in the first auction and this high bid is divided, however, is much more complex. The lowest bidder drops out first, receiving the difference between the price paid for the item in the first auction and his low bid, divided by the number of pool members still in, which in the case of the lowest bidder would be all the members. The next highest bidder is paid off in a similar manner, with the cost being adjusted to make up for the money paid to pool members who have dropped out, until only the highest bidder is left.

If, for example, a pool of five members bought an item for $100 and then submitted the following bids: A bid $200; B and C both bid $250; D bid $300; and F bid $600, the split would be as follows: A would get $20, which is one-fifth of $100 which is the difference between what the pool bought the item for and what A bid. B and C would each get $32.50, which is one quarter of the difference between $120.00, the new cost of the item— $100 plus the $20 paid to A—and their bid of $250 ($250 minus $120 divided by four). D would get $57.50, which is one-half of the difference between the new cost, which is $185 ($100 plus $20 plus $32.50 plus $32.50), and his bid. The total cost to E, consequently, would be $242.50 though he had bid $600. If a round-robin had been used, A, B, C, and D would have each gotten $100, which is one-fifth of the difference between the cost of $100 and the high bid of $600, and it would have cost E $500 for the item.

Clearly the round-robin auction is the simpler of the two. The prevalent use of the English knockout highlights the communal tensions that surround most rings. If there is a high degree of mutuality and trust among the members of the ring, the participants will normally elect to utilize a simple round-robin knockout in their private auction. There are times, however, when such mutuality and trust do not exist. Some members of the ring may feel that others have joined in just to get a piece of the action rather than out of mutual self-interest. In these cases, they will opt for the English knockout, which serves to limit the profits that a free rider might hope to get.[19]

Rivaling the English knockout in its complexity is a system generally attributed to the economist William Vickrey, in which, in a sealed bid auction, the highest bidder wins, but at the price bid by the next highest bidder.[20] This system may sound unnecessarily complicated, but there are mathematical reasons, given certain logical assumptions, for believing that such a format results in higher bids than the straight sealed-bid format if all bidders act rationally. The idea is that everyone will be willing to bid all the way up to their limit in an attempt to win while maintaining the hope that they won't have to pay more than the next person was willing to pay. People will bid higher in order not to lose an item, and there remains the possibility that they won't have to pay as much as they bid.

I might be willing to pay $100 for an item but be hesitant to make such a bid if I think that no one else is likely to bid more than $60. In such a situation I may only bid $70. On the other hand, if I know that I won't have to pay more than the second bid—if my assumption is correct, that would be $60 in this case— I might be willing to enter a bid of $100 to ensure that I win. If there are a number of people thinking the same way, this system may generate a number of high bids that more accurately indicate the value of the object to the bidders.

What is of particular interest here is that this format, though mathematically well supported, is practically never used. The reason normally given is that it is too complex. Yet the more complex English knockout system flourishes. The true reason for its disuse might well be that the aim of this system is to maximize bids, whereas the purpose of the English knockout and other systems used in real auctions is to ensure fairness to all participants.

The extent to which any and all of the procedures and techniques discussed in this chapter are used varies from auction to auction or, more correctly, from type of community to type of community. Sometimes the major aim of auction practice is to ensure that no one oversteps community-sanctioned behavior. At other times the problem is to ensure that no one in the community is unfairly denied access. And, at other times, the problem is to assure the rights of the community against outsiders. There are times when all three motives operate, as is the case with most liquidation-forced auctions such as farm foreclosures and estate sales.

In most such auctions there tends to be a community of friends or family who feel that they have a right to bid on the items in question. One elderly farmer remarked that in many ways he would have been just as happy to sell off most of his things privately, but he knew if he did that a lot of his old friends would be upset with him.[21] Any business or household is part of a larger community and when, for one reason or another, it is liquidated, there will be members of that community who feel that they have a right to participate in the determination of its remains.

In addition, there is likely to be a community of fellow professionals—be they other farmers, machine die operators, gun collectors, or carpet wholesalers. For them, the issue is to ensure that none of their fellow professionals "steals" anything that will afford them an unfair advantage. The function of these professionals is to reabsorb the items being auctioned in such a way as to cause the least disruption in their ongoing enterprises. Finally both groups—family and friends, and professionals—attempt to limit the input of participants outside their communities to ensure that the dissolution entailed in the auction causes the least harm to their respective interests. The auctioneer, however, will often attempt to include such outsiders, since they are often the persons willing to pay the most for specific items that they fancy.

There are times when whatever sense of community exists is largely dependent upon the auctioneer. This is the situation in many country-style auctions, in which most of the participants are strangers not only to each other but to the auctioneer. In order to draw these casual buyers into the auction, the auctioneer must create the ambience of a community. Without this sense of community, there is unlikely to be either the sense of trust or the social dynamics of mutual contagion which are necessary for a successful country auction. Buyers are likely to be very wary and to refrain from bidding. To generate a sense of comradeship, it is common to introduce and name the various persons who are assisting the auctioneer. If they are family members all the better. Humor, stories, and self-revelation are also useful strategies. Family jokes, like this one from a Jack Bitner auction in southern Vermont, make use of all of these techniques simultaneously:

> And that's my lovely wife over there by the cash register where you should all pick up your bidding paddles. She's a great gal and an auctioneer's delight. Not only has she kept the girlish figure she had when I married her forty years ago, she's doubled it.

Food helps to create a feeling of a comfortable, trustworthy community. The best arrangement is to have a grange or a church group selling home-cooked goodies. If that is not possible, a simple hot dog vendor will do. The point is to make participants feel at ease and trusting. It is important to make everyone "part of the family" if they are expected to enter into the spirit of the auction. The effort to hold the community together is what most auctions are all about.

Although holding a community together generally means strengthening interpersonal ties, there are exceptions. There are times when the relationships between particular members of a group may become so entrenched that they work against the interests of both the individuals and the community. We are familiar with such occurrences within families and social groups, be it the overprotective mother or the clique. With collectors and dealers operating outside of auctions, the most common manifestations of this process are the individual who insists that a friend sell a specific item only to him, the fellow dealer who after making a purchase wants to return it, the buyer who wants an adjustment in price because the item wasn't as good as she thought, and the close friend who feels that it would be unfriendly of you to make an offer on a piece he is thinking of buying. In such situations, the long-term needs of both the community and the pressured individual may require an increase in the social distance between participants.

One of the more remarkable features of auctions is that they can serve both to decrease and increase the social distance between participants, sometimes simultaneously. Auctions not only bring people together, they also provide some insulation from the pressures and claims of personal relationships. As one thoroughbred breeder remarked:

> I know all of these people pretty well. If I sold them a horse directly, I'd never see the end of them. If the horse got lame or turned out to have no heart, they'd be back at me, expecting me to make it up to them somehow. If the horse turns out to be a winner they won't share their purse with me, but if there is trouble, I'll know. I'd never be free of that horse. This way [an auction], once it is sold it is sold. I've sat next to a friend while he was actually bidding on one of my horses. He got her. I said congratulations and good luck with her. Turned out she couldn't run worth a damn, but he never said a word to me about her.

An automobile dealer at a wholesale, dealers-only, auction expressed a similar sentiment:

> I sometimes don't like the hassle of the auction, but when I sell a car here, no matter to whom I sell it, best friend or enemy, it's sold. I'm not going to get a call the next morning that he's changed his mind or he wants something in addition.

Much the same sort of thing can be heard from furniture, gun, stamp, book, and print dealers.

The need to increase social distance in some auctions points up the fact that while communities arc common to all auctions, there is considerable variation in the number of distinct communities to be found within a given auction as well as the way these various communities are interrelated. There can be a strong community of buyers, as in the New England Fish Exchange; a strong community of sellers, as in thoroughbred auctions; or a strong mixed community of buyers and sellers, as in wholesale automobile auctions. There may similarly be secondary communities, such as the community of fish captains present in fish auctions; thoroughbred owners at horse auctions; and the loose, temporary community of casual buyers present at most art and antique auctions. While the need to maintain a sense of community is common to all auctions, it is this specific mix of communities that accounts for the specific rules and practices of each auction.

Although communities of varying sorts dominate auctions, there are buyers who attend auctions as purely self-interested individuals with a desire to buy certain goods for less than their assumed value. These buyers, in part because of their indifference to the communal dynamics of the auction, seldom get the items they want at their price and are usually disregarded by the regulars. While these individuals clearly exist, their relevancy to the whole auction process remains minor because their low bids do not hinder or interfere with the communal process of determining value and allocating goods.

There are other self-interested individuals, however, who can disrupt the process, namely bidders who are willing to overpay for an item simply because they want it. There are even times when a collector or a dealer may act on such highly individualistic reasons, as when a decorator wants a particular piece to finish up an entire room. The communal price may be of little consequence here, since not only can the decorator pass on the price to the client, but the cost is likely to be incidental in comparison to the overall cost of decorating the room. Much the same situation might exist if a dealer has been commissioned to buy a piece for someone, or knows of a customer to whom he or she can resell a piece at almost any price.

Even such buyers, however, seldom upset the consensual character of an auction. While they may be successful in purchasing the items they want at what may be considered inflated prices, their purchases are commonly minimized and excluded from the definitional process. This happens because the other professionals attending the auction recognize the particularistic and deviant nature of the purchase and discount it. When dealers and collectors become aware of the fact that an item is being bid up over its normal price, they attempt to see who is bidding. If they see that the bid is being run up by two nonprofessional buyers, they are likely to ignore the whole process. If they see that one or the other is a professional, especially if the professional is identified with the type of item being sold, they are likely to assume that the professional has a specific client for the item. Having identified the bidders, it is not unusual to see the other professionals exchange knowing glances, followed by a return to their previous look of indifference, which indicates that they have wiped out the whole transaction from their own calculations.

The situation with sellers is fairly similar. There are times when an item is put up for auction because the individual believes it to be very valuable and intends to maximize income. Like the bargain envisioned by our low bidder, the expected high bids normally do not materialize, leaving our seller with the item unsold if too high a reserve was set, or sold for much less than initially expected if no reserve was set. In either case, such actions have little to no impact on the communal evaluation of the item. At other times, people offer things for sale through an auction simply to get rid of them quickly. There is often no real interest in determining the true (communal) value of the items, or perhaps even little interest in the moneys received. While such goods are normally bid up to a reasonable level by the dealers present to ensure that no one gets a steal, they may be sold for significantly less than normal if there is no, or only one, dealer present with any interest in the item. Again, these situations are the exceptions.

The possibility that there may be very few, if any, dealers or collectors at a given auction relates to another possible auction scenario; namely, the auction as, in effect, a private treaty transaction. This occurs when there is clearly only one real buyer and the seller elects to bid on his or her own item, or the auctioneer decides to enter bids using a "flexible reserve." In these situations the other potential buyers serve as little more than an audience. The private treaty aspect may be even more institutionalized. A buyer may have approached a seller or sometimes the auctioneer and negotiated a price for a given item prior to the auction. The item is then put up for auction with the understanding that the buyer will pay the difference between the negotiated price and the price he or she is able to buy it for at auction if the latter is less. If the item goes higher, the amount above the negotiated price (or some part of it, depending on the form of the agreement) also goes to the buyer. This practice is known to exist in most types of auctions dealing with one-of-a-kind objects, from horse to antique auctions.

In the situations just noted, it is usually the buyer who approaches the seller or auctioneer. There are also situations, however, in which a seller will use an auction format to draw people in. He or she will negotiate a price and then auction the item against this negotiated price. Sometimes such auctions mask what is really a fixed-price system. The seller has a predetermined price at which to sell the item, and all of the preauction discussion isn't even true negotiation but merely a means for determining whether the buyer-customer is willing to pay the fixed price.

These situations are again exceptions. While it is not unusual for specific individuals to make highly individualistic bids, or even for such bids sometimes to be the winning ones,[22] most bids—especially most winning and consequently defining bids—reflect a collective judgment regarding the value of an item at that moment. This collective judgment is not a mere aggregation of the revealed preferences of the individual participants but is rather the product of a collective decision-making process that unfolds within the auction itself. It is specifically this ability to confer, not reveal, value on items without a clearly defined value that makes auctions such attractive sales vehicles. The true power of the auction is that its attribution of value represents the collective judgment of the auction community.

One of the reasons that auctions are used so often to raise money for charitable organizations is that the auction format is able to put the strength of the community behind the solicitation. A case can obviously be made that the auction format is often favored by a charity because the items being auctioned are of unknown value. How much is the eighteenth-century portrait of Aunt Helen, an afternoon on Joe Green's yacht, or the services of Greta and Jim Brown as cook and butler and chauffeur for a day *really* worth? In many cases, however, the value of the items auctioned is known almost to the penny. In fact, they are often announced with their retail cost. "I have here a lovely barbecue, donated by Harry's Hardware, which I am told lists for sixty-nine ninety-nine. Who will start it off for me at fifty dollars?" Why doesn't Harry simply sell the barbecue and donate the cash he receives?

There are, of course, a number of different reasons why not, including the fact that with an auction two people have the opportunity for a tax deduction, although not legally. More important, such auctions tend to be good fun, creating a pleasant communal atmosphere. People are drawn into the auction. They relate to each other as they attempt to work out what the next item will go for. It is this genial communal feeling that successful charitable auctions seek to generate, because it can be used to increase bids and hence money raised. The auctioneer can enlist the support of the community to push each bidder higher than he or she intended to go.

Given that in a successful charity auction, items will sell for more than their retail price—this is only fair considering that the buyers are often taking tax deductions—it is clear that fair value is not the sole issue. What is more often at stake is communal status. This is clearly the case when honors such as the right to lead a parade or go to dinner with a celebrity rather than material goods, are auctioned. It is also clearly the case, however, when the material goods auctioned are of intrinsically no value, such as the Christmas logs auctioned by Monty Roberts each year for hundreds of dollars. People aren't bidding for fire logs, they are bidding for social status that can only be bestowed by a community; a community that in this case is produced by the auction.

It is one thing to argue that auctions are inherently communal processes and that prices are set by a type of consensus, and quite another thing to explain why this is so. It is clear from the empirical evidence that participants are generally more concerned in maintaining a sense of a community of shared interests, values, and interdependence than in maximizing their own economic position. The question of why this is so remains. Why is the community so important?[23]

To some extent this question has already been answered. Communities are important because they are the basic source of all meanings and definitions. Communities, however, serve not only to generate meanings, but to legitimate such meanings and associated practices.[24] For individual participants, who are the agents that actually produce and maintain these communities, it is the desire for such legitimacy that is commonly crucial. They support and utilize auctions because they are seeking a means of bestowing legitimacy on their transactions. Objects are reborn in auctions. They acquire new values, new owners, and often new definitions. Sometimes they even acquire a new history. For these new identities to be accepted as legitimate, they must be seen as having a communal sanction. It is this search for legitimacy that underlies the communal character of auctions.

Chapter 4

The Search for a Fair Price
The Primary Objective

To many people, including most economists, the idea that auctions function to establish a "fair" price is incontrovertible; by their definition, the auction price is both correct and fair since it is the price at which market supply and demand curves cross. This particular view of fair value, however, only has meaning within the economic paradigm. "Fairness" for most people connotes something more; it implies a governing principle of legitimacy grounded within the community. It is not merely the product of rational individual decision makers, it is a social goal.

Social goals and norms are not part of the economic model. The only pertinent rules are those contractually accepted by individuals to serve their own self-interests; rational self-interest not only explains what people do but what they should do. According to the broader sociological view, this is not the way things happen. Practices are judged proper insofar as they conform to communal standards rather than rationally calculated individual self-interest. Auction practices are no exception. Fairness is not an unintended consequence of numerous individual auction decisions, but it is an explicit, if not always conscious, objective of the auction community.

Although legitimacy is a central concern of all auctions, both its form and means of implementation vary depending on the structure of the community. Of decisive importance is the relative cohesiveness of the auction community; the more cohesive the community, the less manifest the concern for legitimacy. The reason for this is that legitimacy and community are not only mutually dependent upon each other, but given their intrinsic connection, substitutive for each other. The more salient the one, the less pressing the explicit need for the other. When the sense of community is strong and decisions are seen as embodying communal judgment, the question of the legitimacy of the decision generally does not explicitly arise because it is implicitly assumed. In relatively tight communities, such as those found in most commodity-exchange auctions, for example, the members feel no need to justify the price or the allocation of goods. The fact that it is an exchange decision is sufficient. The legitimacy of the price is taken for granted.

When the sense of community is diffuse, however, there is commonly a felt need for explicit rules and regulations in whose terms auction decisions can be judged.[1] Participants are more apprehensive and seek greater assurance that auction determinations are properly and fairly executed. The auction itself, rather than the community that supports it, becomes the perceived means for establishing legitimacy. This is most commonly the case in sales auctions in which the sense of community tends to be most attenuated because of the relatively high percent of nonprofessional participants and fewer extra-auction business ties among the professionals who do attend. At a typical summer weekend country auction in New England, over half those in attendance are likely to be tourists and another quarter nonprofessional locals. Most of the collectors and dealers will know each other from past auctions, but few will have had specific business relationships with each other. Everyone will be monitoring what happens to ensure that all rules are followed.

Further support for the inverse relationship between community cohesiveness and concern with legitimacy is offered by dealer-dominated auctions. The more closed to outside buyers a dealer-dominated auction is, the more it operates like an exchange auction; the more open it is, the more it resembles a sales auction. While dealers attending a jewelry auction in a suite at the Waldorf-Astoria accept their mutual evaluations without question, a jewelry auction at Doyle's or Christie's requires estimates and extensive information on size and quality of the stones. Similarly when third parties—individuals who do not actively participate in an auction but have some economic, legal, or fiduciary interest in the process—are significant to an auction, be it a publisher

critiquing the performance of a subsidiary rights manager, a
bank officer reevaluating repossession practices, or a judge re-
viewing an estate liquidation, legitimacy concerns tend to increase
as compared to similar auctions without third parties.

Auctions of subsidiary rights of literary works, for example,
are normally confined to a tight-knit group of rights managers
and editors. The primary purpose of such auctions is to ensure
that everyone in the community has an equal opportunity to acquire these rights. There is also a desire to establish a consensual
evaluation, especially when the author has no established track
record. (The subsidiary rights of established authors are more
often sold privately, since there is often a communal understanding, if not a legally binding contract, that the previous purchaser
of this author's subsidiary rights has an option on such future
rights.)

While such auctions satisfy the need to ascertain value and
allow equal access to all, these are not always their most important
function. In many cases, there is a high degree of consensus regarding the value of the property; in other cases, there may be little
or no interest in the work; while in yet other cases, the rights
may have been sold informally based on a special relationship
between editors. Nevertheless, an auction will be held. In part,
this posturing serves to ensure that communal rights are maintained even though no one seems interested in exerting them.
Often more important is the need to legitimate the price and
choice of paperback publisher to the author, the author's agent,
and even the directors of the buying and selling publishing houses.

The rights managers and editors seldom have a need for such
justification. The determination of the final price as well as the
eventual purchaser of the subsidiary rights is accepted as fair by
those involved insofar as it reflects their communal judgment as
ratified by auction. Participants in such auctions often discuss
whether the price was high or low, whether one house or another
would have been better for the book, whether one assessed the
dynamics accurately, but they don't normally talk about whether
it was fair. Having followed their own established procedures for
making such decisions, they accept the decision as reflecting their
best collective judgment. The auction is valued as a means for
verifying this consensus.

Authors, literary agents, and publishing executives do not usually participate directly in either the pricing or allocation of subsid-

iary rights. They are not part of that literary community and consequently not ready to trust its decisions. But they do trust the auction process. Even if the price realized through the auction proves to have been low—the book becomes a best-seller—the publisher is not likely to blame the rights director providing he or she went through the proper auction procedures. Even if the auction produced only one bidder, the publisher can defend the legitimacy of the transaction. "An auction was held and that was the top price." Authors and literary agents usually accept this view.

Third parties accept auctions as means for establishing a legitimate price rather than merely as reflecting a communal judgment in other auctions. In New York as in a number of other cities, if an automobile gets a sufficient number of parking tickets that are not paid, a default judgment may be made against the car. When this happens, a city marshal can take possession of the car and tow it away if he or she can find it. There are a number of marshals who, working from lists of default cars, with addresses, will scour different neighborhoods looking for cars, especially late-model expensive cars, with numerous tickets. Once such a car is spotted, the marshal will call a tow-truck operator who will pull the car in; most marshals work with specific tow-truck operators. The city runs a similar, though less picky, operation of its own. Once a car is taken, the owner is informed and given the opportunity to pay the fines plus the towing and storage fees to reacquire the car. If the owner fails to do this, the car can be auctioned to pay off the charges. In either case, the marshal gets a percentage of the moneys, and the tow operator gets his towing and storage fees. The city meanwhile gets its fines paid. (Sometimes, especially with older cars with many fines, there may not be enough money to cover all of these charges. In these cases, it is usually the city that ends up not getting its full share.)

In a given week in New York City, there will be an average of six such auctions. Most buyers tend to be mechanics and persons interested in using the cars as sources of auto parts; there are also small dealers who buy and sell inexpensive cars and trucks. There are also a good number of persons interested in buying one of the better cars for themselves. While prices can vary considerably, most cars sell for less than they could be bought for elsewhere. In fact, it is probable that more money would be realized if the garage–tow-truck owner were allowed to set a price on

each car and to sell it off by private treaty. Clearly other considerations are involved. As a major tow-truck operator revealed:

> Sure, the city would probably end up with ten to fifteen percent
> more if the cars were sold one on one. But you couldn't do it.
> There'd be too many problems. There are a lot of regulars here.
> If I sold a car to one guy, another guy might come in the next
> day and say "Hey, I hear you've got a 1983 red Caddie." I'd
> answer "No more. Vinie bought it yesterday." Right away he
> would start to bitch. "What did you sell it to him for?" "A grand."
> "A grand?" he'd answer. "Hell, I would have given you that
> much. You know I have a thing for Caddies. It's not right, you
> should have given me a call."
>   It is just not worth it. The next thing, someone from down-
> town would be calling to find out if there was monkey business
> going on and if I was selling cars for less than they were worth.

The quote reveals some of the subtle differences in the attitudes
of the various participants. The garage owner clearly feels that
there is a sufficient consensus among dealers and mechanics to
enable him to determine a reasonable price on most cars. He
isn't concerned that dealers will complain about the prices he
would set, but about being denied access to cars they might fancy.
On the other hand, he sees the auction as protecting him from
accusations of unfair pricing from government officials responsible
for impounding the cars to pay off tickets. Concern with legitimacy
is seen as coming from auction outsiders, "someone downtown";
the regulars are perceived as interested in maintaining their communal rights. The auction achieves both ends.

Bank-automobile-repossession auctions serve a similar purpose, though the participants are slightly different. The bank
takes possession of the car in an attempt to recapture the money
owed on an unpaid loan. The cars in repossession auctions tend
to be newer, with the result that more of the buyers are private
individuals looking for a personal car; there are fewer auto strip-
pers—mechanics and dealers interested in the cars for their parts—
than at police auctions. The dealers present are primarily interested in buying the most expensive cars for resale. Often they
have come to buy one or two specific cars that have been advertised.
This mix of buyers is much less cohesive than that found at most
police auctions. The auctioneer, consequently, spends more time

attempting to establish a sense of trust. The rules are more explicitly stated; often there is a printed copy of the rules.[2]

Because the cars are newer, the auctioneer, dealers, and banks actually have a more specific idea of the value of each car. Most of the buyers, in contrast, being nonprofessionals and not part of any community of buyers tend to be highly uncertain of the value of the cars. Such a situation would seem to favor a system whereby the banks in collaboration with dealers and auctioneers would simply set minimum prices for all cars. Nevertheless, banks still favor auctioning repossessed cars because the process insulates them from disgruntled ex-owners. As an auctioneer who sells these automobiles almost exclusively puts it:

> The banks could probably get more money for their cars if they sold them privately through a dealer, but then they would be exposing themselves for all sorts of trouble. Here they pick up a year-old Buick with an outstanding loan of seven thousand bucks. The blue-book value on the car is eleven thousand, but that is a retail price. There is no way that a dealer will give more than eight and a half grand for that car. At auction it may bring only seven and a half. If the bank takes the eight and a half, however, the guy who they took the car from will start to bitch that the bank did him out of two and a half grand because the blue-book value of the car is eleven thousand dollars. If he takes the bank to court, they may have a hell of a time convincing the judge that they really got the best price, especially if they have regular dealings with this dealer. If they auction it, they have no problems. They simply tell the judge that they put the car up for auction with a recognized auctioneer who advertised the auction, and that is the price that the car brought.

In both types of car auctions there is no question on the part of most participants that the cars are worth more than they will bring at auction. The auction is not seen as maximizing the return. The sense of legitimacy attributed to the price in each case, therefore, is clearly not due to the fact that the auction reveals the true economic value of the cars. Rather the legitimacy in each case is due to the public manner in which the price is determined. The price is legitimized by the community of active participants much as punishment is legitimized by a jury.[3]

The similarity between auctions and juries runs deep. In both situations there is a properly constituted group that has the ability to establish communal guidelines and to determine a final outcome be it a price or a sentence. An especially revealing story that illustrates the commonalities between the auction and the jury is told by auctioneer Tom Caldwell:

> One day Tom's father received a call from a judge he knew. The judge had been presiding over a divorce case involving one of the richest men in town, who was married to a woman of considerable wealth in her own right. The divorce proceedings had moved ahead quite easily until it had come to the division of the joint property. It had been agreed to divide the property evenly, but all attempts to work out an equitable division had failed. The judge had brought in a whole range of different experts to value this and that, but sooner or later both husband and wife refused to accept the evaluations offered by the various experts. Only they knew the true value of what they owned, and they couldn't agree.
>
> The judge proposed that Tom's father hold a two-person auction at which he would auction off everything they jointly owned, and when it was over they could settle up the difference. If one bought $10,000 more worth of goods in the auction than the other, that person would have to give the other $5,000 to even things out. Everyone agreed to this plan and the next week, after going through all the items as he would have in a normal sale, Tom's father set up his stand in the courtroom and proceeded to auction off the joint property. It took the whole day, but the commission was sizable. The auction had been used to establish fair prices when the distrust of the people involved made other more established means for assigning value unacceptable. What is particularly poignant about this particular auction is that it functioned as a marriage substitute, enabling the couple to reclaim their ability to make mutually acceptable joint decisions in order to dissolve their marriage.

In most marriages or families, if disagreement or simple uncertainty regarding the value of some item occurs, the interested parties will normally discuss the matter. In effect, this means that a joint effort to define the item correctly and from this definition to deduce its value is being made by all interested participants. If this cannot be done, due to a failure to agree on criteria of value or a lack of trust, outside experts are likely to be called in.[4] In the case of a divorce, signifying the breakdown of the family and hence normally the end of the family consensual base, reliance on outside experts to resolve disagreements and uncertainties is common. Tom Caldwell's story is so arresting because even though the divorcing couple has elected to dissolve their own particular "community," that is, their marriage, they will only accept this community's (their own) judgment regarding the value of their joint property. They rely on the judgment of exactly the community they are dissolving. It is nevertheless a communal judgment on which they are willing to rely rather than their individual self-interests, which are seen as suspect.

If the purpose of the auction were to reveal the "true" value of each item, there would be no need to restrict the auction to the couple. The more interested parties the better for arriving at an objective estimation of value. If, on the other hand, the auction served only to reveal the particular subjective value of the items to each of them, it could not work, since many items with a high market value might go for relatively little (if only one of the two were interested in it) providing grounds for later controversy and thereby further complicating the final division of goods.

The success of this auction was that it revealed the value of items as they related to the two of them as a couple. In the case of some items, one or the other of them drove the price up even though they had no interest in the item. They did so knowing that the other really wanted it. In other cases, items went for a tenth of what they were worth. It is important to realize that while this process clearly was influenced by the preferences of the parties involved, the prices reached did not reflect these preferences in any logical way. The prices rather revealed the complex joint values of the items in question, determined by the couple's collective evaluation. This collective evaluation was not a simple composite of their individual evaluations, but a unique product of their respective evaluations and expectations concerning each other. The final evaluation and outcome was not an aggregate phenomenon but a product of their psychological and social interaction.

The above example demonstrates that auctions are capable of generating a sense of legitimacy normally associated with collective decisions, even when those participating in the auction may not feel as if they are part of a communal process. Admittedly, in many auctions, including most exchange auctions, the legitimacy of auction determinations is quite clearly linked to an explicit awareness that such decisions reflect the consensus of the group. In others, including not only the couple just described but most sales auctions, acceptance is dependent on following auction procedures. Participants accept as fair the highest bid for a specific item, be it a horse or painting, often unaware of its consensual character. To them it is simply the winning bid according to the auction rules. The fact that these procedures have become institutionalized specifically because they insure that the decision will be a consensual decision is often not realized. It is a case of people believing in specific rules even though they no longer grasp the reason for the rules. The more manifest the community, the more likely its decision will be accepted at face value. The more attenuated the community, the more likely the need to establish the legitimacy of the auction process separately.

Despite these differences, there are also similarities in the way participants interrelate within both types of auctions. In both cases, there tends to be a high degree of apprehension associated with the interpersonal relationships. In sales auctions, this apprehension is commonly due to ignorance about the intentions and resources of other participants. In exchange auctions and other auctions where there exists a cohesive community, the anxiety is linked to the awareness that while the members of the exchange are united in certain respects, they are also in direct competition with each other. Trust is consequently always limited. Participants may be willing to take each other's word, but they would prefer it if the word was spoken publicly. It is such interpersonal uncertainty—as much as uncertainty of value, price, and allocation—that promotes and supports auctions.

This uncertainty is reflected in the response of the director of a major art museum when questioned about the relative value of auctions as compared to private transactions in acquiring and dispersing museum works. He said that while he had and would continue to make selective purchases for the museum at auctions, he normally sold museum property privately. He admitted that auctions could bring very high prices for some items, but that he dealt almost exclusively with items of known value and in such situations auctions tended to bring slightly less than he could arrange privately. It was specifically because the types of items he was interested in tended to bring slightly lower prices at auction that he would buy at auctions.[5] The only exceptions to this policy were situations when he had to sell through an auction for interpersonal reasons:

Some years ago I discovered that we were overloaded with paintings by a good but fairly minor late-nineteenth-century painter.
I, with my board's approval, elected to sell half of our holdings.
I knew a very reputable dealer who was interested in this man's
work and felt I could get top dollar from him for two of the
paintings. For the third, I had arranged an exchange with another
museum.

Unfortunately, in the middle of my negotiations, I received a
telephone call from the son of the gentleman who had originally
donated the painting to the museum. In discussing the matter
with him, he became very upset, not with the fact that we were
going to sell the painting, but with the price I had negotiated.
He felt that the painting was worth considerably more and ever
so gently questioned my relationship with this particular dealer.
I called the dealer as soon as I hung up and withdrew the painting.
Next, I called Sotheby's and arranged to have the painting auctioned. It was sold three months later for significantly less than
I had been offered by, I believe, the same dealer. There was
no way I was going to get involved in that sort of mess. Since
then, I have probably sold a half dozen objects at auction and
all but one were sold that way for the same reason. Someone,
somewhere was questioning the legitimacy of a private sale I
had arranged.[6]

In auctioning a particular painting this museum director
sought to legitimate and justify the transaction to a donor's son,
an outside interested party. He knew the auction process would
protect him from the ire and criticism of the donor's son much
in the same way that the subsidiary rights director was able to
protect herself from the ire and criticism of her publisher. The
rights director, however, chose the auction mode not only to protect herself from her boss, but to maintain group cohesiveness
by ensuring access for all, and to resolve any uncertainty surrounding the value of the particular rights being offered. If not for
the donor's son, the museum director would probably have arranged a private sale because he felt that the value of the painting
was known. It was this interpersonal uncertainty rather than value
uncertainty which required the legitimating powers of an auction.
   The legitimating power of auctions is evidenced in other situations, including charity auctions. It is specifically the ability of
auctions to legitimate prices that explains their popularity at charity functions. As in the museum director case, fairness in most
charity auctions is more tied up with interpersonal relationships

than the items themselves. The question often is not what a particular item should sell for, but rather how much should different individuals pay. In these cases, it is often third parties who use the auction format to legitimate their price to the actual bidders rather than vice versa. Where the museum director used the auction to justify the price he received for the painting to the donor's son, the members of charitable groups often use the format to legitimate the comparatively inflated prices they expect from donors. Not only can they urge prospective bidders on, they can join in the bidding themselves, simultaneously raising and legitimating the higher price.[7] Just the fact that someone else made a ninety-five-dollar bid can be used to justify a hundred-dollar bid.

An important ramification of this process is that it serves to produce self-legitimation. If one buys through an auction, one can always rationalize a high price by observing that others were willing to pay almost as much. The same justification can be made selling through an auction; the price may be low, but that was all that anyone would offer. Even such self-legitimation is grounded in a social context, since the process is totally dependent on the social interactions intrinsic to the auction and cannot be explained in terms of individual self-interest or rationality.

This need to establish the legitimacy of price and allocation informs auctions from top to bottom. The significance of fairness is surprising given the common belief that auctions are places where the buyer must beware. In reality, the buyer probably is better protected at most auctions than in many department stores, to say nothing of most flea markets. The continual warnings associated with auctions are, in fact, often the result of attempts on the part of auctioneers to ensure that the highest degree of fairness will be attained.

The effort to ensure that the price paid is fair starts before the auction actually begins. In nearly all auctions, items are sold under strict conditions concerning faults, returns, and refunds. In most cases things are sold "as is." In most commodity-exchange auctions this fact is simply assumed; it doesn't have to be spelled out because everyone knows the rules. In sale and dealer auctions, where such knowledge of rules and practices cannot be assumed, it is presented continually in various ways. They are not only printed in the catalogue but announced at the beginning of most auctions and at regular intervals. There is, in addition, generally a preview where the items can be inspected. Despite all these safeguards, most professional auctioneers will ensure that items are held and shown with defects apparent and will more often than not indicate the defect before starting the bidding. If it is a car auction, liens and known defects will be announced. At horse auctions, a special light on the tote board, where the bids are shown, flashes on to indicate whether the horse is a "cribber,"[8] while past operations, broken bones, bleeding, and other illnesses are announced. Even at Luther's—where the sums of money tend to be minimal—the rabbit's blind eye and the pony's skin rash are noted. Admittedly, some things may not be noticed or reported, but such omissions are more the exception than the rule.

The extent to which the search for a "fair" price governs most auctions is revealed by a number of other practices. Despite the rule that all items are sold as is, and the previews scheduled before the auction, if a bidder changes his or her mind immediately after purchasing an item because the item isn't what he or she thought it was (or it is more damaged), most auctioneers will take it back. (Such a situation is only likely to occur in sales or dealer auctions and is unlikely to involve a regular. If it does, the auctioneer is not as likely to be so understanding.) The auctioneer may refuse to accept a bid from that person for the rest of the auction, but he will nevertheless normally take back the item. In short, professional auctioneers are seldom guilty of the type of "sharp" practices that are commonly attributed to them.

To say that auctioneers are not generally guilty of sharp practices does not mean that such practices do not occur. More often than not, however, the guilty party/parties (normally such sharp practices are carried out by teams) are sellers and buyers.[9] Perhaps the most common practice of this sort is "pool" buying by dealer rings noted earlier, in which a number of dealers agree that they will not bid against each other. In this way they hope to keep the bid down. Afterwards they hold a private auction among themselves, with the difference between the price paid at the formal auction and the price finally paid in their private auction divided among the pool members. Here again, however, we find a situation in which an apparent breach of a principle proves otherwise.

At one level, pools would seem to be a violation of fairness. By refusing to bid against each other the members of the pool are supporting a practice that would seemingly lead to unfairly low prices. Auctioneers obviously do not commonly approve of this type of activity. On the other hand, they often tolerate it, providing the item is sold at a price that the auctioneer feels is fair. This may seem to be an impossibility by definition. How can such pools and fair prices exist side by side?

The apparent paradox rests on the fact that in such situations we are often dealing with both an established community and outsiders. If the price set by the pool is seen to be a fair dealer's price, and the number of outsiders is few and they are not regulars, an auctioneer is unlikely to make a big fuss. Most of the items are going to be bought by the dealers, and provided they give the auctioneer their fair price, he or she will not complain. A private agreement between a few dealers, in fact, may be experienced as less disturbing than a bidding war among two or three dealers, which results in a highly inflated final price for one item, which serves in turn to make other items seem underpriced.[10]

Moreover, an auctioneer may actually make use of such a pool to get rid of some items that would otherwise be difficult to sell. He or she may actually address the members of the pool directly and ask them to buy the item. "Hey, come on guys. You know this is worth more than I have here. One of you give me a bid and take it off my hands." If the auctioneer has treated the pool fairly, more often than not they will cooperate when so propositioned.

Sometimes when nearly all the buyers are dealers, "agreements" among buyers are sufficiently open and spontaneous that it is questionable if they really constitute a pool, even when items bought at the auction may be exchanged and resold afterwards. In some midrange jewelry auctions, for example, which are often held in hotel suites and attended only by dealers, it is not unusual for the auctioneer to suggest a single bid and have it met by one or another dealer with no other bids. Dealers openly remark to one another, "I know, you like that sort of stuff. Remember though, the next item is mine." On the other hand, one dealer may approach another after the auction and purchase the item at a price that gives the first buyer a small profit. If questioned about the equity of such actions, these dealers would be taken aback. As one commented:

> I'm not sure I know what you mean. We know what the items are worth and we are paying good money for these items. No one is going to steal anything here. We won't let anyone do it, and even if we wanted to the auctioneer wouldn't let us. He

has his own responsibilities. On the other hand, we aren't going
to run the price up on an item just because two of us like it.

In more open auctions, such cooperation is not as spontaneous.
Pools, when they exist, tend to be more formally organized. The
particular form of the pool can vary. It can be organized as either
a round robin, where the payoff is equal for all members, or an
English knockout where payoff is proportional to bids made in
the knockout auction. (For a description of the two forms, see
pp. 70–71.) This difference has nothing to do with the relationship
of the pool to the formal auction. It is a purely internal matter
and is a reflection of the inverse relationship between group cohesiveness and the need for explicit rules to ensure legitimacy. When
the members of the pool constitute a strong community with a
high degree of mutual trust, most are willing to use the round-
robin method, which assumes equality of members. When the
pool is less cohesive there is more likely to be a move on the
part of some members to use the English knockout, where the
rules explicitly recognize differences in the members' bids in the
distribution of profits.

Provided pools function to ensure stable prices within an acceptable range, they tend not only to be tolerated but are often
quite inconspicuous. Things get slightly more complicated when
there is a sizable group of outsiders and the pool acts to inhibit
the emergence of a new consensus. In these cases auctioneers
may become more than a little testy, no matter how well they
know the members of the pool.

The acceptance-nonacceptance of auction rings, both formal
and informal, is just one example of the various types of accommo-
dations and adjustments common to auctions. The social flux
and context of auctions requires flexibility from its participants.
In practice, different types of auctions give assorted advantages
to distinct players. Sometimes the auctioneer is allowed to maintain
a reserve against which he or she may bid, which normally favors
sellers. Sometimes sellers and buyers are permitted to enter into
such preauction arrangements as the use of floor bids in publishing
or similar agreements in which buyer and seller negotiate a price
subject to modification in the auction. Sometimes sellers are able
to withdraw their goods after the auction is over such as the
right of fishermen to take back their entire catch if they feel the
total price received for the catch is too low. Varied situations

require giving the parties different handicaps if a "legitimate" price is to be determined; no single set of rules can do this in all situations. Nowhere is this better demonstrated than in the way split bids—that is, bids that offer a smaller increase over the last one than normal or requested by the auctioneer—are handled.[11]

Split bids force auctioneers to earn their keep. Judging the acceptability of a bid lower than what was called for presents two potentially conflicting principles: On the one hand, it is the auctioneer's responsibility to get the most he or she can for any item; even if the split bid offers less than was requested, it is higher. If no other bids are forthcoming, it may well be the highest bid. On the other hand, it is the auctioneer's responsibility to run an orderly auction in which everyone feels fairly treated; this generally entails the use of standard increments, since a bidder who has been required to increase the bid by one hundred dollars in order to acquire the bid will feel cheated if another bidder is able to take the bid back with an increase of only ten dollars. The specific increments used vary from auction to auction, but the common practice is to use increments of between 5 and 10 percent of the last bid, adjusting such increments to "round" figures.[12] These percentages will vary at very low and very high prices, with larger increases normal in the former and smaller percentage increases in the latter.

The bidding on an antique chest of drawers at Sotheby's, New York, for example, could well go as follows: "Will someone start it off at $2,000? $2,000? $1,800? $1,500? $1,300? I have a bid of $1,200. Will someone say 1,300? I have 1,300! 1,400?" The bids may then go 1,500, 1,600, 1,700, 1,800, 1,900. 2,000 but then jump to increments of 200: 2,200, 2,400, 2,600, 2,800, 3,000.[13] If the bidding is brisk, the increments may be jumped more rapidly. The following sequence of bids on a yearling colt at a Keeneland select sale is an example of this. "$100,000, I have 100,000! 120,000! 130,000! I have 140,000 out back, and 150,000! Will you give 175? 175! 200? 200! 250? Will you give me 250?"

With used cars, bric-a-brac, jewelry, and real estate, the rhythm is very similar. The question is what happens if someone offers $145,000, $142,000, or $141,000 when the auctioneer is asking for $150,000? There is no fast rule on this; it will depend on the type of auction, whose bid it is, where in the bidding the split bid occurs, and the particular mood and judgment of the auctioneer at that moment. In some cases, the auctioneer him- or herself may introduce such a bid. Having increased the bid by increments of a thousand dollars, for example, an auctioneer may ask for an increase of only five hundred dollars if he or she cannot get a thousand and the bidding has dried up. In nearly all cases, however, the practice selected appears to make the process fairer to all concerned.

In commodity-exchange auctions, for example, where split bids are so common as to be the norm rather than the exception, they provide the fine tuning required to ensure that goods are allocated in accordance with communal needs. Since all buyers end up paying the same price, such bids do not serve to give one buyer an advantage over another. They may serve to benefit the sellers somewhat, but given the overall disadvantage of sellers in most commodity-exchange auctions, this is not considered unfair. On the other hand, it is sometimes difficult to label a bid as a split bid in such auctions even if it is technically less than would be expected, because normal increments tend to be quite small. The bids on many commodities increase by a cent or less per bid.

This, of course, is not the case when dealing with prize livestock, be it an Angus bull or a thoroughbred yearling colt. In these cases, the increments may be sizable. Although such commodity auctions are more correctly seen as sales auctions rather than exchange auctions, split bids will in most cases also be accepted. The bidding at Keeneland, for example, may commonly drop to the minimum thousand-dollar increment[14] after reaching a quarter of a million dollars by jumps of twenty-five thousand dollars. The auctioneer may take the opportunity to poke fun at a bidder making such a bid, but he will take it. "Oh, come on now. What are you doing to me? You're offering me a thousand more? Daddy told me there'd be days like this. Okay, I've got 251,000, anyone offer me 275,000? I'll take 260 if it will make it any easier on anybody." This is not likely to happen at Sotheby's or Christie's, or any other major art-antique auction house. The response is much more likely to be, "The bid is $250,000. Will anyone say 260?"

This does not mean that split bids are never accepted at Sotheby's or Christie's. A half bid, that is, an increment of $5,000 when a $10,000 was requested, which still represents a 5 percent increase will normally be taken if the auctioneer feels that the bidding is reaching its upper limits. A $1,000 increment to a $300,000 bid, however, would not be accepted. In this respect, Sotheby's and Christie's are more representative of auctions in general than are Keeneland and Fasig-Tipton. Even at the end, Sotheby's and Christie's are not likely to take increments of less than 5 percent, whereas many smaller art and antique, "country," estate, and liquidation auctions will.

In many instances these differences seem to be a matter of past practices and tradition. Horse auctioneers often say that though they don't like taking split bids, they have always been allowed—providing they meet the minimum—in horse auctions. Liquidation auctioneers describe their auctions as similar in this respect. In contrast, auctioneers for Sotheby's, Christie's, and other high-market art-antique auction houses have indicated that such bids are demeaning to the whole process and have traditionally been avoided.

While tradition and related practices clearly are significant in determining what is acceptable—the practice of accepting split bids in select livestock auctions is in part a carryover from the more conventional agricultural commodity auctions—there are other factors at work. Horse auctioneers, for example, will commonly add that their job is to get the most they can even if it is only another thousand dollars on a quarter of a million. In contrast, art-antique auctioneers, especially at the more select houses, defend their policy of not taking split bids by arguing that it would not be fair to the other buyers who have been playing by the "rules."[15]

The policy of attempting to get the last dollar in auctions of prize livestock, even at the risk of irritating buyers who may feel that they are being nickled and dimed by the process, is not surprising when it is remembered that these auctions are organized and run primarily by the sellers. Keeneland and Fasig-Tipton are sales organizations. The same thing can be said for many liquidation, estate auctions, and most real estate auctions, which are also organized to benefit the seller. In some cases, such as farm liquidations, there may be additional communal sympathy for the seller. In these situations, anything which can bring in a little more for the seller is legitimate and tolerated by the auction community.

In contrast to these auctions, the dominant community in most collectible/dealer auctions is constituted by the buyers. This is also often the case in regular liquidation and estate auctions run by an auctioneer with a significant following of professional buyers. The same can be said for many if not most mid-range art and antique auctions. It is the community of dealers and collectors that makes these auctions possible. The sellers tend to be liquidating individual holdings and are unrelated to each other. They tend to be neither auction regulars nor well known to the auctioneer.

The buyers, in contrast, are regulars and are known. They have their own rules that govern who gets what. To allow one of them, much worse an outsider, to "steal" a particular item with a split bid is seen as illegitimate. In addition, such bids introduce an element of haggling that can work to the detriment of the auctioneer. They not only can serve to "cheapen" the process but can take a good deal of time for little substantial increase. In these cases split bids serve the interests of neither the auctioneer nor the more important members of the auction community. It is not surprising, consequently, that they are seldom tolerated.

There are, of course, always exceptions. Auctioneers will themselves sometimes ask for a split bid toward the apparent end of a bidding sequence. This is quite common when the increments have been substantial but are petering out and the auctioneer believes a drop in increments may help extend the bidding. There are other times when a sensitive auctioneer will keep the increments below their normal level because he or she senses that bidding may cease if the increments are jumped in a normal fashion.

In the case of John Lennon's Rolls-Royce, at two hundred thousand dollars, when the increment would normally have jumped from ten thousand dollars to twenty-five thousand, it was decided to stick with the ten-thousand-dollar increment. This remained the increment all the way up to the final bid of two million three hundred thousand dollars. Under normal conditions the increments would have been minimally a hundred thousand dollars.[16]

To summarize, split bids are routinely accepted in commodity-exchange auctions, but the small increments common to these auctions, coupled with the fact that all buyers generally end up paying the same price, tend to make them a nonissue. In contrast, they are an issue of major importance in most dealer dominated auctions, where they are commonly seen as illegitimate, especially if they are used against the dealers. (If the bid has been increasing by increments of ten dollars and the bid is presently held by a dealer, the auctioneer is not supposed to accept an increase of two dollars from a chance buyer. On the other hand, if the present bid is held by such a chance buyer, the auctioneer may accept such a split bid from a dealer.) The situation in sales auctions will depend on the relative powers and rights of buyers and sellers. In art and antique auctions, in which buyers tend to dominate, they are discouraged. In most select livestock, real estate, and liquidation auctions, in which sellers are in charge, they are commonly not only accepted but encouraged, especially near the end of a bidding sequence.

Attitudes toward split bids relate in an interesting way to attitudes toward pools. In many cases, tolerance of buyer cooperation, if not collusion, is seen as offsetting the relative advantages of buyers and sellers as reflected in the use of split bids. Cooperation among buyers at select livestock sales, for example, is not only common but quite open. It is almost as if the sellers' advantage is understood and the buyers are given an offsetting right. In contrast, pooling is not allowed in most art and antique auctions. When, in fact, it does occur, it is often justified by those in the pool as being necessary because the auctioneer is refusing to respect their rights as buyers.

There are a number of variations concerning the acceptability of split bids related to other bidding practices. In Dutch auctions, for example, the issue really doesn't come up because the decreasing bid is usually tied to some mechanism that moves down in a continuous fashion. This is consistent with the nature of Dutch auctions, which are nearly always commodity-exchange auctions. In silent auctions—that is, auctions in which bidders write their bids on a bidding pad attached to each item on display—which are commonly used in charity auctions, minimum increments are built into the rules; each new bid must be so much more than the preceding one. Most charity auctions are run by an in-group of sponsors-buyers who prefer not to lose an item to a guest for a penny or two.[17]

Auctions that use sealed written bids are slightly more difficult to locate on a buyer-seller-favored auction spectrum. The fact that only one bid is allowed would seem to place them more with buyer-dominated auctions, since there is no way for the auctioneer to "milk" the buyers for just a little bit more. On the other hand, bids that are only slightly higher than others may be submitted, resulting in a higher price for the seller. In some cases, such as bond auctions, the whole issue becomes academic, since bidders that close together are both likely to "win"—that is, to receive their share of bonds, or lose. (In this respect, they are very much like commodity-exchange auctions, which, of course, is exactly what they are.) Moreover, they will end up with rates very close to each other or actually the same if that is the form of the auction.[18] It is difficult to see how such minor differences favor either buyers or sellers.

When such bidding is used to award contracts, in contrast to bond or other high-multiple items, there is usually only one winner. Theoretically, this should put additional pressure on buyers to increase their bids, since it is not sufficient, as it is when there are multiple winners, to have one of the higher bids. This is not surprising, given that sellers tend to control such auctions as in the letting of government contracts. In actuality, if the bids are very close, the rules may allow the auctioning party to treat them as identical and to enter into further negotiations. This relaxes somewhat the pressure to be the high bidder, but it also gives the seller an additional opportunity to increase the bids.

All of these factors would indicate that such a system in the long run favors the seller. Often, however, buyer-bidders in such auction are organized since they are commonly fellow professionals—for example, building contractors, suppliers, or maintenance companies. If they perceive the auction as favoring the seller, it is not unusual for them to engage in collusive practices. The seller is unlikely to feel that this is legitimate and may well retaliate by claiming that buyers are engaging in price-fixing. What commonly emerges from such disputes is a system of checks and balances which both parties feel protect their interests.

THE use and acceptance of reserves raises many issues similar to those raised by the question of legitimate increments. Again, there are differences among auctions, and the deciding factor seems to be the relative rights and responsibilities of those involved. When strong communities exist, the particular practice, whatever it might be, is commonly accepted. When such communities do not exist, there is more concern with legitimating the practice.

In most commodity-exchange auctions, for example, sellers

normally retain the right to reject any final bid, though they seldom employ formal reserves. If the last bid is not acceptable to the sellers, they can in some cases simply withdraw their goods. This is the dominant practice in most fish auctions, where it is know as "scratching." In other commodity situations, especially those where buyers have more control, the seller may be allowed to buy back his or her offering. This technique is quite common in horse sales where it is called simply a "buy-back." The seller who withdraws goods is normally still liable for a commission or equivalent charge, though there are often discounts for such scratches and buy-backs. Restrictions may also be placed on the future sale of the withdrawn goods, such as not being able to reauction them for a period of time.

At the higher end of livestock auctions, the auctioneer usually knows what minimum price will be accepted; moreover, he will usually act as the seller's agent in supporting such a reserve. He will generally not bid against the reserve himself, which is common practice in most art and antique auctions; that is, though he will not sell for less than the reserve, he will not continue to enter his own bids in order to reach the level of the reserve. If the last real bid is not sufficiently high, he will put in his own bid and, in effect, buy the item back. In scratches and buy-backs, the auctioneer normally does not know ahead of time what the seller's minimum acceptable bid will be. In most such cases, even the seller often hasn't thought out ahead of time what this minimum will be. The decision to scratch a fish catch may be made up to a half hour after the auction. Many buy-backs are quite spontaneous and more than a few are unintentional; the seller makes a bid intending to push the bid just a little higher and ends up buying his own horse.

These situations entail a range of compromises between buyers and sellers. The buyers would prefer not to give the seller the added leverage offered by a flexible reserve. On the other hand, they realize that they have to provide the option of withdrawing from the process altogether. This is the situation that holds in most exchange-type auctions. In those cases, however, where sellers have more power, they normally preserve their option of controlling the minimum bid by bidding directly on their goods. When this happens, however, the seller is normally also part of the community that is buying. It is a situation in which buyers and sellers overlap. When this is not the case, and buyers are in control,

it is important for the auctioneer to develop a special relationship
with the sellers to ensure their trust. This is clearly what happens
in tobacco auctions and many local commodity auctions; in fact,
the need to protect the sellers—or at least to be seen as doing
so—was stressed by auctioneers from the New England Fish Exchange to the tobacco floors of Kentucky.

Reserves are not common in distress and liquidation sales.
Again we have a situation where the buyers are normally in control;
the sellers, as liquidating owners or as agents for such owners,
in fact, may have no alternative but to sell. The professional buyers,
who tend to be dealers, are consequently much less tolerant of
reserves of any sort. In commodity auctions there is a sense in
which the buyers realize that the sellers are also professionals
and need some protection. In liquidation and distress sales, the
buyers' attitude tends to be that they are there as a service to
the seller and the goods should be sold to the highest bidder.

In commodity auctions, in which basically identical goods are
sold on a regular basis, it is possible for auctioneers to work with
flexible, unstated reserves. What commonly happens is that the
auctioneer will buy for his or her own account anything that
seems to be going for much less than it is worth—and then attempt
to sell it at a later auction. This option is normally not available
in liquidation auctions. What the auctioneer can do, however, is
attempt to solicit the cooperation of specific buyers to offer equivalent minimum bids by accepting them when offered in response
to a direct appeal. In doing this, it is not uncommon for the
auctioneer to address the buyers by name and literally tell them
to up their bids:

> Come on now, men, you know that this press is worth a lot
> more money than that. [Bidding has stopped at a price which
> the auctioneer feels is too low.] John, you paid five hundred
> more for one not nearly as good last week. Someone give me
> $2,000. John? Okay, thank you. $2,000 sold to number 158.
> Sorry, too late. [John responds to the request and makes a bid,
> and then others elect to bid also, since the price is on the low
> side, but the auctioneer ignores their bids and takes John's solic-
> ited bid of $2,000.] You had your chance.

This dialogue aptly reflects what often happens in these situations. At the request of the auctioneer, a dealer puts in a higher
bid. Then, after some hesitation, another buyer makes a higher

bid. In part as a reward to the first bidder for responding to his request, the auctioneer sells the item out for the two-thousand dollar bid although he could have kept things going. If the winning bidder really doesn't want the item, he or she may be able to sell it privately for a profit to the late bidder. That is a reward for helping out the auctioneer.

The seller's preference for a reserve and the buyer's disapproval carries over to the more common country and art and antique auctions. Buyers have come to buy, and they feel that items should be sold without reserves. This also tends to be the view of most auctioneers. Auctioneers realize, however, that there will be no auction without sellers and that the sellers will normally want some sort of protection. The question is whether the seller is in a position to demand such protection. Over the last few years it appears that those auction houses dealing with more expensive items have begun to switch the balance more toward the sellers. For one thing, the practice of officially charging the seller only half the commission and the buyer the other half is fast becoming standard.[19] The other practice that has become common is the reserve. Moreover, in these auctions, it is quite normal for the auctioneer to aid the seller by bidding against the reserve throughout the auction in an attempt to raise the bid, moving through a series of artificial bids below the reserve price before taking a real bid just at the reserve level.

The increased use of reserves has produced its own counter-reaction from buyers. There is growing concern among buyers that they have been misled. It is one thing, they will argue, for an auctioneer to enter a single bid above their bid if a previously determined reserve has not been met. It is something else to bid above the reserve or to orchestrate a series of bids. In many cases buyers' concern with this has led to a new practice of announcing the underbidder—the last bidder below the winning bidder.

IN a further attempt to balance the rights and privileges of buyers and sellers, a variety of practices has sprung up to inform the public when an item has not sold. These practices range from announcing the fact at the moment—"$350? Will someone say $350? I'm sorry, $325 is not good enough. The item is withdrawn"—to noting the fact in a follow-up auction report. The former practice is becoming more common at art and antique auctions; the latter practice is standard in horse auctions where the sales summary published soon after the auction notes which horses were not sold. The practice is to put either a "Not Sold" or an "RNA" (reserve not attained) notation next to the horse's hip number where the sales price would normally be. These practices serve to ensure that buyers are not misled into believing that items have been sold for prices higher than they were able to bring. It also protects other potential sellers from overestimating the value of their own goods, though it can hurt them in deflating inflationary expectations that drive prices up.

Other practices used to disclose to all or to a specific subgroup whether an item has been sold or not include knocking or not knocking the auction hammer on the lectern, specific statements such as "sold," or code words known only to the regulars. In horse auctions, for example, the practice is not to announce non-sales at the auction, since it is felt that nonsales may prove contagious, depressing future sales. The people working the auction, however, need to know immediately in order to determine whether they need the signatures of the buyer, which not only legally commits him for the money involved, but also transfers ownership and all associated liabilities. If the horse drops dead on the way back to the barn, it is the buyer's loss, not the seller's. Changeable codes, consequently, such as repeating the name of the "spotter," the auctioneer assistant, who has apparently taken the winning, are used by the auctioneer to indicate a nonsale.

One of the most interesting and idiosyncratic systems of reserves, increments, and disclosures is the use of floor bids common in literary auctions. A floor bid is an initial bid by a potential buyer made and announced before the auction begins; it is, in short, a guaranteed minimum bid. In return for making an acceptable floor bid—to be acceptable it must be sufficiently high to start the bidding at a level that would be judged a reasonable final bid—this bidder gets the option to top the final bid by 10 percent. If, for example, the floor bidder makes an opening bid of $100,000 and the bidding then goes up to $250,000, the opening bidder will have the option of acquiring the rights for a bid of $275,000 (the last bid of $250,000 plus a 10 percent increase of $25,000). The floor bidder does not participate in the bidding except for the first and the last bid. Before going back to the floor bidder, however, the seller will normally ask the high bidder among the other auction participants if he or she wishes to increase the bid. The present high bidder might raise the bid in an attempt to discourage the floor bidder from exercising the topping privilege.

The high bidder may feel that the floor bidder is willing to go up to $300,000 but no more. He or she may, therefore, put in a bid of $275,000, knowing that the floor would have to counter with a bid of $302,500. This will be the high bidder's last chance to enter a bid. There will be no opportunity to enter a higher bid if the floor bidder chooses to execute his or her option.

ON the surface this seems like an overly complex system. But it makes perfectly good sense when we remember that in literary auctions buyers and sellers are part of a very close-knit community. It is a community in which private treaty transactions are as normal as auction transactions. This particular system allows a type of private treaty within an auction framework. It allows the seller to establish a minimum and buyers to know ahead of time what that minimum is. It further protects buyers from having a book in which they are interested "stolen away," since they know the winning bid must be at least 10 percent higher. The floor bidder, meanwhile, receives certain privileges for making the first bid and allowing the seller to publicize it before the auction. Such bids are extremely valuable to the seller as an expression of confidence in a relatively unknown commodity. A reasonably high floor bid from one publisher will generally attract the attention of other publishers and get them to take a closer look at the book.

Floor bids highlight the fact that different types of auctions occur within specific contexts rich in their own meaning. The rules of a literary auction only make sense within the framework of that particular community, with its particular relationships and history. The same can be said about most other auctions. In one major standardbred auction in Pennsylvania, for example, problems arose because the seller was not only a breeder but also a trainer and racer of horses. Buyers were suspicious that he was selling his less promising horses and keeping the best for himself. To deal with this problem, the seller instituted a practice of bringing two horses into the ring simultaneously. When the bidding ended, the winning bidder could choose either horse. The other horse would be kept and raced by the seller. In this way the breeder-trainer was able to reassure his buyers and yet offer only half of his yearlings for sale, keeping the other half to be trained and raced by him. His adaptation, like that of the literary auction, was aimed at demonstrating his fairness while protecting his own self-interest.

ALL these practices and decisions concerning reserves, split bids, buy-backs, disclosures, scratches, and nonsales are continually subject to review and modification according to relative fairness toward buyers and sellers. In all instances, their existence testifies to the ongoing awareness and need to sustain the community's faith in the fairness of the process. This is not to deny that buyers and sellers are apt to press their advantage. Even here, however, they are likely to do so only insofar as they feel it is appropriate and acceptable to the community. A recent series of laboratory experiments confirmed this.[20] In simulated auctions, student subjects did not utilize their advantages in a bargaining situation when they saw such advantages as being arbitrarily conferred. They only pressed their advantages when they believed that they had been earned based on their earlier performances. Their sense of community fairness took priority over their individual self-interests.

The sense of fairness operative in an auction can be quite particularistic, reflecting similarly particularistic conditions that pertain to the specific situation. Such idiosyncrasies underscores the communal character of fairness in auctions. In thoroughbred auctions, for example, it is considered perfectly fair for sellers to do all sorts of things to make their horses look better and sounder. This is crucial since the most important quality of a yearling horse, besides its bloodlines, is its soundness. A thoroughbred that stays healthy normally makes its owner money; unfortunately for owners, many of them go lame or break down some other way.[21] In buying a yearling horse that has never raced, it is most important to try to determine if there are any signs that the horse may not prove sound. Buyers carefully watch the way a horse walks and stands in order to detect any misalignments in the legs which could create the type of extra pressures that would lead to lameness.

Sellers are, of course, aware of this practice and will often doctor up a horse to correct for any such misalignments. One way to do this is to carve the front hoofs of the horse in such a way that a leg that is actually slightly twisted in or out looks as if it is facing directly forward. Another more radical technique, especially if such misalignments are caught early, is to operate on the horse and put in splints which will straighten the leg. Both of these practices are considered fair and it is up to the buyer to detect them. (Here we again see the relative power of the sellers in these types of auctions. In fish auctions and many types of commodity auctions, where sellers are in a much weaker position, the buyer may very well refuse to accept goods that are later shown to have been doctored in a similar manner.)

It is not legitimate, however, for the seller to dye the front legs of an animal that has had splints in order to cover up the small telltale white marks caused by the splint operation. Although this may in part represent a communal compromise on the use of splints (they can be used, but the telltale signs must remain), it is more likely related to the very strict rules bearing on markings to ensure that racehorses are not switched, enforced by the Jockey Club. In contrast, in auctioning an antique chair, the use of a small amount of stain to cover up a slight crack in a leg would be acceptable, whereas replacing the leg with a new leg would not be acceptable. In car auctions, it is considered legitimate to change all the oils to cover up mechanical difficulties, but cheating to change the odometer. An argument could be made in each case that there is something wrong with what is considered fair and unfair. What is evident is that much that is considered fair in an auction reflects the traditions and history of the specific auction community.

The fact that a number of auction practices considered fair within specific auctions appear on reflection to be ethically questionable, reveals a somewhat paradoxical facet to the way community cohesiveness and explicit legitimacy concerns complement each other. The more manifest the need to establish an aura of legitimacy and fairness, the greater the possibility of exploitation.

Deliberate exploitation, in contrast simply to profiting more from a transaction, requires that the manipulating party know the value of the items exchanged. Given that auctions occur primarily in situations characterized by value uncertainty, it follows that auctions would be insusceptible to such practices. The greater the uncertainty, the greater the immunity. All auctions are not subject to the same degree of uncertainty, however. There are auctions—for example, automobile, jewelry, and estate—in which many of the regular participants have quite definite knowledge of the value of the goods being auctioned. It is often the need to satisfy interested third parties that prohibits them from entering into private treaty transactions.

It is specifically these auctions in which, because of the interest of third parties, the aura of legitimacy is most consciously developed. Where there is true uncertainty and ambiguity, coupled with community cohesiveness, legitimacy and fairness are taken for granted as ingrained in the auction process. The primary concern among participants is to resolve both the price and the allocation uncertainties. It is assumed that the auction process, especially as it is embedded in the community, does so in as fair a way as possible. When the rules seem peculiar and no one appears particularly concerned about fairness, the probabilities are high that no one is taking advantage of anyone else. On the other hand, it is when everything makes sense, and great effort has been taken to assure everyone that everything is above board, that the buyer should truly beware.

In auctions things are often not as they appear. Economic, psychological, and social concerns combine in a myriad of ways, both producing and reflecting the complex social context of the auction processes: the show itself.

Chapter 5

The Show
Putting It All Together

W HATEVER else an auction might be, it is generally a good show: the intense emotionality, the expressive gestures, the plots and counterplots, the dreams, the despair, the dialogues and repartee, the interactions, the disclosures, the buildups, and the climaxes. The actors, staging, props, audiences, and scripts may vary, but all auctions are public dramatic performances.

For social theorists who see social behavior in general as embodying and revealing such dramaturgical features, this is not surprising; for them the dramaturgical paradigm is commonly capable of identifying, organizing, and explaining facets of behavior that other paradigms, such as the rational economic man paradigm of neoclassical economic theory, either cannot accommodate or simply ignore. In its most general form, it emphasizes the mutuality of social life and public performances expressed in Shakespeare's line, "All the world's a stage, / And all the men and women merely players."[1] It conceives of human behavior as contextual, both reflecting and constrained by social expectations, governed more by expressive aims than instrumental tasks, more emotional than rational, and more interactive than self-directed. Perhaps most important, it views social behavior as requiring the interpretive skills of knowledgeable performers; social life requires not only that social actors comprehend the meaning of the various situations in which they find themselves but that they are able to renegotiate such meanings with others. Successful performances entail the joint interpretation and modification by performers of scripts and stage directions.

This view has been forwarded and systematically articulated by a number of social scientists, the foremost being Erving Goffman and Rom Harré.[2] They have analyzed the various ways in which everyday activities are structured as performances; the use of costumes and props, anything from a waiter's apron to a salesclerk's pencil; the way some spaces, such as lecture halls, dining rooms, and sales floors, function as formal staging areas whereas others, such as teachers' rooms, kitchens, and back offices, are used for preparatory activities; teamwork by performers to generate specific impressions for particular audiences, as parents do for children or salespersons for customers; and the way social interactions are organized with beginnings, middles, and closings. They have examined broad philosophical issues such as the use of emotions and rhetorical forms, the function of meaning and inconsistency, and the balance and tensions between individual and communal performances, as well as the more limited technical ones such as different uses of lighting, sound, and timing.

All these issues pertain to most auctions, where they clarify and illuminate much that might otherwise be overlooked. Auctions, in turn, provide a wealth of empirical evidence that supports and augments the explanatory power of the dramaturgical model. The affinity between auctions and the dramaturgical paradigm is sufficiently strong, in fact, to endow auctions with an explanatory capacity of their own.[3]

An auction is seldom simply held; rather, it is staged. Place, setting, and props are arranged to reinforce the ambience and sense of community appropriate to the particular auction. These factors convey, among other things, different degrees of affluence, seriousness, glamour, order, separation, formality, tradition, and risk. They also put constraints on who can participate. To understand how, it is necessary to be aware of the specific ways in which different auctions are staged and the various factors that favor one form over another.

A number of factors can affect the staging of an auction. One of the most basic is the nature of the items being auctioned. In some cases the items being auctioned make it necessary to bring the auction to where the items are. Commonly the case with real estate auctions, this can also be true for liquidation and estate auctions. When this occurs, the staging has a temporary quality to it, reminiscent of a traveling circus; such auctions are usually held under a large tent. If the items can be moved, and if they are to be sold through an established auction, it is more likely that they will be auctioned within a permanent auction edifice of some sort. If the items being auctioned are commodities raised or grown in a particular area, such permanent sites are very likely to be found in the vicinity where the items are produced.

In other cases, including most fine art and collectibles auctions, the initial location of the items generally plays little or no role in the location of the actual auction. In these cases, the auction's location is more often determined by where buyers are expected to be found. Sometimes this converts into traveling auctions, such as those commonly held for rugs and jewelry; more often, it leads to established auction houses in various major cities. Whether auctions are temporary or permanent, however, their ambience can and does vary considerably.

Sotheby's main gallery, the New England Fish Exchange's auction room, Keeneland's main auditorium, and Luther's Commodity Exchange auction pit are all permanent sites, but they have very little else in common. Each is set in a very different milieu, which sets a tone that carries over into the auction.

Sotheby's main New York gallery is on the Upper East Side in one of the more expensive neighborhoods of one of the most expensive cities in the world. Limousines and expensive foreign sports cars fill the streets. Most other major art and antiques auction houses are in similar areas. Just to enter one of these galleries is to become part of the Upper East Side scene. The young women who serve as receptionists are universally attractive and well dressed, and the patrons no less so. In winter furs abound.

The New England Fish Exchange, in contrast, is set right at the end of a dock in Boston Harbor. The air smells of salt and fish. Trucks outnumber cars by at least three to one. There are few people around, and those who are about are not window shopping or relaxing; they're working. Except for the manager of the exchange and one assistant, there are no women to be seen.

Luther's Auction Barn is also set in a simple and unpolished setting: a dozen acres of undeveloped land alongside a state highway in Dutchess County. The area is clearly rural, though there are clusters of houses that make up small towns. Though there are a number of farms in the immediate area, you have to travel further north before you get into real farm country. There are also some roadside restaurants and bars, gas stations and garages, and a number of equipment-machinery stores. The barn and auction room open up onto a football-size field that serves as a combination parking lot and outdoor auction area for the larger livestock. The tone is less serious than that of the fish exchange. Many more women and families are present. For many people there it is clearly an outing; in this respect it is more like the art and antique auctions described earlier.

The Keeneland and major Fasig-Tipton sales pavilions have elements in common with all three of the auctions described. Like the New England Fish Exchange, they are located within a setting that symbolizes and reflects the industry of which the auction is a part. Within walking distance there is usually a race track, while the whole Lexington area is dotted with scores of horse farms. The ambience, however, has the affluence of Sotheby's and Christie's coupled with the festive feeling characteristic of Luther's.

The settings within these different auctions also vary. The major art and antique auction houses normally have numerous items on exhibit. The halls are carpeted. The chairs are comfortable and arranged in a manner which calls to mind a music recital or guest lecture sponsored by a prestigious club, or a small theater. There may even be a few private rooms which overlook the main auction hall reserved for major buyers and consignors. The auction hall of the New England Fish Exchange, in contrast, projects an image of disarray. Chairs of varying types are scattered about, paper signs and sheets are on desks and tables, and the windows need washing. The ambience is much like that of the union hiring hall depicted in a number of movies in the 1950s.[4]

The sales halls of Keeneland and Fasig-Tipton are probably the most impressive of all. If Sotheby's projects the image of a well appointed small recital hall, the major thoroughbred horse sales pavilions with their hundreds of upholstered seats arranged in permanent, terraced, circular rows project an image of a formal stage or sports production. The seats at Luther's are also terraced and permanent, but their condition, the steepness of the pitch, and the decaying condition of the room are more reminiscent of the cheap balcony seats in the old vaudeville theaters.

These differences in ambience are not accidental. Each setting is designed to convey a set of particular values, attitudes, and expectations. The elegant reserved seats and theatrical ambience of the major thoroughbred auctions convey the message that a performance of superstars is in process in the central arena. All

who participate in or are related to the performance share in
the celebrity. The auctioneers and announcers are stars. The
horses are stars. The multi-million-dollar bidders are stars. Moreover, you can be a star too. All you have to do is bid. The cameras
are rolling; the photographers are shooting pictures; the reporters
are scurrying around. Sotheby's and Christie's can often generate
a similar feeling at their fine art auctions, but they seldom achieve
the same degree of theatricality that is common at a select sale
at Keeneland, Fasig-Tipton, or Matchmaker. Everything tends
to be more subdued and understated.

There is a deliberate attempt to create an atmosphere that is
not only affluent and theatrical in these auction arenas, but also
quite detached and distinct from the everyday world. The theaters
of Keeneland, Fasig-Tipton, Sotheby's, and Christie's deliberately
have no clocks in view to remind the attenders of the external
world of time and responsibilities. The only numbers one sees
are the numbers on the tote boards. Generally there are no windows in the hall to concern people with the weather or the onset
of evening. Pay telephones are discretely located near the toilets.
The telephones being used by various staff persons at art and
antique auctions are one way affairs; they allow buyers who cannot
be physically present to call in and participate. They are not there
to connect anyone inside the auction to the outside world. The
furnishings and the formal seating arrangements serve to underscore the impression that this is a complete and sufficient world
unto itself where those present are capable of carrying out the
process and determining results independently.

The plush and elegant surroundings, and the presence of
attentive and attractive service personnel, further serve to enhance
the participants' sense of their own significance and self-suffi-
ciency. At Keeneland and Fasig-Tipton, the sumptuous dining
rooms which provide a wide selection of delicious foods to potential
bidders while enabling them to watch the auction on closed circuit
television, further reinforces the sense of mastery. Just by attending one of the auctions, it is possible to feel that one has the
resources and judgment to make a sizable purchase. The management of these establishments admits to deliberately fostering this
privileged, world-apart atmosphere. "Hey, this is never-never land;
we don't want people worrying about the time," said one vice
president. "When you come in here, you are supposed to leave
your everyday concerns at home," said another. "Do you find

any clocks in Vegas?" The very high prices that the items at these auctions bring require a setting of comfort and indeed luxury to encourage expansive bidding. The high risks involved, especially in thoroughbred auctions, also require self-confidence and the ability to ignore some of the realities of life.

Most commodity-exchange auctions, in contrast, are staged to create a more mundane, commercial, and cluttered appearance. The grubby, unkempt look characteristic of most agricultural commodity exchanges serves to instill a business-as-usual, no-frills attitude. The conspicuous presence and use of telephones on the walls and desks, the large clock on the wall, the auction clock on the counter, the recurrent concern with time, and the colorless and routine manner of bidding, all function to emphasize the commonplace, non-personal character of the process. The whole process serves to minimize and camouflage individual decision making. The participants are merely accomplishing one task entailed in carrying on their respective businesses. There is minimal second guessing of the prices generated.

The auctioneer presiding over a liquidation also seeks to project a businesslike atmosphere, but one in which bargains are to be found for those who are astute. There is seldom the feeling, common at the major sales at Keeneland, Sotheby's, and similar auction houses, that one is surrounded by potential treasures; most items to be auctioned are likely to be commonplace and of known value. Ideally, however, there should also be the hope that there may be a few hidden prizes. The best setting for a liquidation auction, consequently, is one that conveys a sense of disorder, fostering the hope and belief that there may be treasures here that no one has yet discovered. This requires that the bulk of the items auctioned be seen as quite ordinary. Rather than plush seats and flowers, this auction will offer folding chairs and a run-down warehouse. If, as is common, the auctioneer is selling the goods from their place of origin, he will arrange things only to the extent necessary to run the sale, leaving room for a sense of search and discovery.

The settings of country auctions, provincial art and antique auctions, and collectible-estate auctions are more varied. While exchange auctions are organized to emphasize the collective processes of establishing prices and allocating goods, and sales auctions to emphasize the interests of individual participants, these auctions are commonly arranged to enhance the sense of a sociable community. From the way items are stacked about the auction hall or tent to the food stand in the back, there is commonly a party-gathering atmosphere that is quite deliberate. Things are often staged to create subspaces within the larger auction, where smaller groups can congregate and that allow individuals to move about. The greater informality and accessibility of space generates greater participation and involvement.

One common way of structuring space is to assign specific areas for more formal public activities and others for more private preparatory activities. Goffman analyses such differences in terms of his distinction between frontstage and backstage. As applied to auctions, this distinction not only accurately separates the auction proper from supporting practices but also recognizes that particular areas are designated for particular activities. Nearly all auctions, for example, have office space that serves as backstage areas for the auctioneers and is off-limits to all others. In addition, many auctions have particular viewing areas where goods to be auctioned can be inspected before the auction. Sometimes, especially with smaller auctions, this space may be the same one where the auction will be held, creating an interesting situation where the same space serves both as backstage and frontstage at different times. With horses and livestock there are the barns where the animals are kept, while Sotheby's and Christie's maintain viewing galleries where the goods are displayed preceding an auction. It is here that buyers inspect goods carefully and record specific pieces of information in their catalogs. It is also time for buyers to determine whether there are any other buyers interested in the items they favor. If sellers are present, as in most horse auctions, it is their chance to access the market for their horse. Preliminary jostling may occur with buyers and sellers attempting to solicit additional information while at the same time seeking to hide their own plans.

There are often secondary front- and backstage areas as well. There may not only be a formal frontstage, such as the auction floor proper, and a distinct backstage, such as backroom offices or paddock areas, but a backstage area of the frontstage and a frontstage area in the backstage. A quiet corner on the auction floor may serve as a meeting place for two bidders to negotiate a private deal, while the backstage may be used to stage particular happenings, be it the "discovery" of an "original" invoice attached to a chest of drawers or an early morning inspection of a racehorse by a major trainer, in the expectation that knowledge of them will work its way into the auction. The greater the mix of front- and backstage areas, the more likely that a given participant may believe that he sees something that no one else does, which, in turn, may induce him to act on his own judgment.

However an auction may be staged, it is commonly comple- mented by particular costumes in the form of specific dress codes for auctioneers and audience. Similarity of dress among the buyers, like the formal dress common to many charity auctions, not only enhances the communal character of an auction but also sets a desired tone. At the select yearling sales at Saratoga, the Match- maker season-and-share dinner auctions, and particular fine art sales at Sotheby's and Christie's, such formal dress is currently reserved for the auction staff. Even when so restricted, the formal attire says this is a special occasion where money isn't a problem and is likely to be spent liberally. In contrast, the work clothes visible at most commodity auctions, including tobacco, cattle, fish and other livestock exchanges, give just the opposite message: This is a bread-and-butter business and every penny counts. The cowboy hat and boots affected not only by cattle auctioneers but many Midwestern and Western general auctioneers serves to au- thenticate their auctions by introducing a historical and traditional element. The most graphic use of this particular costume is dis- played by television cattle auctioneers, who sell cattle over closed circuit television from a studio but still dress in their cowboy outfits.

While dress normally serves to eliminate differences among auction participants, it may also be used to accentuate such differ- ences. The clearest example of this is the auctioneers and spotters who often dress in a distinctive manner to set themselves off from bidders and sellers. Specific buyers and sellers, however, may also dress in particular ways to support an image they are trying to project. Sheikh Maktoum of Dubai, and those in his entourage regularly dress down in dungarees when attending the select thor- oughbred auctions in Kentucky. Initially, the purpose was no doubt to disguise their wealth, but now that most everyone recog- nizes them, it has become more a personal statement than anything else. Other major buyers affect idiosyncratic outfits from Bermuda shorts and plaid shirts to bright-colored pants and shirts. Such outfits, however, are nearly always worn either by newcomers unaware of acceptable attire or major players announcing that they are leading actors in the drama. The range of dress in major art and antique auctions tends to be less extreme, but even here any unusual costume will generally belong to an outsider or a major player. (Two or three very casually dressed dealers are normally found at Sotheby's and Christie's.)

Auction dress is as self-conscious and deliberate as any costume in a performance and varies with the play. Many antique dealers who dress casually in slacks and an open shirt for most non–New York auctions automatically put on a jacket and tie for a major New York auction. They will just as consciously remove the jacket and tie for an auction of more modestly priced items even if it is in New York. One California horse dealer consistently wears slacks and an open shirt except for the select Keeneland Yearling sale, when he switches to a tie and suit. Participants' sense of appropriate dress is an integral part of all auction environments. Such dress not only reflects the ambience of particular auctions but also creates it.

Though settings and costumes play an important part in defining most auctions, they are secondary to the actual performances of the participants, especially that of the lead actor, the auctioneer. The auctioneer, who in nearly all instances is the star of the show, remains the heart of any auction. He or she is the focus of all activity. Figuratively and literally, the auctioneer is at center stage. In some auctions, he or she is not only the star but also the producer and director. In others, these roles are shared. Even as the star performer, however, what the auctioneer does varies with different types of auctions. Some introduce the items to be sold; others don't. Some recognize all bids; some don't. The one thing they all do and what can therefore be considered the key function of any auctioneer, is to request and announce the flow of bids. The common technique for doing this in many auctions is the auction chant.

NOTHING symbolizes an auction more than the auction chant. The chant is the theme song of the performance. It is so closely connected with auctions that even a fairly poor rendition by an amateur will normally be sufficient to be recognized. Even auctioneers who do not use a formal singing chant tend to call for bids in a rhythmic manner that has a chantlike quality. Whether or not a formal chant is used, the actual repetition of bids is normally only part of the auctioneer's overall performance. What is more, in most cases where a sophisticated chant is used, very few people are able to understand everything said. All that many people can grasp is the actual bids, and many others cannot even determine those. This is not as disastrous as it might appear, since a tote board is normally used, which allows participants to see what the present bid is. Yet the chant, or its equivalent, retains its importance.

The truth is that the importance of the chant does not lie in its role as price monitor. Its major function is rather to orchestrate the auction rhythm. The chant controls the temporal order of an auction, the movement of the bids. Its importance is underscored when we remember the extent to which auctions are ripe with uncertainty and ambiguity. The chant introduces form where it is sorely lacking. It is a basic structure around which other meanings, namely price and allocation, can be built. The key to a good chant is not only to monitor the bidding but to establish the cadence of the bidding. It does this by controlling the size of bid increases as well as their timing. It manages to take what is a very erratic, disjointed process and meld it into an ongoing, comparatively harmonious process. Like any music, it provides a unifying rhythm or theme.

A chant is only part of the offering process. In the classic case of the tobacco auction, the warehouseman approaches a new bale of tobacco and gives the auctioneer a starting price. Not only does everyone hear that price, but in most cases everyone already knows what that price is likely to be on the basis of previous sales. Once the first price is announced there is only so much time for the buyers to indicate their interest in that bale by offering a higher price. If one or more buyers have indicated a willingness to pay the asking price, it will be sold to the preferred buyer within a short period of time. If no one accepts the first asking price, the auctioneer will normally drop the price a penny or two at a given rate till he has reached the price at which the warehouse man will buy the bale himself. If a second or third price is accepted, he will attempt to move the price back up.

All of this happens very, very quickly. What the chant does is tell the knowledgeable buyers where they are in the process. The particular rhythm of the chant, and the use of filler—that is, words or sounds used between the actual bids, such as "give me" or "right now"—indicate when the auctioneer is about to act one way or another. Like the music in a dramatic movie, tension is built and relieved by the rhythm and its variations.

The buyers know from familiarity with the chant when the auctioneer is going to say "sold American." A layperson not familiar with the process wouldn't, but the buyers who travel around the country with the auctioneers know the style of each. They are keen to pick up any changes in the rhythm that might indicate something unusual, such as an imbalance in the expected allocations or an adjustment in instructions from the warehouse owner. They will also note when slight changes in chant are being used to speed things up or to slow things down. Without the chant the key players at tobacco auctions would not be able to function as efficiently and knowingly as they do.

The chant functions similarly in other types of produce commodity auctions, which deal in high multiples of similar goods such as cattle, eggs, and produce. It takes on a slightly different function when the goods for sale become more singular, such as a thoroughbred auction. Again the chant is not crucial in informing the buyers of the price. It provides the auctioneer, however, with a good deal of discretion in the time he allocates to each horse, and more leeway in the way he uses filler and the types of increments he can solicit. For example, with a bid at $175,000, he may ask for a bid of $200,000 for a while and then drop back to ask for a bid of $185,000. He also can interrupt his chant with additional comments or invite the announcer to comment. Such breaks, just because they *are* breaks, serve to catch people's attention—much as switching channels on the television can wake someone who has dozed off.

The greater leeway afforded auctioneers by the chant, the greater the responsibilities he must shoulder. Not only does the chant require more attention and control on his part, but it requires expert skill to maintain an engaging chant. The tobacco auction itself will generally go on for hours, but each specific chant is relatively short, ten to twenty seconds. In a horse auction, or even more so in a real estate auction, the auctioneer may take up to fifteen minutes to sell a given item. Three minutes of chanting, however, is usually the limit without a break of some sort. Even three minutes is a long time to keep the attention of buyers. The rhythm of the chant plus the use of filler help to do this job, and the more skilled the auctioneer at exploiting the chant, the more successful he'll be.

To a large extent, it is more the sound and cadence of the chant filler that manages to capture attention than its content.

Many people can't make out the actual words of the chant even though their meaning manages to be communicated. A good example of this is Chris Caldwell's filler, "Will you give more to the buyer?" which he inserts between bids in such a way that one "feels" the request even if one doesn't hear the words. The whole phrase is said in less than a second in what sounds like about four syllables: "Willlyrgivmr ferdebyr?" Other auctioneers will spice their chants with more clearly heard comments like "I'm gonner sell her!" or simply "Let's go!" or "Right quick!" Fillers, whatever their particular form, are used to move the auction along and participants depend on its rhythms to situate themselves in the process. Only when there are no bids and the auctioneer feels that the present price is unacceptable, will he stop his chant, break the rhythm of the auction, and comment, thereby jostling the players into a new, and hopefully more productive, round of bidding, which will be accompanied by a renewal of the chant.

The variable rhythms of a chant are particularly useful because they allow the bidders time to consider what they want to do, while at the same time setting limits on their deliberation. In the case of a tobacco auction, the time limit may be no more than a few seconds; in the case of a thoroughbred racehorse or a ten- to twenty-thousand-dollar antique, the time is more likely to be two to three minutes. With a rare masterpiece or a large estate, the bidding may last for fifteen minutes. The shorter the period of time, the greater the saliency of the bidding practice; the longer the time allowed, the more the significance of the individual buyers. What is central in all cases is that the auctioneer maintain control over the timing and sequence of the bids and keep potential bidders aware of the process of bids and eventual sale. Like a Greek chorus, or a master of ceremonies, he is responsible for overseeing the auction process and relaying and interpreting it to the audience.

Even when there is no formal chant, which is the case not only at Sotheby's and Christie's but at many country auctions, liquidation auctions, and even commodity auctions, the auctioneer's comments, requests for bids, and announcements of bids function in a similar way. Prices will be stated and requests for increases will be made periodically, augmented by comments quite similar in content to the fillers of chants. The key fillers are, "I am going to sell it," "Do I hear any more?" and the most famous of all, "Going, going. . . ." In some exchange and dealer-dominated auctions, the auctioneer may actually address individual buyers by name in making a request for a higher bid. There is an orderliness to the process, however, which is quite similar to that produced by the auction chant.

The use or nonuse of a chant in most cases is a matter of tradition. Chants are used in thoroughbred auctions in the United States but are not used in similar auctions in England. There are situations, however, where the requirements and structure of certain auctions preclude the use of a chant, even when other factors may lead one to believe that a chant would be appropriate. Given that fish auctions are primarily allocation processes that deal with multiples of like items, they would appear to be well suited for chanting. They're not. The reason for this lies in the necessity for more than one auctioneer. The chants of two or more auctioneers would vie with each other and cancel each other out. Instead, the two auctioneers work in tandem. First one calls out bids on his boats, and then the other calls out bids on his boats. The time orchestration that would be provided by a chant is handled by the use of a clock. A two- or one-minute warning is given before the end of bidding, ensuring that everyone knows just how much time they have to enter their bids.[5] It is reminiscent of candle auctions of the past where bids were accepted as long as the candle remained lit.

A clock is commonly used to control the declining price sequence of a Dutch auction. A Dutch auction, it will be remembered, is one in which the price starts high and proceeds to drop until someone enters a bid at the present market. The key in such an auction is to be able to time one's bid so that it comes in at the price one wants. This, like many ascending commodity auctions, requires that one be in rhythm with the auction. In most Dutch auctions, the timing is controlled by a real clock visible to all participants. In ascending auctions, this function is served by the rhythm of the auctioneer's chant and call.

The performance of the auctioneer, of course, entails more than the chant or call. The chant or call merely serves to bring order to the bidding process. This organizing process, however, is itself only part of a more complex and encompassing orchestrating process. The participants must be managed and given their cues. This is not a major problem in most exchange or dealer-only auctions, since here the participants are familiar with their

roles and the script. In sales auctions, however, there is a greater
need to manage the bidders, whose preference and needs might
not be commonly known. The auctioneer must try to keep all of
the active bidders involved while maintaining a lookout for any
other bidders who may be interested in becoming active. At exchange and dealer-dominated auctions, where the participants
are generally all active and known entities, the good auctioneer
can focus all his energies on the bidding itself. He may not only
note who has the bid at any given moment but urge specific
buyers to get back in the bidding or be more aggressive:

> 250 is the bid, say 275. Come on, Lady (to a woman who had
> the bid at $225 and is hesitating) don't lose it for $25. 250!
> 275? 275 anybody? I'm going to sell it. Lady, you stayed with
> it up to here. One more bid might do it. 275? 250! 275? 275!
> Thank you, madam. I have 275, 300?

The task of managing the participants, of course, starts before
the bidding even begins. The key to a successful auction is to
get all potential bidders actively involved in the process. This is
most commonly a problem in sales auctions, especially auctions
of medium-priced goods where there is considerable uncertainty
regarding the items being sold. (In up market sales, at Keeneland
or Sotheby's, there may be considerable uncertainty over the price
of the items, but the items themselves are generally known.) The
auctioneer in these situations must establish a sense of community
and trust. The most common strategy for achieving this is through
the use of humor and stories. Through laughter and sharing,
the auctioneer establishes a general ambience conducive to participation in the bidding. Creating such an ambience often requires
a virtuoso performance of an auctioneer.

The auctioneer's performance can range from the benign to
the aggressive. Rather than waste time entreating bidders to increase their bids, an auctioneer who feels that the bidders are
holding back, especially if they are dealers, may elect to sell certain
goods quickly at the low bid offered. This will often serve to
galvanize the other bidders to act out of fear that they may end
up with nothing while others walk off with bargains. While this
strategy often works, it can be expensive for the auctioneer and
is generally used only as a last resort. Most auctioneers would
much rather activate the bidders by offering them items they
cannot ignore. This is clearly not an option in most commodity

auctions, where there is only one thing to sell with perhaps several different grades.

In sales auctions where items tend to be more idiosyncratic, however, it is possible to manipulate the order of items offered to maximize interest. The experienced auctioneer begins with enough good things early in the auction to generate some high bids, while keeping back enough good things to ensure that bidders stay around. He or she will also attempt to alternate the type and price of things being sold, and to group items in a manner that will allow the good stuff to carry the bad rather than allowing the bad to bring down the good, much as a master of ceremonies tries to order the various acts of a performance. The outcome of the auction will depend on how successfully these things are done.[6]

These practices are part and parcel of the auctioneer's performance. Although some items may sell themselves, they are more the exception than the rule. It is more often the case, to use the old Madison Avenue line, that people buy the sizzle rather than the steak. Though a good performance by an auctioneer can go a long way toward creating this sizzle, however critical, it is not the whole production. Buyers and sellers must also play their roles. In fact, for many buyers and some sellers, the opportunity to be part of the auction production is the main reason for participating. They are drawn to auctions as amateur thespians are drawn to amateur community theater groups. (It may be argued that this is also true of some auctioneers, but given that professional auctioneers make their livelihood through auctions, they would have to be compared to professional actors.)

The feeling of being onstage and part of a performance in which you are expected to know and play your part well is widespread among auctiongoers. It is seldom enough to know what specific things are worth. Many potential buyers admit that they are more nervous about not playing their role properly than the economic consequences of making a poor buy. The classic fear of scratching one's nose at the wrong time and having this taken as a bid arises more from the possibility of embarrassment over acting inappropriately than concern with financial loss. Many auction novices admit it is not likely to happen yet cannot avoid the anxiety: "I would be so humiliated."

Though some are intimidated by being part of a performance, most regular attenders love the collective venture. It isn't just the glamour and celebrity status associated with the grand sales auctions that attract them. Neither is it the opportunity for self-expression and the sense of personal power, although these, too, may be attractive. It is rather the sense of belonging to a creative community which attracts them. As one amateur auction enthusiast responded when asked what he liked best about auctions, "It's being part of the action. You get a chance to put your two bits in."[7]

Whatever the feeling—fear of humiliation or exhilaration of being an active participant—these buyers are caught up in the theatrical tenor of auctions. To a large extent they are puppets in the auctioneer's production, but most participate willingly and happily, even when they realize that "playing their part" is likely to be expensive, as it is in most charity auctions. It is such pressure that makes auctions such an attractive fund raising program for many charitable organizations. The wealthy businessman who makes a contribution to his Lower East Side Orthodox synagogue on Purim, by bidding for the right to read or have someone else read the story of Esther, confronts not only the charitable expectations imposed on the wealthy but also the auction expectations that "stars" are expected to be the highest bidders. Similar pressures exist in the black-tie Junior League auction dinner, where charitable inclinations are heightened by self-images that must be maintained in the competitive frenzy of the auction.

While theatrical expectations normally serve, as in charity auctions, to support aggressive bidding by potential buyers, sometimes, primarily in exchange and dealer-dominated auctions, they serve to constrain bidding. In part such constraints result from peer pressures rather than dramatic expectations. There is also a sense, however, in which professionals feel that they must try not to become too enthusiastic. Collectors and amateurs are allowed to go "wild" and let their emotions run away with them, but it is somewhat unseemly for a dealer to do so. As a consequence, many a dealer has dropped out of bidding on an item that he later wished he had bought, just as many amateurs have bought things they wish they had stopped bidding on.

There are occasions when even lay buyers may experience constraints on their enthusiasm that are grounded in the auction script rather than in either their personal resources or interests. Some buyers, for example, will fall out of the bidding when they see that they are bidding against a major buyer, not because they are intimidated—though this is sometimes the reason for such actions—but because it strikes them as inappropriate, as it seemed to the woman who wouldn't bid against the university. The decision to bid or not to bid, in fact, more often than not reflects the part and play that the bidder perceives him- or herself to be in.

Not all performance are individual matters. Many require the cooperation of others in a way which might be considered as "team" playing.[8] In horse auctions, the announcer and auctioneer constitute a very important team. Each acts to complement the other's performance, often by apparently redirecting their attention to each other. A temporarily frustrated auctioneer not able to solicit the bids he wants may break off his chant to ask the apparently unbiased announcer what he thinks of the bidding.

> I have 250 thousand, 250. Anyone say 275? 250. 250. Let's go. 275? 275? Tom, can you believe only 250 thousand for this colt?

> To tell you the truth Walt, I can't. It seems we have much more horse here than money. Some of those people out there just must be asleep. This is a full half-brother to a multi stakes winner. A real nice looking horse.

> OK. Let's see if you were able to wake any of these people up. I have 250. I'll take 260. Thank you! 260. 260. Give me 275, 275?

In art, antique, and collectible auctions, the auctioneer may engage in a similar type of banter with a range of persons including his assistants, other employees, or even a particular buyer. The purpose, however, is nearly always the same, namely, to generate some dialogue that will indicate that the present price is too low.

THE auctionner is not the only one to engage others in such team play. Buyers, especially dealers, will do the same thing. While such team play may occur during the auction itself with one yelling to another that he or she is bidding too much, it is more likely to occur before the auction, when in front of the auctioneer or the seller one will indicate to the other that the item is somehow flawed or otherwise really not very good. A number of rug dealers, who often travel in groups, are notorious for coming up to a prospective buyer who is examining a rug and, either singularly or in pairs, indicating that they don't think much of that particular rug. Such performances often serve to convince an amateur buyer

not to bid as high as he would have otherwise, making it possible
for a confederate dealer to purchase the rug for less money.

Buyers may also engage in more formal teamwork. The act
of forming a buying pool or ring is perhaps the most extreme
instance of this. In some cases, including most antique and art
auctions, such pools may be illegal. In other auctions, however,
they are permitted. Whether legal or not, there are significant
differences in how structured such teams might be. In a fish auction, a buyer with a larger allocation than he wants at a particular
price may quite informally make a deal with another buyer nearby
who has lost all or part of his allocation. Similar informal agreements regarding specific items may occur among dealers who
run into each other during a preview before an auction. Other
rings may be sufficiently established that a member may receive
his share of a secondary ring sale even when not present. There
are also instances of informal agreements, where a successful buyer
discovers after purchasing an item that he has a "partner," and
other cases where an inactive bidder becomes half owner of an
item he never even examined. It may be a horse trainer buying
a yearling and bringing in other buyers later, an antique dealer
assuming an associate will split the costs of an expensive item,
or a rug dealer after the sale claiming part ownership in a particular
rug bought by another dealer. Such occurrences often function
as plays within plays. The principals and a select number of knowledgeable observers are aware of the subdrama unfolding, but
most participants are not.

It is the teamwork between buyers and sellers that is perhaps
the most intriguing as well as the most ethically questionable. At
the simplest level, some sellers work out agreements with particular
buyers to bid up their goods to a specific level, hoping to induce
another buyer to step in at the higher level. If the accomplice
ends up owning the item as a result, the seller will normally agree
to take it back or give a partial refund. At other times, a buyer
and seller may agree to bid against each other without trying to
rope in a third buyer. The buyer may be an agent working on a
commission who wants the bid to go up so that his commission
will be bigger. He may also be a collector who wants to maintain
the price of the item.

There are also more complex arrangements, in which a buyer
and a seller may actually agree to a price before the auction with
all money above that price belonging to the buyer. If the buyer

ends up with the item, he in effect owns it at the agreed price. If someone else ends up the high bidder, the first buyer receives the surplus over the initially agreed price. Sometimes buyers and sellers will agree to split the surplus over a given price. In this way the buyer will only be paying fifty cents on every dollar he bids above the agreed-upon price, but the seller will still profit if the price keeps going up. As might be expected, most of these arrangements are not looked on with favor by other auction participants, and as such are done secretly. On the other hand, the use of floor bids in literary auctions could be seen as such a public agreement between seller and buyer.

What is relevant about these buyer-seller arrangements in the present context is that they create particular impressions of what is happening in the eyes of the other auction participants. The principals in these cases are often more motivated by calculated self-interest than by social norms, but they are nevertheless keenly aware of the performance aspect of what they are doing as far as others are concerned. The main players in these situations make no attempt to force others to bid one way or another. They are content to create an illusion which will in turn induce others to act in particular ways. They are practices, like most dramaturgical routines, whose purpose is to generate particular meanings, values, and expectations.

THE art of creating and projecting a particular view of things, of course, is not limited to the theater. It is also the stock-in-trade of the con man and the charlatan. Erving Goffman clearly recognized this fact and gave due attention to such characters. This link between the theater and charlatan models is evident in many people's response to auctions. Those who engage in what others might consider questionable auction practices, defend themselves by arguing that they are just doing what everyone else is doing: "Hey, most of the people who come here are motivated by hope and greed. They want to believe what they want to believe. I don't force them to do anything." Others will forcibly argue that there are clear differences between putting the best face on an item and misrepresenting it. Whatever the case, the extent to which auctions are perceived as crooked in some way can be traced to the very high dramaturgical component of most auctions. That truly questionable practices are primarily limited to marginal auctions, and even then not the norm, is due to the primary concern with establishing prices considered legitimate by the entire auction community.[9]

The prominence of hope and greed reveals another similarity between auctions and theatrical performances, namely the high level of emotionality. One of the major assets of the dramaturgical paradigm in comparison to the rational-economic-man paradigm is its capacity to incorporate expressive aspects of behavior. Although the model stresses the ways in which settings, situations, and roles are defined and interpreted, it also recognizes that how actors perform in given situations will be affected by their emotional state. This is clearly revealed in most auctions where we find not only greed, but fear, hope, and even generosity influencing the way people bid. People are emotional as well as thinking actors.

Although all auctions include an expressive component, they vary considerably in its significance. Not surprisingly, it is those auctions that allow for and encourage the greatest degree of individuality, namely sales auctions, which tend to be most subject to emotions. In exchange auctions, the constraint to conform to the consensus of the group limits the possibilities for personal expression. The major emotional outbreaks that do occur are normally in response to an attempt by someone to go against the consensus; they tend to be collective responses. While there is considerably more room in dealer-dominated auctions than exchange auctions for individual response, such responses tend to be more cognitive than emotional; participants attempt to determine how ongoing actions modify existing interpretations. It is in the sales auction, where personal taste, self-aggrandizement, and individual resources play major roles, that individual passions emerge as relevant. At times, in fact, these emotions may appear to dominate all else, as evidenced by the introduction that John Marion, the head of Sotheby's, received one evening: "And here is John Marion, the prince of the Passion Palace!"

The dramatic character of auctions is revealed yet again in the customary presence and importance of the audience. Generally, neither fixed-price nor private treaty transactions occur before an audience. They tend to involve only those directly party to the particular exchange. This is not the case with auctions, where there is always a public. Sometimes, as in most exchange and dealer-only auctions, this public is made up almost exclusively of other buyers and sellers. At other times, as in most sales auctions, most of this public functions exclusively as an audience. They are not there to buy or sell. They are there to observe and to be entertained. Their presence in the drama of the auction and the performance of its participating members, in turn, is acknowledged and used when necessary to move the auction along and generate desired outcomes.

What holds the audience and enables them to be used in this way? At times, the glamour of the scene and the attenders may suffice. There is the thrill of being part of all that money. There is also the vicariously experienced emotional high of the intensive competition among bidders, including the exhilaration of winning and the apprehension of defeat. In most cases, however, people are there to observe a performance and have a story told. The attraction varies with the spectator. For the out-of-towner, the infrequent auction visitor, it is all new. The performance may be in its tenth year but to them it is fresh, fast-moving, and impressive. For the frequent attender, the major attraction is the comfort of seeing a familiar production done well. They are interested in seeing who will shine, and if there will be deviations from the script and precedent. The veterans have their eyes open for new big bidders or the very skilled auctioneer who may appear on the horizon. In short, whereas the infrequent observer tends to be immersed in following the plot and keeping all the players in the production separate, the regular is more interested in seeing how the production is being managed and reproduced. And if both observers are pleased, they will break into applause at the proper moment.

It is significant that customers do not clap in department stores or flea markets. Individual buyers and sellers may smile. A passerby or two may nod in response to a particular transaction they have observed. To understand why people clap at auctions, it is necessary to understand why people applaud in the first place.

People applaud a performance that up till then they have not had any opportunity to acknowledge. Their applause underscores the fact that during the performance their silence and lack of engagement in it made them invisible. The actors respond to each other, not to the audience, as they engage in a process of creating a "reality," though clearly a symbolic one. The audience is "ignored" because they are not part of this created symbolic reality, and to allow them to interfere during the performance proper would only disrupt the process.[10] It is only when the performance is over or is in recess that applause is considered proper; that is, that the audience can participate by showing their feelings.[11] Through applause, the audience also manages to indicate to all that while they may have been silent through the production, they are part of the production if not the performance proper.

If by definition the audience is not part of the performance, how can they be part of the production? What have they possibly been able to gain—or give—through their attention? A range of vicarious experience is often possible, as well as emotional support for the performers. More important, however, is their presence at the creation of another reality, a distinct vision or worldview within which all the behavior and activity is given meaning. The "great" performance is one that is capable of generating a "reality" of particular significance for an audience. Whether it be Shakespeare, a ballet, a magic show, or a professional tennis match, the applause generally acknowledges that the audience has experienced a particular reality through the performance that they could not have experienced without it. Their applause expresses approval and acceptance of what has transpired.

Auctions can function in much the same way. Admittedly, it would be very unusual for bidders at the New England Fish Exchange to break into applause. On the other hand, a record sale of a horse at Keeneland or a masterpiece at Sotheby's will nearly always be followed by applause. In fact, whenever an item sells for considerably more than its apparent economic value there is likely to be applause. A new "reality" has been created. Be it a high price for the footstool made for Rock Hudson by Elizabeth Taylor or a record price for an old duck decoy, the audience realizes that they have seen a mundane item transformed into a valuable social object. As in the theater, the performance by those involved in the auction has secured the audience's approval and acceptance of the new value and meaning given to an item.

To characterize auctions as "reality"-generating processes is to restate the thesis that auctions are primarily processes for dealing with ambiguity and uncertainty by generating socially legitimated definitions of goods. Performances are similar "reality" generating processes. The power of both the theater and the auction arise from the fact that people depend on such social enterprises to give order and definition to activities that would otherwise be seen as inchoate and meaningless. The show must go on because to interrupt the show is to allow the reality and meanings that are dependent for their very existence on the show's performance to crumble. Meanings cannot exist by themselves. They exist only insofar as they are embodied in social practices that are acknowledged and understood by a community. Without the auction there would be no transactions, and without the transactions there would be no attribution of value to objects whose value was previously unclear or ambiguous.

There are theatrical elements, beside scripts and roles, which reinforce the dramaturgical imagery; some are present long before the actual sale takes place. Notices and advertisements are sent out. The sponsoring house in most cases will have put together an impressive catalog that will not only list the items but will attempt to hype the sale as a whole. In many cases there will be a whole array of stories as to how the successful house managed to get the consignment. The extensive publicity—which included a ninety-five dollar catalogue, television appearances by John Marion, and extensive previews—given the Andy Warhol auction is perhaps the most extreme example of this process. The items to be sold are themselves prepared to be shown. Livestock is tended and groomed by the owners in the backstage barn area. Most objects are similarly spruced up unless there is a deliberate attempt to maintain the "buried treasure" look. Special care is then taken in the way the objects are shown. Nearly every horse that goes through a major auction ring is made to look like a champion by the professionals who show the horses during the sale. Much the same can be said for the way furniture and paintings are shown by professionals.

Other theatrical practices occur only after the sale has ended; the most striking of these is the auction review. The very fact that such reviews exist underscores the theatrical nature of auctions, especially since they are normally carried in the entertainment or arts and leisure sections of a newspaper rather than the business sections. Such reviews seldom report the prices of all items sold. Specific items are selected; specific participants and the most exciting sales are noted. There is also likely to be some background information as well as some general local-color comments. We are often told who said what and what changes, if any, the auction reflected. It is social rather than economic factors that are noted and stressed and for which the dramaturgical paradigm is ideally suited.

It is these social factors that are embedded in the real world that differentiate auctions from most other theatrical performances. Their ambiguities and uncertainties are supplied by everyday concerns such as the price of haddock today, ownership of a Van Gogh masterpiece, the definition of an automobile classic, and value of a colt by Secretariat. They need not be dramatically invented in order to give direction to the performance. Similarly, most of the performers remain deeply enmeshed in the everyday world and are motivated by everyday concerns. Auctions make good theater, but they are also very practical affairs. The ability to reveal the theatrical aspect of everyday life and the practical side of the dramaturgical paradigm is one of the striking strengths of auctions.

Chapter 6

Bargains and Bonanzas
Structures and Strategies

AUCTIONS are more than theatrical processes for resolving
uncertainties of price and allocation, maintaining communities
of interest and trust, and establishing the legitimacy of value determination; they are places for making and saving money. In fact,
auctions have the paradoxical distinction of being the site where
both the highest and the lowest prices are found; they are the
home of both record-breaking prices and bargains.

As with most everything else about auctions, the primary factors that determine whether prices are bargains or bonanzas are
social in origin. In many cases, they are structural; that is, they
relate to the various options open to buyers and sellers in different
types of auctions and the relative bargaining advantages these
options give buyers and sellers. In other cases they are due more
to specific strategies adopted by buyers and sellers, some of which
include private agreements that transcend the formal jurisdiction
of the auction. Though the decision to employ such strategies is
often an individual matter, such strategies are always subject to
a wide range of social constraints that vary depending on the
type of auction.

Whether structure or strategy, bargaining advantages for buyers or sellers are due to a combination of alternative options,
better information, greater financial resources, collaboration of
others, and more intense personal investment. These factors are
themselves commonly related to where in the distribution process
the auction occurs. Wholesale auctions, that is, auctions where

the buyers resell what they buy to a network of secondary distributors, generally favor buyers since they are often the only outlet
for the seller. In contrast, retail auctions, where there tend to be
many buyers purchasing for their own use, often give the seller
an advantage. What is crucial in all cases is not what is exchanged,
or even the aspirations of individual participants, but rather the
relationships between and among buyers and sellers.

Commodity-exchange auctions are nearly all wholesale auctions that favor buyers. As in fish and tobacco auctions, the major
objective of buyers is to ensure that none of their number obtains
an unfair advantage over the others by either paying less for
the same-quality goods or by obtaining a larger share of goods
than is seen to be that person's fair share. While buyers are interested in pursuing their own self-interests, they are more organized
than sellers and more apt to cooperate with each other in present-
ing a unified front to sellers, who for the most part participate
in the auction as lone individuals. This generates peer pressure
among buyers to keep prices as low as possible while ensuring
that everyone gets the goods they need to stay in business. On
the other hand, as middlemen who are in a position to pass on
their costs to their buyers, they need not seek the lowest possible
price, providing it is the same price for all, which gives them
added flexibility in negotiating price.

As middlemen, buyers also tend to be more knowledgeable
than are sellers about the markets in which they trade. Sellers
are normally first and foremost producers of the goods they sell,
and their overall knowledge of the market is normally limited to
the specific auction transaction in which they participate. The
buyers, in contrast, buy from a range of suppliers and resell to
a number of different retail and commercial outlets, which gives
them a much better overview of the broad market. This gives
them alternative sources of supply and markets. The seller has
to sell goods within a relatively short period of time and through
the few markets accessible to him. All these factors put the seller
at a great disadvantage; it is the buyers who control things, which
enables them to keep a lid on price. (The situation is somewhat
different in exchange markets, such as stock and futures markets,
where many sellers and buyers are primarily traders who participate both as buyers and sellers. These situations are discussed
in more detail below.)

Given this situation, the question isn't why prices tend to be low, but rather why anyone would be willing to sell in such circumstances. The reason is quite simple. As bad as things may be in such an auction for sellers, they are normally better than they would be in a private treaty situation. Here the seller's relative impotence is partially offset by the competitive tensions among the buyers concerning their shares of the market. In auction settings such as the New England Fish Exchange or the New Bedford Fish Exchange, buyers act to ensure that other buyers are not able to "steal" a catch. This serves the interest of the sellers, even though their interest is of little concern to the buyers. Tensions among buyers seldom, if ever, become so great as to allow a divide-and-conquer strategy on the part of sellers, but the visibility and openness of auctions generally protect sellers from instances of extreme greed or exploitation on the part of buyers. While these factors limit the powers of buyers somewhat, most buyers willingly accept them to ensure that they will not be faced with a competitor who can seriously undersell them.

Despite the general acceptance of the auction by both buyers and sellers of commodities as the best possible means of pricing and exchange, its tendency to effect low prices is reflected in recurring dissension among and complaints by sellers. This distress is commonly aggravated by buyers who use their position of power to extract even greater concessions from sellers. Buyers may refuse some goods bought on the grounds that the goods are not as represented; after the auction, they may argue that fish bought as large are really mediums or that produce is of a lower grade.[1] They may also play games with weights and counts. In many commodity auctions, goods are sold at approximate weights and counts; actual weighing and counting occurs later. Buyers are sometimes in a position to influence both weighing and counting.

Sellers obviously resent such behavior. Negative reactions to such alleged behavior has contributed to actual physical violence in some cases, such as at the New Bedford Fish Exchange, where a few years ago a number of people were injured, resulting in the temporary closing of the auction and its eventual movement to a different location. In other cases the response takes the form of sellers simply refusing to auction their goods even if this means taking a little less in an individual private treaty transaction. More than one fishing-boat captain has asserted he'd sometimes rather take the penny or two less than go through the pain of getting pushed around at the auction.[2] Such sentiments reflect awareness

of the balance of power tipping toward the buyers at auctions
and the fishermen's need to assert their own power to step outside
that relationship.

There is, however, something ironic about such reactions and
responses. Not only is the price they get for their fish through
private sale set by the auction price determined that morning in
Boston, but the relative harmony of these nonauction transactions
is dependent on the auction. The types of hassling that occur at
auctions, in fact, really have nothing to do with auctions but rather
reflect the advantages that buyers have. The same exploitive practices can be and are used in private treaty transactions. They
are less common because there is less need for them. The fact
that prices paid through a private treaty transaction tend to be
a few pennies less than the price set at auctions means that the
buyer doesn't need to steal an extra penny. There is the added
fact that if he gets a reputation as being difficult, fishermen are
unlikely to sell to him. Once the price is set in Boston, they can
get the same price from another buyer who won't hassle them.

While the fishermen who avoid the fish auctions are nevertheless constrained by these auctions, their refusal to sell through
an auction commonly does generate some benefits for them; it
limits the number of fish brought in for auction and hence acts
to push prices up. It also can be a corrective to the seller's sense
of impotence in the power relationships of the auction. But the
fact remains that the relatively straightforward pricing practices
and hassle-free transactions in a nonauction sale are made possible
because of the benchmark prices established in the auctions. Without such auctions, in fact, such private treaty transactions would
probably be more exploitive than the most exploitive auction. It
is only because of the auction that the dealer can say, "Haddock
brought one twenty-five this morning in Boston, I'll give you
one twenty-two and a half."

While wholesale auctions of perishable commodities, such as
fish, tend to epitomize the buyer-dominated auction, there are
auctions of other commodities—such as government securities
and contracts, which are put up for sealed bids—which are quite
similar. Government agencies are normally thought of as fairly
powerful, but when it comes to raising money they are generally
at the mercy of the large banks to whom they make their initial
offerings. Similarly, while bonds are not perishable items, they
are commonly sold under severe time constraints due to a need

to meet various fiscal deadlines. Government agencies are also
often at a disadvantage when it comes to letting contracts of various
sorts. It is true that normally there may be only one "item" being
offered at a given time, which theoretically should create greater
competition among the "buyers." Over a period of time, however,
there tends to be a multitude of similar items, be they highways
to build or pencil sharpeners, to be shared by the relatively small
community of bidder-buyers, which not only enables them to cooperate but encourages such cooperation. Moreover, the seller—
that is, the government agency—is generally less knowledgeable
about the costs entailed in the project than are the bidders. These
factors tend to give the bidders a decided advantage in setting
the contract prices, in this case inflating such prices, in a manner
that serves their best interests. Furthermore, they are usually in
a position similar to that of commodity buyers to maintain control
over any of their fellow buyers who attempt to deviate from the
norms of the group by denying them information that the others
have, collectively undercutting them in other situations and
spreading negative accounts of their operations.

Given the apparent advantage of the buyers in these situations,
one may again ask why government agencies use auctions to let
contracts. The answer is again that it is generally better for the
seller than private treaty arrangements, where the advantages
of the buyers may produce worse results. The seller, meanwhile,
is seldom in a position to set a fixed price. If the price is set too
low for the buyers, they are likely to ignore it. On the other
hand, if through ignorance the price is set too high, they are
likely to find too many takers.[3] There is the added factor that
government agencies are often subject to criticisms from interested
third parties, for example, voters, legislators, and other potential
bidders. Auctions provide protection from such attacks by virtue
of their open access and public proceedings and the belief that
they encourage buyers to compete with each other, generating a
better price for the seller. In actuality, of course, what normally
happens is that the buyers act to solidify their communal interest
through legal cooperation and peer pressure, or, as we learn regularly from our newspapers, by engaging in illegal collusion and
price-fixing.[4]

The disadvantages under which the seller works in each of
the cases described are by and large beyond his control. The
highly perishable or at least time-dependent character of the com-

modity, the lack of alternative outlets, the greater knowledge of
market conditions of buyers, and the greater solidarity of buyers
are inherent in most commodity-exchange auctions. To say that
prices in such auctions tend to be low, therefore, is somewhat
misleading. The prices are low as compared to the prices that
these same goods will demand later in the distribution cycle, but
they are not low in comparison to comparative wholesale prices.
Neither can they be considered bargain prices, because most people do not have access to these goods at these prices.

Where time is not so crucial, or where sellers have better
knowledge of market conditions and consequently clearer expectations of what their goods should bring or what services cost, the
disadvantage of the seller is lessened. This is the case in a number
of situations, including auctions of more stable commodities, such
as tobacco, furs, bonds, and other fiduciary instruments, and auctions of used manufactured goods. While generally not as vulnerable as the producers of highly perishable commodities, even these
producers-sellers tend to work at a disadvantage to the buyers
in terms of both their resources and their knowledge of the secondary markets. This is due to the fact that most of these auctions
also function as wholesale auctions, which means that the buyers
are generally better connected to alternate suppliers and a wider
range of secondary distributors.

At wholesale auctions the prices are necessarily low in comparison to the retail prices they will later acquire. While sellers may
complain about such low prices, most are aware of these factors
and accept the differences although they do complain when they
feel the differences are too great. If there are grounds for their
complaints and a sufficient number of sellers withhold their goods
in protest, they are likely to obtain slightly better prices. Meanwhile, the retail buyer who can make a purchase through one of
these auctions can generally obtain a significant bargain. It is,
however, often difficult for such buyers to have access to these
auctions.

At some auctions of this sort sellers accept the prices dictated
by buyers more in agreement than under duress. This is most
likely the case when sellers know the secondary retail markets
well and there is general agreement between buyers and sellers
as to what constitutes a fair markup between wholesale and retail
prices. In these situations, the question of whether the prices
are high or low has little meaning to either buyers or sellers. In

fact, the whole auction process in these situations is often little more than a ritualistic exercise that overlaps and merges with a private treaty transaction. The decision to go through with an auction, in fact, is more often than not tied to the need to satisfy persons not directly involved in the transaction of the fairness of the price. This is often necessary when such third parties are only familiar with the retail price of goods and might see the wholesale auction price as too low, as may happen when repossessed automobiles, furs, and household goods are sold subject to court order. Without such third parties, the auction may actually function as no more than a place to hold private treaty transactions that occur openly or through a wide range of private deals worked out between buyers and sellers before the auction.

Where interested third parties are the actual owners of the goods and the sellers are acting as their agents (as occurs when owners elect to liquidate their holdings through an auction company or through a stock brokerage firm that is an actual member of the stock exchange), a slightly different situation is created. If these third parties were able to or had chosen to participate in the auction directly, they would, for the most part, be in the same position as the captain who brings his fish to market. They would be less knowledgeable than the professional traders, have fewer resources, and be working under greater time constraints. This is the major reason why people are often willing to pay a commission to let a professional trader represent them. The professional traders, in turn, will favor the auction format even when their transactions are in effect private treaty transactions to protect themselves from owner suspicions.

What is significant about all of these transactions is the fact that though the prices may seem low to persons only familiar with the retail price of the goods auctioned, auction buyers and sellers tend to accept such prices as "fair" wholesale prices. Given uncertainties of supply and demand, such prices fluctuate, but the highly integrated markets within which most commodity auctions function, coupled with the rapid dissemination of information among buyers and sellers, serves to limit price extremes. For those actively engaged in such auctions, there tend to be neither bargains nor bonanzas.

There are other factors that serve to limit price fluctuations in such auctions. Key among these are the preauction negotiations that are common and that may produce formal agreements such as the floor in literary auctions or the agreed price in tobacco auctions. In other cases, sellers may enter into a preauction agreement whereby they will sell their item conditionally to one of the buyers based on any of a number of complex arrangements. They may agree, for example, to sell an item for a fixed price with anything above this price reverting back to the buyer; on the other hand, they may agree to split such surplus—this is often called "going halves"—with the buyer. It is not even necessary for the potential buyer to end up being the high bidder. Buyers have been known to enter into such agreements, to let another buyer outbid them in the auction, and then simply collect their portion of the final bid. These practices all serve to constrain extremes in price fluctuation insofar as they tend to reflect agreements between buyers and sellers based on past transactions.

Continuity of price is also supported by sellers withdrawing their goods from sale if they find the price offered too low. Because sellers in most commodity-exchange auctions are part of the same community as the buyers, they can buy back their own goods if they feel the price is too low. Depending on the auction, sellers can do this in a number of different ways. In some auctions, for example, fish and most livestock, they can simply withdraw, or scratch, their goods. In other cases, they can bid on their own goods. Although such practices are clearly the exception, they serve as a check on prices, guaranteeing that no one can "steal" an item, or get too great a bargain.

The conditions for both bargain and record prices are quite different in sales auctions, be they at Sotheby's, some less-known art–antique auction house, Keeneland, Fasig-Tipton, or any auction where buyers are likely to be buying for their own use. Prices set in these auctions are usually final, retail prices. Sellers, meanwhile, tend to be more knowledgeable than buyers, and to exercise more control than buyers over the auctioning process itself for exactly the same reasons buyers dominate in commodity auctions— namely, they are the professionals with more contacts in other markets. On those occasions when retail buyers are as knowledgeable as sellers, they are still generally at a disadvantage, since the commonly most knowledgeable participant, the auctioneer, serves as the seller's rather than the buyer's agent. It is further in the auctioneer's interest to push prices higher in these auctions since he is paid a sizable percentage of the final sale price in these auctions—5 to 20 percent, whereas in most commodity auctions he is paid per item or at a lower percentage. All these factors combine to increase prices in sales auctions.

Although the social relationships surrounding sales auctions favor sellers and hence work to increase prices, the specifics in each case vary. In thoroughbred and standardbred horse auctions, it is the actual owners who are both knowledgeable and organized. They tend to be more knowledgeable for the simple reason that they have both bred and raised the horses being sold. As fellow breeders, often living and working within specific geographic areas, they also tend to be more tightly knit as a community.[5] Breeders know each other, interact with each other, share all sorts of information, and, perhaps most important, control through memberships on different boards most horse sales organizations. It is their industry. An outsider may manage to purchase a horse and race it successfully. If such an individual becomes highly successful and knowledgeable, however, he or she is more than likely to end up a breeder him- or herself. Successful buyers, in short, generally become sellers, further reinforcing the control of sellers.

IN the case of the major art and antique auctions, sellers tend not to be as knowledgeable nor as well organized as those in horse auctions. Their representatives, the auction houses, possess the knowledge and organization required to maintain their position of control. There are, of course, exceptions; major dealers and collectors, both private and public, are generally highly knowledgeable and quite well connected. Whether it is the actual owner or the auctioneer who is in the know, the fact remains that the selling party tends to be in the more dominant position in an art auction. This position of strength is greatly augmented by the fact that the auctioneer will generally protect the seller by setting a reserve price at three-quarters the minimum price expected.[6] In some cases it might be lower, but in other cases it could be considerably higher, especially if a low estimate was publicized to entice potential buyers to the auction.

Given the apparent control of sellers in art and antique and other one-of-a-kind retail auctions, it could be asked why they do not simply establish a fixed-price system or minimally utilize private treaty transactions, where their apparent advantage could be fully exploited. The answer is that they do. A number of auction houses operate separate "tag sale" rooms, where customers can either buy items as priced or negotiate around such "suggested" prices. There are many antique stores throughout the land, in fact, which started out as auction houses and have become fixed-price–private treaty stores.[7] A similar question arises as to why buyers would purchase anything in such auctions, given the apparent advantage of the sellers coupled with the reserve. To a large extent, the answer is the same as that given to explain why sellers are willing to sell in buyer-dominated auctions. It is better than the alternatives, which preclude a collective consensus being arrived at competitively and publicly. Given the absence of comparative prices and the idiosyncratic nature of the item, there is always the possibility of a lack of interest and a low price. Another reason to buy such items at auction is that may be the only place where they can be found.

The possibility of a real bargain coupled with the more idiosyncratic nature of the items auctioned is what gives these auctions their distinctive quality. Despite sellers' knowledge and control, these auctions normally deal in items that maintain their own inherent indeterminacy. It is not so much that the value of each antique chair or yearling thoroughbred colt is indeterminate as it is that the overall level of indeterminacy is sufficiently high to create the possibility of one or two major surprises. It is the possibility, if not the probability, of a major surprise that makes the auction format attractive to both buyers and sellers in these situations.[8]

When asked why he preferred to sell his horses through an auction rather than privately, a thoroughbred breeder shrugged his shoulders and said, "That's the way we do it. That's the way we have always done it." But when queried whether he thought that he got higher prices through the auction than would be possible if he sold them privately, he stopped what he was doing and enthusiastically explained:

> I'm not sure if I get the highest price through the auction or not. That is where the market is and that is the way we normally do it, though I've sold more than a few horses privately over the years. If I had to guess, however, I'd bet we could probably do as well if not better with most horses by selling them privately, but you'd give up that shot at hitting the big one. When one of your horses, especially if you have a good one, walks into that ring, there is always a chance that two or three of the big spenders will like him. If they do, they can run the price up two to three times what you had been hoping for. Admittedly,

it's a gamble, but that is what this business is all about anyway. Taking a chance. Going for the big win.

Most breeders would agree with him.

For the buyer, the idea is to find a yearling with "family" that has raced successfully, which looks as if it has the conformation and spirit to race successfully itself, so that others will be convinced that its offspring will also be able to race successfully and it can eventually be used in breeding. The last point is crucial, since in nearly all cases the real money can only be made if the horse is seen to be a good breeding animal itself.

The possibility of the really big sale is in some measure related to the nature of horse racing, which itself is based on uncertainty. As of July 1, 1987, 167 thoroughbred yearlings had sold for over $1,000,000. Of these less than 20 have so far earned $100,000 or more racing. Most of these 20 plus a few others, however, have actually made a profit for their owners through syndication as stallions or as broodmares.[9] Nevertheless, the owners of at least three-quarters of these 167 million-dollar horses are unlikely to recoup their investment. On the other hand, Seattle Slew was sold for $17,500 at auction in 1975 and within a few years was worth over $150,000,000. Few other bargain yearlings have done as well, but for every million-dollar yearling that did not work out, there have been one or two bargain horses that have.

It is hard to document the extent to which the possibility of making a fortune on a relatively modest investment with a race-horse lends a gambling quality to horse auctions. Horse racing is itself a gambling business. Whatever the linkage, the horse auction clearly radiates with possibilities of the big win. It is this possibility that leads many of the most experienced bidders to complain that they always pay more for a horse in an auction than they intended. The extent to which they do bid more than they initially intended is hard to document. It is clear, however, that it is commonly believed that they often do, and it is this factor more than anything else that makes the auction so attractive to sellers. "It is a simple case of giving up a little in the hope of really hitting it," explains a breeder, when asked why he would sell his best horses through an auction even if he could get 10 percent more through private treaty sales.

On the face of it, it is a long way from the auction rings of Kentucky to the auction rooms of Sotheby's and Christie's in London and

New York. There is no racetrack on which to test one's judgment when it comes to an antique chair or masterpiece. There are no syndications, no parimutuel bets. There is, however, still the long shot, the gamble. The items auctioned tend to be seen as unique individuals, but individuals with a pedigree of their own as in the case of the Cadwalader wing, "hairy-paw" chair that brought the all-time record for a piece of furniture of $2,750,000. Before the sale, the chair's "family and relations" were featured much as the relatives of a yearling colt are featured before a yearling sale. Here again you have buyers trying to judge the past performance of the "family"—that is, how this type of item has sold— and the future performance of the "family"—how this type of item will sell in the future. As with horses, each individual must test itself against other individuals. Here, however, the test isn't on a racetrack but in the opinions of future buyers.

If sellers, or at least the auctioneers, generally know the likely prices of various works of art and horses, how can there still be such dramatic fluctuations? The fact is that such dramatic fluctuations are more the exception than the rule. The lack of criteria for determining either inherent value or supply and demand, however, introduces an element of uncertainty which pervades such auctions even when nothing unexpected happens. The structure of these auctions is such, in fact, that a comparatively few surprises can affect a whole industry. It is a case of the exception proving the rule. The fact that sellers and auctioneers are knowledgeable of their markets and monitor their markets serves under normal conditions to reinforce the stability of such markets, but it also serves, when a surprise does occur—no matter where it occurs—to affect other auctions.

Whereas the dominant strategy in most commodity-exchange auctions is to minimize loss even at the cost of sacrificing major gains, the dominant strategy in many select sales auctions is to attempt to maximize major gains even at the risk of suffering substantial loss. It is this strategy that draws both buyers and sellers in; it is also the engine that produces new record prices for both a racehorse and a painting. It does not, of course, guarantee that the record price paid will prove to be a profitable investment. A good number of very expensive yearlings never race, and the lofty prices of many works of art have collapsed. Similarly, items that may be perceived by the community as having minimum value may later prove to have great value. It is unlikely, however, that items perceived as having high value by sellers or auctioneers will be sold cheaply in such auctions, given the practice of using reserves. Whatever bargains there may be will only be revealed through time.

FOR the average auctiongoer the bargains and bonanzas of commodity-exchange auctions and select sales auctions are only of academic interest. They reflect various social constraints operative in these various auctions, but given that most people have limited or no direct access to these auctions it is of little practical concern. For the average auctiongoer, the action is to be found at the local country or town auction selling almost anything that anyone may have found in the attic, garage, or barn. It is in regard to these auctions, consequently, that the question of bargain or premium prices is likely to be of most general interest. It is also in these auctions that one finds the greatest number of both, due to the heterogeneity of participants.

In an average smalltown auction, there are normally many buyers buying items for their own use. For most of these persons, the price of things, which generally falls between established wholesale and retail prices, will be cheap compared to their fixed-price retail cost. On the other hand, prices may appear quite strong to sellers who, without the auction, would have to accept wholesale prices. If these were the only forces at work, most prices would remain within the wholesale-retail range generating modest bargains and bonanzas. Many people who attend such auctions, however, attend primarily for the entertainment value they derive from the auction; these people are often willing to pay more than normal retail prices just to be part of the action. Other amateur bidders may be vulnerable to playing a hunch or be likely to get carried away by an impulse or enthusiasm.

Though the presence of such amateurs tends to inflate prices, there will generally also be a dealer or two whose actions often serve to deflate prices. Such dealers buy for their own inventory and bid cautiously unless they see an item for which they know they have a buyer. In fact, dealers tend to be more cautious in these sales then they would be if surrounded by other dealers. It is one thing to make a bid against a fellow dealer in whose judgment you have some faith, and another thing to bid against someone who has no idea what the item is worth. Amateurs spotting dealer hesitation may respond with their own caution, believing that to pay more than a dealer is willing to pay is to overpay. As a result, dealers may well end up buying a large percentage of what is sold at comparatively low prices. In other cases, amateur buyers may feel confident in outbidding dealers, believing that dealers will never overbid. This can lead to extremely high prices if the dealer is buying something on consignment for someone else. Where another dealer would realize that the price had become too high and drop out, an amateur may happily keep going.

Further contributing to the erratic character of these auctions is the fact that there are few reserves due to uncertainty on the part of sellers-auctioneers as to the demand they might expect from a primarily nonprofessional crowd. Items may sell very cheaply or quite high. The situation is such that it encourages auctioneers to adapt a wide range of techniques to get the crowd involved and bidding. They can and do knock down some items very quickly to encourage people to get into the bidding early and not to hesitate too long in making their bids; with other items, they may go on and on, telling stories and using humor to bring the audience along with them. Ironically, these tactics may serve further to accentuate what is already a very unstable situation by generating higher-than-expected prices for some items on which a great deal of time was spent, and allowing other items to go more cheaply than usual because of the use of a quick hammer. In either case, they serve to increase the number of both bargains and overpriced items.

Despite these variations and the odd exceptions, the following patterns tend to be the norm at most country auctions. Items sold to dealers tend to be sold at minimally half of what they would cost from these very same dealers. This is generally more, however, than the sellers are likely to get on their own if they attempted to sell the goods, and much more than they would get by junking the goods. Items sold to lay buyers also tend to be low when compared to dealer's prices, though at most sales, at least two or three things are likely to be sold for substantially more than what they could have been bought for from a dealer. Perhaps the fairest way of summarizing most such sales is to say that individual items tend to sell for less than they would bring elsewhere, but that the total return for all the goods sold in a given auction is often quite high. In this respect, such auctions tend to be just the opposite of more up-market auctions dealing in quite expensive and rare items, where many individual items may go for very high prices, but the total returns tend to be more modest.

The overall erratic nature of these auctions is directly related to the comparative lack of an encompassing social structure. Bidders, sellers, and auctioneers are all responding to each other, but they tend not to know each other very well. They also come to the auction with very different interests. Similar conditions hold in most charity auctions and produce similar erratic results. (The participants often know each other quite well, but there is a much greater range of individual reasons for participating, including self-aggrandizement, which plays a minor role in most country auctions.) It is not unusual at a charity auctions, for example, for one very expensive all-expenses-paid trip to some exotic place to be bought for half its cost and another very similar trip to be sold an hour later for double its cost. Every year at the Christmastime charity auction held in California, mentioned earlier, some logs will sell for hundreds of dollars while others will go for very little.

THERE is another type of auction where the question of bargains arises in which the social relationships among participants is quite different from all of the various types so far described. These are auctions—more accurately, pseudo auctions—where the auctioneer is actually the owner of the goods being auctioned and is merely using the auction format to sell his goods. Buyers are all amateurs and seldom even know each other. There are many examples of such operations, from the traveling "Oriental rug auction" held at your neighborhood motel where all the rugs are owned by the so-called auctioneer, to the "auction store" with a permanent address and "auctions" nearly every night of mass-produced goods that are owned by the auctioneer.

Most of these auctions do not qualify as true auctions because the goods are owned by the "auctioneer," who will not sell anything below his or her price. Sometimes such dealers will have stock from other sources which they have been asked to liquidate, but even then they normally will only sell if they receive what they consider a legitimate price, normally a price within 10 percent of the wholesale price of the items. In nearly all cases, a knowledgeable buyer could purchase the items directly from the dealer for the same price as at the so-called auction.

The normal technique with "auction" stores is for the vender to bring the customer into the establishment and to exhibit the goods. If a customer shows interest in a particular piece, the salesperson, for that is what he or she is, tries to get some idea of the price the customer may be willing to pay. If the price is within the acceptable range, the salesperson will inform the customer that that item will be auctioned that evening or later, when the auction is planned. The item is then brought out, and the auctioneer will run the price up taking bids "off the wall"[10] until he reaches his "fixed price," at which time he will drop his hammer and say sold. In those rare situations where there may be two real bidders, the auctioneer will normally produce, within a reasonably short period of time, another, nearly identical object, which he will auction off to the losing bidder for approximately the same price.

Basically this same technique has recently been used in television auctions, which have appeared on various cable channels. (I am not discussing here the auctions run by nonprofit television channels, which are similar to the charity auctions described earlier.) Here the first task is to get the potential buyer to tune into the show. There is normally also a live audience in the studio to create the proper auction ambience and from whom the auctioneer takes his bids. The "auctioneer" knows before the "auction," however, the price at which he will sell the item and then he will offer it at that price to all, both in the audience and at home. The common technique is to run the price up using confederates in the audience to, let us say, sixty-four dollars for a set of china that would wholesale for forty dollars and retail for seventy-five, and then to offer it for forty-nine dollars to all who want such a set:

> What am I offered for this lovely set of china? Will you give me $20? I have 20! 25! 30! I got 35! [It is impossible to tell where he is getting his bids, and if you watch carefully it is quite clear he is often going on his own.] I have 40, now 50. Gimme 55, 60. Anyone 65. No. Okay, I'll take 62, 64. I have 64. Anymore. That's it? $64. But here is what I am going to do. I'm going to give you this lovely set of china for $49. Some buy! And I have some more identical sets that I'll also sell for $49. First make sure that everyone who was bidding on that first set gets a set. Just hold up your paddle if you want a set for $49. [Here assistants begin to call out the numbers being held up.] You people at home can have the same set for the same price. Just call the number at the bottom of your screen.

In these auctions, the auctioneer may not actually be the owner of the goods. He may have been hired by the owner. This clearly is the case in most television auctions. The prices, however, will be set by the owner. This more than anything else distinguishes such auctions from local liquidation auctions where the practice of offering off multiples of the same item for the price set in auctioning one of the items is common. Another major difference in such local auctions is that the price will be set by the auction rather than selected by the auctioneer.

Why anyone would buy items in such an auction is another question. In some cases, it is simply a question of ignorance. In other cases, it grows out of a fondness for the auction form. Many such buyers admit it isn't the bargains so much as the fun that keeps them coming. Moreover, the prices set in such "auctions" are often quite competitive with both private treaty and fixed-price systems.

The reason for this is that the seller in these auctions tends to concentrate his or her stock in a few items that have been purchased quite cheaply. This can often be done because the seller is not running a normal store that requires the maintenance of a broad inventory. He or she can make a large purchase at a "real" liquidation auction. The skill with which goods are sold, moreover, often carries over to the buying, which increases the possibility that he or she will be able to sell the goods at a very competitive price. The auction mode generally serves to lower overhead costs. In some cases such as the traveling auction, it eliminates the need to maintain a store. In the case of the nightly auction store, it allows the owner to cut back both on hours and staff and to expose himself to robberies only during the short auction period, when extra security help can be brought in.

As a result, the prices of goods at most "fake" auctions, be it a Pakistan rug, ceramic lamp, or mass-produced metal sculpture, tends to be in line with the prices paid for similar goods in private treaty and fixed-price transactions. On the whole prices are similar to those one would likely pay for similar items at a discount store. If, of course, a buyer has indicated in earlier discussion with the vendor that he thought the item to be worth more than its discount-store price, many of these auctioneers will oblige him by running the price up by taking phantom bids. Most such operators, however, will be more than happy to get the price they want and attempt to make such a buyer a regular customer. Some rug dealers, for example, have a number of steady customers who follow their auction from one motel to another, buying a throw rug here and a runner there. Even in these pseudo auctions, in short, if buyers are to obtain bargains, it will be due to the social relationship they have established with the seller.

As described, the pseudo auction is much more a selling strategy of an individual salesman than a collective pricing and exchange mechanism that auctions have been claimed to be. As such, the relative advantage that the seller is able to achieve in these pseudo auctions is much more a result of specific actions taken by the seller than structural features of the relationship between and among buyers and sellers as is the case in the real auctions described earlier. The distinction, however, can often become somewhat blurred. The fact is that within the context of real auctions, individual buyers and sellers can and do engage in strategic practices that can dramatically affect the prices paid. Even in these cases, such strategies are both constrained and made possible by social conditions that pertain to the specific auctions. A full understanding of factors affecting bargains and bonanzas requires an explication of these strategies.

SOME of these strategies, including rings, preauction private arrangements, the doctoring of merchandise, the use of phantom bids, and various types of posturing, have already been discussed in other contexts. Each of these practices, however, lends itself to a range of uses depending on the type of auction. Most interesting is the fact that while all of these strategies are initiated by specific individuals and all entail ethically questionable tactics, they are all also subject to fairly rigid communal guidelines. Each auction is governed by standards that specify how much and what type of doctoring of items is allowed. Even when they are the products of such strategies, consequently, most bargains and records remain subject to social expectations and to existing patterns of social relationships.

The members of most rings, for example, don't consider what they do most of the time to be unethical, even when it is illegal. A good number of auctioneers agree. The fundamental question is whether or not their actions serve to generate fair prices. Some will even claim that it is the casual buyer who is the source of most difficulties. As one antique dealer who is frequently a member of such rings stated:

> Look, we are here day in and day out. Not only that, we can be counted on to support the prices we set. Some lady comes in off the street and pays five grand for a table that we would only offer four for. It's nice for the guy who owned that table.

The auctioneer also makes an extra two hundred bucks.[11] There is no way, however, that she is going to be back here tomorrow willing to pay five thousand for an identical table. If we pay a particular price for an item, the auctioneer knows that he can get pretty much the same thing from us tomorrow.

Rings, of course, don't always function in this "constructive" fashion. Rings have been known to spread false information about specific items that they are interested in acquiring cheaply. They may start rumors regarding the authenticity or the provenance of a particular piece. They have been known to put pressure on other buyers, nearly always other dealers, who have refused to cooperate with them. These actions are looked upon as illegitimate by nearly all, including those who engage in them. As one rug dealer said, "Sometimes some things happen that are not very nice." (He was referring to an instance where a rug bought by a small dealer who had refused to join a particular ring was deliberately damaged by someone thought to be a member of the ring, sometime between its sale and when it was picked up.) "It happens."

While rings play an important role in the life of dealers and auctioneers, they are really of minor importance to most casual auctiongoers. Most rings will not interfere with isolated purchases. It is true that a casual buyer may be misled on occasion, but this can happen in both private treaty and fixed-price situations too. Moreover, dealer strategies that depress prices are unlikely to hurt the casual buyer; it is practices that serve to inflate prices artificially that can prove costly to the unknowing amateur. (For the casual seller, of course, ring practices that depress prices are costly; it is here that he or she must rely on the agent, the auctioneer, for protection.)

The practice most used to artificially inflate prices is the practice of inventing bids, earlier referred to as taking bids "off the wall." It is important to distinguish this practice from the legitimate practice of employing reserves. The question which concerns many auction amateurs is whether such practices are common. Perhaps the most honest way to answer this question is to say that it is not as common as many auction cynics would assert but more common than most auction houses would admit. The whole process becomes somewhat more complicated by the fact that while in some cases the auctioneer may be inventing bids, in other cases it may be the present owner who is throwing in bids. The auctioneer may or may not even be aware of what is happening. It all depends upon the type of relationships that hold between auctioneers and buyers and sellers as well as the levels of cooperation among buyers and sellers.

It is not uncommon for buyers and sellers to use a mixture of different strategies to move the price in a particular direction. Many a horse has walked into the ring with a specific reserve known to the auctioneer and an unknown phantom bidder in the back. A reserve might be set at thirty thousand dollars, but a confederate of the owner—it is normally not wise for the owner himself to be seen bidding on his own horse—may have instructions to bid up to fifty thousand dollars. While such practices are not taken kindly by most auction houses, they are normally tolerated providing that such bidders don't disappear if they win the item. If an owner ends up buying back his own horse through a friend for twenty thousand dollars more than the reserve, so be it. The auction house will get a larger commission even if it agrees to charge only a buy-back commission.[12] In short, the auction house will tolerate such behaviors because they are in the position of protecting their own interests. If, however, the bidder refuses to acknowledge the bid or simply disappears, intending to let the legitimate bidder have it at his or her last bid, the auction house may find itself in the difficult position of trying to get the next to last bidder to take the item at his or her last bid without causing this bidder to feel that something funny is going on.

If the underbidder, the next to last bidder, is willing to accept the horse at his or her last bid, the whole matter is likely to pass unnoticed. When this happens, the original owner is likely to feel very pleased, since he or she may well have successfully run the bid up considerably higher than it would have gone without such intervention. The buyer, of course, will have been forced to pay considerably more than would have been the case if the owner had stayed out of the bidding. The underbidder, however, suspecting what may have happened, may elect not to accept the horse at his or her last bid. The auctioneer may then go back to the person who had apparently been the high bidder to see if he or she will acknowledge the earlier bid. It is more likely, however, that he will simply drop the bid back and begin again.

While the practice of bidding on one's own horse is generally considered legitimate, if somewhat nonprofessional (providing one doesn't disappear), bidding and running is considered unethical by all. It is a practice that someone may get away with once but seldom twice. The structure of overlapping social relationships is such that the auction house can normally find out if a regular was responsible for such a phantom bid and take measures to ensure that it does not occur again. The simplest means of control is not to accept the culprit's horses in the future. When, however, the culprit is not part of the industry, little can be done. Some years ago, for example, a woman of striking appearance with two or three younger men in tow appeared at the Fasig-Tipton sale in Saratoga, made the winning bid on several very expensive yearlings, and disappeared. The horses had to be brought back later in the sale and reauctioned. To this day no one seems to know who she was or what she was doing.

WHEN there is confusion regarding the final bid that is not immediately resolvable, rather than attempting to sort matters out between the last two bidders, the practice of beginning the bidding again at a lower price open to all, is preferred for two reasons: The auctioneer may suspect that someone has made a phantom bid and wish to avoid revealing this fact, which would only serve to put the whole process into question; or he may simply want to avoid having the second bidder go through the same doubting process. It could be that the apparent high bidder is a legitimate bidder who has, in fact, really not made the bid attributed to him or her. If the underbidder refuses to acknowledge his or her bid, this bidder may also become suspicious. If the initial high bidder disappears, most will assume that something suspect has occurred. It is generally wiser whatever the circumstances for the auctioneer to back off from such situations after the initial inquiry.

Situations like those just described occur fairly regularly; more regularly than most people realize because of the way they are covered up by a skilled auctioneer. There are many other instances of owners or their agents engaging in such practices but dropping out of the bidding before a winning bid. Some owners will bid below their reserve in order to generate some early action. This can backfire, however. On more than one occasion during the last few years, major buyers have been known to drop out of the bidding when they discovered, or even suspected, that the owner was bidding against them in an effort to raise the price. Provided that owners do not attempt to renege on their bids, such bids are normally accepted as part of the process if somewhat questionable. The crucial variable is the degree to which the protagonist remains subject to social controls. If controls exist, the practices are more likely to be accepted. It seems to be a case of allowing particular buyers to be misled, providing that the integrity of the auction process is maintained by ensuring that individuals attempting to manipulate prices accept the consequences if they fail.

Sophisticated horse buyers have their own strategies to counteract those of hungry breeders and equalize their own powers a bit in these seller-dominated auctions. It is not uncommon for buyers to visit horse farms weeks before a sale to inspect individual animals. During the sale, buyers continue to visit the stalls, where they can have the horses walked for their inspection. During these visits they may attempt to make private deals with breeders. These visits can also help breeders by informing them who is interested in what animals. If a big buyer shows real interest in a particular horse, the breeder may increase his reserve or take a chance of running the bid up during the auction. It is not so much that he believes such big buyers are loose with their money as it is that interest from such buyers indicates that the horse is a good, hence potentially valuable, horse. It is another case of individual actions being used as indicators of collective sentiments.

Professional buyers and sellers take these preauction encounters very seriously in attempting to judge what is likely to happen in the auction. A good deal of positioning occurs, as everyone tries to get the most information they can while revealing the least. D. Wayne Lukas, who is one of the most knowledgeable horsemen in the business, is known to attempt to outsmart breeders during these visits by asking to view both horses he is considering buying and horses in which he has no interest. He has also been known to send back to the stalls in apparent disinterest just the horse he likes best while he continues to study others. As one owner relates:

> He calls for four horses. Two he sends back to the barn in five minutes. The other two he studies for close to a half hour. Comes the sale, I find out he bought both the ones he sent back to the barn and never entered a bid on the other two. A smart son of a gun.

Such actions are considered perfectly legitimate, which is not surprising when they are put alongside breeder practices of carving hooves, the use of splints, and other techniques to enhance the appearance of their horses.

Practices not unlike these can and do occur in other types of auctions. The main differences revolve around the identity of the perpetrators. What gives such practices a distinctive character in horse auctions is the active participation of both buyers and sellers directly in the process. In most auctions, sellers must depend upon the auctioneer to protect their interests. It is the auctioneer who orchestrates everything including the use of phantom bids. Here again, however, such actions are subject to various formal and informal conventions. While these conventions are not only understood by most regular auction goers, but accepted as serving the overall interests of the auction community, the infrequent attender is often ignorant of the practices which raises certain ethical questions. The fact that such questions seldom bother auction regulars simply further underscores the communal character of most auctions; the members of any community seldom accept as legitimate criticism from outsiders though such criticism may upset them.

Most auctioneers, for example, consider it perfectly proper to accept nonexisting bids when they have a higher set reserve. Many will even claim that they are serving the buyer as well as the seller because if the buyer is not urged on to the level of the reserve he or she will not be able to own it. Similarly, it is seen as perfectly legitimate in many auctions, for an auctioneer to take a left bid—that is, a bid left by a person who was not able to attend. This practice is generally not allowed at livestock auctions, but is very common at antique-art auctions. At the more reputable auction houses—and this includes many small country style auctions—it is customary for such left bids to be handled by an auctioneer's assistant. Most commonly, it will be someone at a desk on the side who is keeping a record of the auction transactions. The practice of acknowledging such bids by saying something like, "I have two hundred dollars at the desk, will anyone say two twenty-five?" or, "Helen [the name of his assistant, which is known to most of the bidders] has the bid," is much preferred to acting as if the bid were in the room. Some auctioneers have been known to say, "The bid is against the room," when the last bid is either their own based on a reserve or a left bid.

What is not considered proper by most is when the auctioneer enters a bid on his own that is not tied to a predetermined reserve.

It happens, however, especially when the auctioneer owns the item being auctioned. This is not standard practice in most auctions. There are a number of respected auction houses, however, which will buy large lots of goods outright and sprinkle them through an auction. There are other times when an auction house may give a certain commitment to a seller on what the total sale will minimally bring. The auctioneer in effect has a direct financial interest in the goods even if he is not the owner. In these situations, he may elect to buy the item himself rather than sell it for a price that is less than what he will have to reimburse the owner. Sometimes an auctioneer will bid on an item because he believes it to be worth more than the present bid and he is willing to buy it at that price. Most auctioneers will announce when they have bought an item in this way; some will even indicate before the sale that they intend to bid on a particular item. In many cases, however, the only way of knowing that the auctioneer bought the item is to see where it goes after the auction is over.

WITH the exception of phantom bids made solely to elicit a higher bid when the reserve has already been met, most participants accept these practices as unavoidable if not desired. They are necessary to protect the interests of sellers, who, it is argued, would otherwise be at the mercy of professional dealers, to open the auction up to buyers who cannot attend in person, and to limit extreme price fluctuations which would serve to undermine confidence in the entire system. In short, what might appear to be questionable practices serving the self-interests of particular buyers and sellers are commonly accepted because they are seen as supporting the collective needs of the auction community. The major questions are the openness with which they are done and whether or not bidders should be informed and what they should be told. Obviously, some practices such as taking a nonexistent bid cannot be done openly at the moment, but the fact that such practices are employed can be made public. What is a common practice in one auction may be unusual in another; similarly, what is acceptable practice at one time may become unacceptable later. Again the determining factor is the structure of social relationships characteristic of the auction.

Only a few years ago, for example, David Bathurst was forced to resign from Christie's when it was widely publicized that four years earlier he had stated that three out of eight paintings had been sold at a sale when only one had actually been sold. The story had been well known for some time among dealers and collectors, but it had not caused any uproar since these professionals not only knew that such things occurred but accepted them as necessary to insure a healthy auction atmosphere. Moreover, in the early eighties, the practice of not announcing nonsales was standard practice. Bathurst's undoing was due to two things: He claimed that the paintings had been sold rather than simply saying nothing, and he made the claim to reporters who then relayed the news to a wider audience.[13] In so doing he transposed a practice that was accepted as necessary and legitimate within the auction proper into another area where it lost its legitimacy. Concealing a nonsale during an auction, it can be argued, protects the items yet to be sold; denying a nonsale after an auction serves to misrepresent the market.

Even today, however, it is not standard procedure to publicize nonsales in art auctions, though it has become standard procedure in thoroughbred and standardbred horse auctions. On the other hand, art auction houses will commonly announce the underbidder in major sales where this is not done in horse auctions. These subtle differences reveal delicate differences in the structure of the two markets. The thoroughbred industry contains a greater number of professional buyers and sellers who have to know what the present general market is. They need to know what types of horses are selling for how much. In the elite world of art masterpieces, the players and the major transactions are fewer. Individual buyers are, consequently, more concerned to ensure that they are bidding against a real other buyer rather than the auctioneer or the owner in the specific situation.

While there is a high degree of consensus regarding these various practices within each auction community, changes in the composition of buyers and sellers cause auction houses to continually review their own practices. Keeneland debates whether they should announce underbidders and Sotheby's wonders if they should publish a summary of sales sheets. For most old-time regulars in both types of auctions, these are really not ethical issues because they know what is happening. It is the amateur and new player who is likely to feel that he or she has been mistreated. The question for the auction houses is whether they have an obligation to ensure that these amateur buyers understand what is happening if, as has been the case, the auction houses have deliberately attempted to bring them into their auctions. A tobacco auctioneer doesn't have to concern himself with these types of questions since all his bidders are professionals and familiar with these covert practices. Christie's, Doyle's, Skinner's, and Sotheby's do.

WHILE auction professionals continue to debate the practical and ethical implications of such practices, nearly all will agree that the deliberate misrepresentation of items is unethical if not illegal. Admittedly, goods are nearly always sold as is. The concept of "as is," however, is meant to cover the condition of the item, not its type or pedigree. It is one thing to sell a Louis XVI chair with a crack in a leg and quite another to sell a nineteenth-century copy. If, of course, the chair is not announced as a Louis XVI chair, then the auction house is not responsible. If something is announced as an example of a particular kind, the buyer has recourse if it turns out to be something else. The same is true if it turns out that the seller does not have proper title to the item, unless again the bidders have been warned of the dubious nature of the title, and the item is sold subject to this uncertainty. It is legitimate, in short, to attempt to get the community to value items in a manner that will serve one's own self-interests, but it is not legitimate to misrepresent what the items are.

The average casual auctiongoer generally need not fear being deliberately lied to or misled. On the other hand, no one will feel compelled to explain what is going on or what everything means. It is common practice today to publicly present either orally or in printed form the basic rules governing any auction open to the public, but it is each individual's responsibility to understand the nuances.[14] No set of rules, for example, says anything about the present state of a given market, the status of the major players, or the current "collective wisdom." This is not surprising, given that it is specifically these things which most auctions are engaged in determining. On the other hand, no auction begins with a blank slate. Auctions are reproductive processes; they are engaged in reproducing markets, player positions, and collective wisdom; that is, auctions do not generate values, classifications, social relationships, or reputations anew, but rather modify and sustain the values, classifications, social relationships, and reputations that already exist.

THE link between what buyers and sellers accept as a fair price and the social relationships and composition of these buyers and sellers is perhaps most evident in the emergence of new auctions. In recent years, three qualitatively new auctions have emerged: the Matchmaker Stallion Share and Season Auctions, the New York and New Jersey Port Authority Fish Auction, and agent auctions of original manuscripts. These three auctions represent a new use of an auction format. In each case, the auction was a direct response to what were seen to be changes in the composition of the buying and selling publics which undercut existing exchange practices and created an opportunity for particular types of auctions. In all cases, there was a belief that the existing exchange practices did not generate fair prices for all parties.

The Dutch[15] display fish auction organized by the Port Authority of New York and New Jersey is a quite conscious attempt on the part of the Port Authority to respond to a growing number of fish buyers who were interested in having better selective powers in the fish they bought than was presently possible buying through other dealers or existing auctions. They also felt that such an auction would meet with favor from fisherman because it would give them more control over their catch and a better return for their efforts since better quality fish would bring in higher prices. The authority hoped that the practice of displaying the fish auctioned and including new buyers would entice fishermen to bring their fish into New York.

After nearly two years, the auction has not been a success though proposed changes in its format may yet prove successful. The primary reason it has not worked is that the rules of this auction do not reflect the comparative powers of the various participants. The large fish wholesalers who control the Boston and New Bedford auctions and the Fulton Fish Market simply refused to play by the new rules, which they saw as adversely affecting their interests. Many of the practices recommended could and have worked in sales auctions aimed at a more retail market, but this auction remains a wholesale auction. The difficulties experienced by the Port Authority underscore the fact that what is seen as fair in one context may not be seen as fair in another.

While the Port Authority Fish Auction has faced major difficulties, both the Matchmaker season and shares auctions and agent auctions of original manuscripts have proved highly successful. In both situations, items that were previously sold almost exclusively through private treaty have been successfully auctioned. Success in each case seems to have been due to the emergence of new players, both buyers and sellers, who felt that the existing private treaty arrangements were distorted by too many private arrangements among and between buyers and sellers. As one horseman said:

> Last year I enquired about buying a season in a particular stallion. I was quoted a "going price" and assured that was the price that everyone was paying. Later I found out that, in fact, in three cases the price included either a half interest in the foal and in two other cases a mare had been given in exchange for part of the fee and in each case the mare had been overpriced. What it all added up to was that at least five breeders got to that stallion for a lot less than I paid.

In the case of agents attempting to sell manuscripts, the complaints tend to be more straightforward: "If agents were convinced that they could get a fair price from publishers—and with some you can—there'd be fewer auctions."[16] To get the prices that they believe to be fair, more and more agents are auctioning original manuscripts. They have been successful for the same reason that Matchmaker has been successful, namely, because of changes in the social composition of both industries.

What makes these situations fascinating is the fact that while stallion shares and seasons and manuscripts were traditionally sold through private treaty, many of the parties involved in such transactions are often deeply involved in auctioning closely related products. Yearlings and mares have traditionally been auctioned as have the subsidiary rights of literary works. Nevertheless, these same persons not only preferred not to auction shares and seasons and first rights, but looked on such auctions as anathema.[17]

Why most publishing houses and stallion syndicates preferred private treaty sales to auctions for original manuscripts and stallion seasons and shares, while encouraging auctions of secondary rights and yearlings and mares, is not hard to understand. They clearly have more power in private treaty sales of original manuscripts and stallion seasons and shares than individual authors or small breeders and are in a better position to set prices which benefit themselves. It isn't just a case of their being more expert. They also control the market. The ability of a few agents and Matchmaker to break this control by initiating auctions was due in both cases to a significant influx of money and new players on both sides of these transactions, who often felt as if they were still being treated as outsiders. The auctions that they created are clearly not open, but they are significantly more open than the private treaty arrangements that preceded them. For the traditionalists who were part of the old network, such auctions were not necessary. For the new boys and girls on the block they were. In both of these cases, it was clearly not only a financial decision, though many of the most enthusiastic auction players had doubts about the deals they were getting through the private treaty format. There was also a sense in which the new players wanted to redress what they saw as inequities in the old, exclusive networks.

What it is crucial to recognize is that these inequities only became inequities with changes in the composition of the two communities; moreover, it was these changes in the social composition of these communities that enabled these auctions to succeed. In the case of the Port Authority Fish Auction, where the perceived inequities were not supported by changes in the composition of the community, the auction has not been able to succeed.

Despite all the rhetoric about bargains and bonanzas that surrounds auctions, the reality is that extremes of either sort are much more the exception than the rule. Many prices seem low because they are wholesale prices; other prices seem high because the items are very rare. The real bargains are more likely to be found in someone's attic. Auctions more often serve as the means for uncovering such bargains, but even in these cases the nature of the item has usually been discovered before the auction begins. This does not mean that auctions are free of risk or lack opportunities for major gains. Some items auctioned such as a yearling thoroughbred are high-risk items by definition. Many others are risky because they are subject to changing tastes, definitions, and resulting changes in supply and demand. It is because they are subject to such uncertainties that they are auctioned in the first place. These risks, however, are built into the auction process; they are not commonly subject to manipulation by particular participants.

IT would be misleading to imply that there are no risks for the amateur auctiongoer. One can get carried away and spend more for an item than it is worth, especially if there is another amateur bidding against one. The sums involved in such instances, however, tend to be modest. The single greatest danger of being duped through an auction lies in being manipulated by one's own agent. More than one collector or new horseman, for that matter, has overpaid for an item because of private agreements between his or her agent and the selling party. It is not very difficult for an unscrupulous agent to agree to overpay for an item—that is, to run the price up on an item and then to split the extra with the seller. Auctions, admittedly, lend themselves to this sort of practice, but the chicanery in these cases is not due to anything that the auctioneer or the auction house do but to the actions of the agent.

The other major danger for the individual buyer is to become caught in a larger market manipulation or mania. If a few dealers have managed to corner a particular market and to run the price of items up considerably, a novice buyer might discover that he has paid an artificially high price. Provided the dealer or dealers do not liquidate their holdings, however, such high prices may be maintained for a considerable period of time. If, however, the dealer decides to sell his or her holdings, the novice collector may find that he or she has overpaid. (The dealer can normally sell as the price falls and still come out ahead, since he or she has in most cases bought most of the collection at much lower prices than that paid by our collector.) Such problems, however, need not concern the average auctiongoer.

In the end, the bottom line, bargain or bonanza, proves to be just another part of the collective process known as an auction.

Chapter 7

What Auctions Tell Us about Values

Auctions do many things: They resolve ambiguities and uncertainties; they establish the value, identity, and ownership of items; they entertain; they shape social relationships; and they reallocate vast sums of money. They also tell us a great deal about economic life and social behavior. It is in this latter capacity, as a paradigm of human behavior, that they have had their greatest impact not only on how we think about the determinants of economic value and behavior but rational behavior in general. Unfortunately, the auction paradigm presented by economists has little relationship to the dynamics of real auctions we have explored.

For neoclassical economists, the auction paradigm embodies rational economic man in his purest form. They conceive of auctions as socially uncontaminated mechanisms for matching the individual preferences of buyers and sellers. The goal is exchange, with the determination of the selling price as the means. Participants act in terms of their own known interests and resources with minimal external constraints. The prices and exchanges that result are merely products of the pursuit of individual economic self-interest and preference. The practices, places, participants, and conventions of the auction itself—what could be called its "social structure"—are seen to have no direct causal influence on the auction process and its outcome.

This is not to imply that economists ignore environmental factors or that they do not see interests changing through the auction process. Studies have attempted to show how different

162

conditions affect the decision making of participants. What is not included in the economist's perspective is the way the actual auctioning process serves to create–re-create both social definitions of value and the relationships among participants. Instead, participants are seen as individuals participating in auctions with their own predetermined price expectations. Auctions are conceived neither as ongoing processes whereby participants appropriate values that are concurrently being socially generated nor as means for generating and maintaining social relationships.[1] The critical expressive and social concerns of participants and the constraining and enabling social relationships that characterize real auctions and the concurrent determination of values are ignored.[2]

It is specifically these social aspects of auctions that are central to the auction's meaning. Real auctions—in contrast to theoretical models—are not exclusively or even primarily exchange processes. They are rather processes for managing the ambiguity and uncertainty of value by establishing social meanings and consensus. The particular significance of concrete auctions, however, is not that they are complex social processes capable of generating social definitions. Fixed-price and private treaty transactions, to say nothing of noneconomic transactions, are likewise complex social processes capable of generating social definitions. Where auctions differ is that they are *explicitly* concerned with generating and maintaining their social contexts as a means of determining value. Auctions provide us with a rich array of situations for examining the ways in which meanings, values, and practices are mutually determined; the complex social process can be seen unfolding before our eyes.

By showing how the views and interests of individual participants, the influence of time, place, and situation, and the importance of past and ongoing practices, all play a role in establishing values, auctions support a "realist" conception of human behavior. While underscoring the importance of the interpretive component of human behavior, a realist view sees human behavior as constrained by a reality that exists independent of human consciousness, a reality grounded in time and space, and subject to physical forces.[3] Auctions offer us an overview of how values are determined through the exercise of personal interests, the weight of collective interpretations, and the repetition and modification of social practices, all orchestrated dramaturgically but grounded in a real world.

The very existence of an auction means that conventional

methods for determining value have failed for one reason or another. It may be an inability to ascribe to goods meaningful cost or replacement values because of (1) doubts regarding the inherent value of the goods; (2) uncertainty over supply and demand; (3) problems of classification; or (4) some combination of the three. Whatever the specifics, the source of the difficulty resides not merely in the minds of the persons involved but also in the character of the goods. This explains in part why auctions tend to be used extensively and primarily with highly perishable goods, used goods, goods of questionable origin, and goods seen to possess certain artistic merit. In all of these cases, there is a relatively high degree of value ambiguity because the goods can't be related easily to a standard market or a standard accepted formula for evaluation.

Whatever the particular source of the uncertainty, the function of an auction is to establish values using whatever means it can. Auctions differ from each other for the simple reason that different types of auctions have different resources at their disposal. Some auctions rely primarily on the tastes and interests of buyers; others rely more heavily upon the collective judgments of recognized experts, while others base value primarily on past transactions. In revealing when these different methods are most likely to be used, auctions tell us a good deal about the way values are determined. In fixed-price systems, and to a slightly lesser extent in private treaty systems, these various factors tend to become enmeshed in a manner that makes it difficult to distinguish one from another. The value of auctions is not that they are the "purest" example of economic behavior, but rather as an improvised alternative form they more clearly reveal the seams and cracks that allow us to distinguish the discrete elements that contribute to the value-determining process.[4]

The extent to which different types of auctions make use of different resources in their search for acceptable values is reflected even in the way we commonly refer to different types of auctions. The New York Stock Exchange, for example, which is strictly speaking a double auction,[5] is commonly referred to as a "stock market" rather than a "stock auction," which reflects the importance of the transaction itself. Most bond offerings, in contrast, are referred to as "bond auctions," which stresses the decision-making role of the large banks that dominate these sales, though secondary sales, which are to smaller investors and more dependent on past transactions, are commonly referred to as the "bond market." People enquiring about what happened on a given morning at the Boston Fish Exchange will normally ask about the "market," given their interest in the actual transactions, while people enquiring about a particular horse sale at Keeneland's will ask about the "auction," given their interest in the decisions taken by buyers and sellers. Auctions at Sotheby's, on the other hand, are normally referred to as "sales," emphasizing the importance of the major purchase, while dealers at a wide range of dealer-dominated auctions often talk about "buys," which underscores the significance of acquiring stock for future resale.

The relative emphasis given individual preferences, collective definitions, and past and ongoing transactions in determining value relates to other factors including how emotional, how rational, how individualistic, how collective, and how predictable the auction is. The fact that no one had any idea how much some movie fan might be willing to bid for a crudely made footstool given to Rock Hudson by Elizabeth Taylor explains why hundreds of people at Doyle's burst into applause when it sold for $1200; it was seen as a highly personal and expressive act deserving of an expressive response. In contrast, the sale of a diamond brooch for over $40,000 in a dealer-dominated jewelry auction in a suite at the Waldorf-Astoria caused hardly a ripple, because the dealers present expected such a bid as reflecting the collective judgment of what the piece was worth on the wholesale market. The importance of individual desires and tastes in determining values at a select sale at Keeneland or Sotheby's also explains why the emotional pitch is often high enough to churn the stomachs of all in attendance, while the high predictability of prices and lack of personal involvement at many exchange auctions often seem to cause buyers and sellers to fall asleep.

THE primary reason that different resources, be they individual desires or past transactions, are stressed in determining values in specific auctions is because differing auctions provide us with particular types of information. In most sales auctions, for example, especially the more select ones, little is "known" about the item—due to the very idiosyncratic nature of the items offered—and less about past sales since there may never have been any. The only things that can be determined through the auction process are individual likes and dislikes. In contrast, dealer-dominated auctions normally handle less idiosyncratic items and have a commonly accepted "shared wisdom" as to the value range of particular "types" of items, based both on the experiences of "professionals" and the views reflected in their professional publications. This consensus will be the most important determinant of value in these auctions as individual preferences are in sales auctions. In most exchange auctions, there is considerable knowledge of both past transactions and other ongoing transactions (that is, the "market"), making such transactions the most important value-determining factor.

The emphasis given to individual taste and judgment in sales auctions explains why prices are apt to fluctuate more in such auctions than in others. Comparatively unfettered by collective judgment and previous transactions, prices are able to fluctuate in accordance with the whims and hunches of different bidders. The more idiosyncratic the item, the more subjective can be the bid, though the tastes of even the most egocentric bidder are subject to some forms of financial constraint and various internal checks. Even these restraints, however, are attributes of individuals. To understand most sales auctions, consequently, it is normally necessary to understand the motivations and constraints operating on individual players. In such auctions, psychological-biographical explanations of how value is determined commonly prove most informative.

In dealer-dominated auctions, collective judgments are the most important factors determining value. This consensus of opinion is the product of ongoing discussions among experts and commonly formulated in professional journals. Individual members will often have their own opinions, but these are normally dependent on the collective view. Admittedly, a particular individual may, through his or her own bid or action, determine the price of some item at a given time and override the collective judgment. He or she is unlikely, however, to be able to sustain such prices over time. The fact that there are multiples of the items sold through these auctions means that the individual must either have the resources to impose his or her value judgment in all cases, or eventually defer to the collective judgement. A particularly active individual may be successful in redefining this collective wisdom, but it will be the collective wisdom, somewhat modified, which will determine the value.

The situation in exchange auctions is quite different. Here

there is a relatively continuous series of transactions, "a market" in like commodities, which clearly determines both the individual and the collective view. In these situations the public consensus of the moment is subject to the external constraints of ongoing practices—that is, the transactions of the market—in much the same way that individual judgments are subject to the collective view in dealer auctions. The situation is actually somewhat more complex since these past practices themselves incorporate and reflect past expectations and past practices. It is, however, the dominant role of ongoing practices in determining value that distinguishes exchange auctions from other auctions.

ALTHOUGH the behavioral practices that constitute such markets reflect past expectations, these expectations as embodied in such practices acquire the force of tangible fact. It is no longer the case that yesterday twenty members of the New England Fish Exchange "thought" that haddock was worth $2.25 a pound; rather it is the case that haddock "sold" for $2.25 a pound yesterday. The same thing could be said for IBM stock or silver bullion. Once embodied in practices, judgments acquire an "objective" status similar to the "accepted" status opinions acquire when published. Values thus established commonly have more weight than individual or collective opinion.

Another way of describing the differences between sales, dealer-dominated, and exchange auctions is to say that definitions of value are rooted in different soil. In sales auctions they are rooted in individual psyches; in dealer auctions, in various publications and face-to-face interactions; and in exchange auctions, in patterns of behavioral practices. These different contexts have their own impact on the way ideas, desires, and behaviors are related. Individuals are commonly able to maintain desires that are behaviorally inconsistent, such as the need to own an item but not pay a lot for it, while the market price of an item may fluctuate on a given day in a manner that would be considered irrational if it reflected the opinion of an individual.

The weight and effect of values differ according to the contexts in which they are rooted. Evaluations emanating from an individual have less power of persuasion than those that come from a community, and both, in turn, have less than those that are embodied within behavioral practices. It normally helps an individual to quit smoking if he or she desires to quit, but peer pressure to quit is an even more powerful inhibitor. Nothing helps stop the practice of smoking, however, as much as the act of stopping.

Nevertheless, there are always exceptions. There are times when wanting to stop is the most important thing. There are other times when peer pressure may make one quit even if one didn't want to. Similarly, just not smoking for a period of time may work to "break the habit" in some cases, but only serve to increase the desire and practice in others. The weight of each factor cannot be accurately predicted for all situations, but generalizations can be made.

Although the relative importance of individual preferences, collective wisdom, and behavioral practice in determining values varies from situation to situation in everyday life, it is difficult to evaluate each factor except in auctions. In most evaluative situations, group views reflect ongoing practices and individual opinions, individual opinions reflect group views and ongoing practices, and ongoing practices reflect both group and individual opinions. It is only when this interconnected system for determining value breaks down, resulting in the need for a new mechanism to determine value—as occurs in auctions—that we can isolate and examine each factor. What we discover is that there exists a natural priority of social practice over collective opinion and collective opinion over individual preference.[6]

The New York Stock Exchange is an auction, but one characterized by ongoing highly visible and continuous transactions. As such, the "market"—the ongoing collective transactions—dominates. Decisions concerning value are made within the limits set by the market. Individual investors may and do attempt to determine what they believe to be the correct value of a company by engaging in all sorts of research and analysis. Such analysis may lead them to want to buy or sell a particular stock at a particular price. At any given moment, however, the price they will pay or accept will be determined primarily by the market at that moment. Much the same conditions hold for many commodities where there is a daily market.

The situation is very different when no such ongoing market exists. Few collectibles—be they automobiles, rugs, clocks, coins, or guns—are auctioned on a continuous, regular schedule. In these cases, the participants of a particular "auction" are likely to be seen as more important in setting values than the "market."[7] The auction is commonly reflective of some social consensus or shared knowledge, which is usually contained in a professional publications or organization. Such media often serve to bridge the gaps between sales by keeping the community aware of current events affecting the value of items. They remind the reader of what value was determined at the last auction while introducing any new relevant information that may have influence over future sales.

It is normally only when neither ongoing practices nor shared knowledge are sufficiently stable to be used as guidelines that individual preferences are able to play a deciding role in determining value at auctions. This is likely to occur in the case of more idiosyncratic items, where neither ongoing sales or practices nor collective opinion have any relevance. An individual's strong preference can determine value in such cases. Individual preferences, collective opinion, and ongoing practice are generally all present to some degree in determining value, but often one factor is far more important than the others. This explains why we talk differently about different types of auctions.

Even very sizable transactions in the stock market are normally seen as transactions in the market rather than as individual purchases and sales—"two hundred thousand telephone at the market" even though some individual or institution had to initiate such a transaction. A major yearling purchase, on the other hand, is likely to be perceived in much more personal terms—"Maktoum just paid two and a half million for the Windfields' Danzig colt." Cookie jar and duck decoy collectors, meanwhile, are more likely to talk of last week's sale at Skinner's or Doyle's and in many, if not most, cases their comments will be reflections of what they've read in the *Antiques and the Arts Weekly* or the *Maine Digest*, testifying to the weight of shared experience and knowledge in their auction-collector community.

The way people refer to auctions in their speech tells us something about the dynamics—the way different factors mutually affect each other—at specific auctions. It tells us something about how we see auctions functioning, though often we may not even be conscious of what we are saying.

FEW auctions better reflect the dynamics of "markets" than the stock exchange. In recent years we have seen the Dow Jones[8] average rise from below 800 to over 2700 in about five years, only to drop 1000 points within a few weeks and recover approximately half the loss over a period of months. Given the comparatively modest changes in the overall economy—changes in interest rates, unemployment, balance of payments, and federal deficit have been much more modest—such stock market movements seem extreme. What caused them? Was it radical transformations in the way individual buyers perceived the market? Or was it rather dramatic changes in the shared view of the market as embodied in the *Wall Street Journal, Barron's,* or other financial publications? Or, finally, was it something internal to the trading practices themselves?

Clearly all three factors played some role, but the evidence strongly suggests that ongoing practices were the decisive factor. Both individual and collective interpretations were formed primarily in response to changes in the market that were due to trading practices that were themselves intertwined with other trading markets. That is, trading decisions in one market were often in response to transactions that had occurred in another market, which were themselves influenced primarily by practices in yet another market. A great many of the most significant "buy" and "sell" decisions were not made in response to either individual or collective judgments about particular stocks or the market as a whole, but rather in terms of other "buy" and "sell" decisions. Many of the key "decisions" taken, in fact, were taken by computers programmed to respond to specific indicators such as changes in interest rates and capital flow—the movement of funds between different types of securities, which could include not only bonds and stocks but different currencies and precious metals.

The extremes of the last few years, and especially the collapse of October 1987, were greatly enhanced moreover by the introduction of new computer-based trading programs that made use of financial futures and option contracts that didn't even exist before 1980.[9] In combination, what these new instruments enabled investors and speculators to do was to create various complex trading programs both to hedge, protect, other investments and to exploit what were seen as discrepancies in different markets. It created the opportunity to buy and sell "risk," since it was possible to make someone else responsible for extreme moves either up or down. If I own a stock at fifty dollars but buy a forty-dollar put option, someone else will have to make up the loss if the stock goes below forty. The variations rapidly became very numerous.

What is important in the present context is that specific buy and sell transactions no longer functioned merely as a buy or a sell, reflecting an individual's value judgment, or even a communal value judgment. They could be tied into another hedging transaction that for the buyer or seller completely offset what was apparently happening. It was possible, for example, to buy stocks, even very speculative stocks, as part of a program that was intended not as a speculative venture but as a "fixed" return investment. On the other hand, one could also buy options and futures of very conservative stocks and bonds that, because of the leverage, were extremely speculative investments. In combination, this produced a degree of overlapping and mutual dependency between different markets that did not exist before. And since the markets were interrelated, specific purchases and sales did not reflect the individual or collective evaluations that such transactions would indicate if taken by themselves, but rather the fact that another set of transactions had occurred. That is, a particular program was set off, resulting in the sale of a large block of stocks, because another transaction occurred in a completely different market.

A decision might be made, for example, to sell a million dollars' worth of stock not because the seller thinks that the stock is overpriced but because such a sale is part of a program linked to buying an offsetting stock future. The decision to initiate this program may have been set off by a short-term discrepancy between the price of the stocks and the stock futures. More specifically, the stocks may have been trading at a sufficient discount relative to the future that such a program would generate a fixed return higher than currently available from similarly secured bonds. The interest rates of these fixed bonds, meanwhile, may be down because of a decision to lower interest rates in a foreign country, creating an influx of foreign funds into the U.S. bond market, pushing domestic interest rates down. The decision to decrease rates in the foreign country, in turn, may have been triggered by trade figures.

The fact that no one seemed to understand what was happening until after it had happened, and the fact that what was happening wasn't consistent with the "accepted wisdom" of the moment—the positions reported in the financial journals by the financial experts—is not particularly surprising when one realizes that neither individual judgments and preferences nor collective interpretations and wisdom played much of a role in determining what happened. The auction stock market was not responding to either individual or collective opinion; it was responding to what was happening in other markets.

The situation is quite different when auction transactions take place irregularly and such "markets" do not exist. Here, some recent events occurring in thoroughbred auctions are informative. In 1985, the all-time record for a thoroughbred yearling was set at the Keeneland sale in July. $13,100,000 for one horse. This sale represented a peak in the price for thoroughbred yearlings. The next year the highest price paid was $3,600,000, and in 1987 it was $3,700,000. What caused these variations? While there have been changes, primarily increases, in the size of race purses as well as changes in the tax laws, the single most important factor in these price fluctuations was the competition between a few major buyers, namely the sheikhs from Dubai and Robert Sangster, a leading British owner. It was the head-to-head competition between these two buyers that generated the $13,100,000 price in 1985. It was their subsequent "partnership" that excluded such prices in succeeding years.

Something quite similar occurred in January 1987 when two bidders drove the price for a two-hundred-year-old Philadelphia Chippendale "hairy-paw" chair to $2,750,000. The reputed winning buyer (though not the winning bidder since he had an agent bid for him) was Philadelphia collector Richard Dietrich. He was particularly interested in obtaining the chair because he had a matching table that he had bought some years earlier for considerably less. The auction prices for special items such as the Chippendale chair are commonly determined by a very small number of interested buyers, bidding for very personal reasons, such as ownership of a matching table. Here the individual is clearly more important than any other factor.

Each bid reflects not only the personal judgments of bidders regarding the value of the horses or chair in question, but their sense of self and their willingness to compete in a "tournament of values." Past sales and the opinions of others are not ignored, but they clearly play a very secondary role. The fact that the "hairy-paw" chair was judged to be one of a kind, and only one horse was sired by Nijinsky II out of My Charmer, the dam of Seattle Slew, made both the market and consensual evaluation of each irrelevant.

WHILE the stock market and Keeneland and Sotheby's probably reflect these two different processes more clearly than other situations, they are not unique. Transactions in most exchange auctions, for example, be they commodity, fish, or tobacco, tend to be highly dependent on past transactions. Moreover, in each case these markets tend to have a life of their own and are caught up in a complex of other behavioral practices, such as fishing, farming, or alternative processes for allocating such commodities. Prices may remain stable for relatively long periods of time or they may fluctuate erratically. What is true in both cases is that individual and collective expectations of what will happen or what should happen tend to be much less important in determining what will happen next than the complex of ongoing transactions.

On the other hand, prices in art and antique auctions—in fact, any auction dealing with one-of-a-kind or very singular items, especially items that lend themselves to high evaluations—tend to be determined by individuals acting on the basis of their own views and biases. What happened yesterday or last week is not important. If two bidders with sufficient resources decide that they both want an item, it may sell for ten times more than a similar item sold for previously. If the number and frequency of similar transactions increases significantly, of course, such individualized behavior is unlikely to continue, because a market of sorts will have been created. The secret in maintaining a high-flying sales auction is to ensure a steady flow of unique and rare items by emphasizing differences between items so that each item can stand on its own. With no market, no basis for comparison, and no means for the collectivity to enforce its judgement (if there is no other like item to sell, the collectivity can't show that the price paid last time was out of line) individuals are free within their financial limits to assign value as they choose.

The dynamics of how value is determined in communal–dealer-dominated auctions are somewhat more difficult to document because of difficulty in exposing the decision-making process. In these cases there tends to be neither an ongoing market nor dominant players. Rather, there is a complex social process involving various forms of communication, including the auction process itself, through which members of a given community generate a shared definition of the situation. Such shared knowledge is normally codified and communicated through collective publications of varying sorts. On a day-to-day level, however, the most common telltale sign of this process of communal definition is the habit of talking about the price or value of particular types of items without allusion to either the market or the individual bid.

When people talk about the price or value of IBM, they are referring to the last transaction or "market" price. When people talk about the price of a particularly renowned thoroughbred or painting they are talking about the value placed on the item by a particular person. When people talk, however, about the value of an ordinary Victorian chair, a piece of old Wedgwood china, or an eighteenth-century tool, they are talking about commonly accepted values as reflected in the communal media. Moreover, as market dynamics and personal dynamics establish values in those auctions in which they dominate, so communal media affect values in those auctions in which *they* dominate.

One of the most significant consequences of such media impact is a tendency for greater consistency in evaluations over time. In this type of auction, significant changes in evaluations are generally a result of larger changes occurring in some other area of economic life. One can contrast the price movements of real estate with those of stocks and works of art. The price movements of real estate tend to be much less erratic and extreme. When extremes do exist, such as the dramatic dropoff of prices in the early 1970s in New York real estate, it is usually part of a larger context of change, such as the perceived bankruptcy of New York City.

So defined, evaluation in these auctions is most similar to the way items are evaluated in fixed-price systems. In fixed-price systems, however, the community speaks through general rules and procedures. In these auctions, such rules remain much more nebulous; what is key is the ongoing dialogue among the members of the community. There also tend to be more shifts in opinion due to the greater number of uncertainties inherent in the situations.

IN summary, though all auctions are definitional processes that establish and legitimate values, these processes are themselves subject to an external "reality," which is multilevel and affected by social and personal constraints such as preferences, opinions, rules, customs, and institutionalized practices. In all cases, the central concern is the resolution of ambiguity and the establishment of legitimate values. The fact that these values are rooted in different contexts—individual minds, media of different sorts, and ongoing practice—suggests that no evaluation is purely rational. Every determination of value is subject to forces that are part of the dominant context. Individual decisions are subject to feelings, habits, and desires. Collective decisions are subject to a variety of norms that govern communication within the group, while practical decisions—decisions that emanate from what occurs—are subject to a variety of constraints that are built into these practices. Daily limits are set in most future markets that prohibit price movements either up or down beyond the set limits for the day; daily quantity limits are set for tobacco auctions.

Individual decision making, which is characteristic of sales auctions, for example, is influenced not only by the views of the particular person, but also by cultural givens. There is no reason to believe that Japanese, English, Arab, and American buyers have the same attitudes toward confrontation and self-aggrandizement central to most sales auctions. Group decision making similarly is influenced not only by group ideology but also by group dynamics and organization. Some groups are more subject to rumor and fads than others. Similarly, social practices are formed and constrained not only by the expectations and meanings inherent in the practices but also by constraints related to the items being auctioned. The production and distribution of fish is different from the production and distribution of gold and subject to very different types of natural forces. These factors tend to give such auctions a sense of being more dependent on nonsocial factors than sales and communal-dealer auctions.

These social, psychological, and environmental complexities of real auctions reveal the limitations and fallacies implicit within the neoclassical economic model. Real auctions clearly do not support a view of human behavior, or even economic behavior, as either rational or individualistic. Real auctions rather support a conception of human behavior that is expressive, interpretive, and social and grounded in behavioral practices; they illustrate a multilevel social reality that incorporates individual beliefs, communal meanings, and patterns of social interaction and reflects a specific time and physical location. The fact that auction participants are motivated by different types of intentions and objectives, including greed, self-aggrandizement, conformity, friendship, and curiosity, also favors a multidimensional view of human behavior. Finally, the manner in which auctions serve as means for the continuing production and reproduction of values and definitions supports a social-constructivist view of social reality; social reality is not something given independently of social actors but is created through social practices and interpretation.[10]

Such a constructivist view of human behavior, and its inherent critique of the neoclassical model, has significant implications given that the neoclassical model has been used not only as a descriptive but as a normative model of behavior. Economic and governmental policies and programs have been promulgated both to foster and take advantage of such behavior. There are many in political science, sociology, psychology, and other disciplines who have argued that the neoclassical auction model and its theory of "rational choice" best exemplify human behavior. To these researchers, the auction model reveals not only what goes on but what should go on.

Accepted as the way "free" exchanges "should" occur, this neoclassical auction model has influenced governmental policy decisions that affect us all. Many free-market policymakers have argued that government should leave the "market" alone and let price be determined solely by "market conditions," by which they mean competition between rational buyers and sellers. Using this same erroneous auction model, others have argued that such social problems as prostitution, drug addiction, and other criminal behavior are merely rational pursuits by individuals seeking to maximize their own self-interest.[11] According to these theorists, all that is required to solve these problems is a change in the reward structure: The way to end prostitution or crime is to increase the costs for the individual. Unfortunately, such simplistic rational models can't explain what people do in real auctions, let alone why a fourteen-year-old girl "decides" to become an addict.

It would be both misleading and unfair not to acknowledge that a number of economists, to say nothing of numerous other social scientists, have also criticized the neoclassical model. Lester Thurow, for example, argues strongly in *Dangerous Currents*[12] that the core problem for economic theory is its dependence on the price-auction model of human behavior. More specifically Thurow argues that the price-auction model, with its built-in assumptions of individual, rational, utility-maximizing actors, is incapable of dealing with human actions that are inherently social, pluralistic in intention, and of questionable rationality. Unfortunately, neither Thurow nor any other economist who agrees with him on this presents an alternative view that matches Giddens's treatment of the way in which space and time, domination, signification, legitimation, and tacit knowledge are incorporated in social practices.[13] Each of these factors, while ignored by the neoclassical model, is reflected in the auctions of the everyday world.

The "irrational" disposition to dominate or be dominated, or what often appears as a "will to possess" or "be possessed," operates in real auctions and effects the determination of value. Without competing wills to possess, there would be no auctions, with the possible exception of a few highly regulated commodity auctions. Conversely, auctions provide a milieu within which participants can freely exercise and exhibit their wills to possess; they are also, of course, a context in which participants' sense of control and power can be threatened, where they can suffer defeat and humiliation. Whether it is the desire to dominate or be dominated, auction values reflect such nonrational concerns. In fixed-price and private treaty situations, it is only one's pocketbook that is open to attack. The question, Do I want to own this item? is overshadowed by the question, Do I want to spend what is being asked for that particular item? In an auction the first question tends to take priority because the constantly changing price puts most stress on the question, Do I want it? Moreover, it is a question that, once asked, must be answered and reanswered relatively quickly. The question, How much? is consequently often effaced by time pressures and doubts regarding one's desire to own the item.

SUCH powerful, emotive, noneconomic factors explain in part why in many auctions price seems to be quite secondary. The question of how much to bid is less important than the question, Do I want it? If a buyer has decided to own the item, he or she may find that there is not enough time to give due consideration to price. The only decision that can be made is to bid or not to bid, with the result that the bid may be considerably higher than will seem reasonable in hindsight. This explains why sellers will often sell through an auction even if they know that more often than not they could do better selling the item privately. They are looking for that buyer, or more correctly those two buyers, who just *have* to own what they are selling and will bid accordingly. The reverse is also true. People go to auctions to find those items that some seller must sell regardless of price.

Instances in which the desire or need to possess an object takes precedent over price are many: the fish buyer who needs to acquire sufficient supplies to satisfy his major customers; the collector or museum curator who must own an early painting by a famous painter; the baseball fan who will pay nearly anything to own a baseball signed by Babe Ruth. In these situations, especially if financial resources are unlimited, the auction ceases to be a matter of economic competition. It becomes an arena for the confrontation of individual wills. It should be stressed, however, that such confrontations would normally not be seen as socially acceptable or legitimate; the participants would be looked upon as irrational, self-centered, and stubborn. Such behaviors and the values they generate are sanctioned only because they occur within the auction setting; an auction by definition legitimatizes such confrontation. In the case of auctions, signification, or what we expect, and legitimation, or what we sanction, are generally also linked to the particular physical setting and its associated meanings as the policeman's role is linked to his uniform. Auction values, in short, are influenced not only by noneconomic concerns of participants and time constraints, but also by meanings associated with the physical setting.

As a man visiting a local shopping mall to pick up a few groceries explained, after he had just happened into a dress store during a liquidation auction and bought three lots of dresses:

> I didn't even know that this auction was going on. I was in the shopping mall to buy some wine. I walk in and I end up buying all these dresses. Oh, well. I have two daughters and three granddaughters; they'll take what they want and I'll give the rest away for a tax deduction. How can you not buy at an auction?

The important roles of space and time, location and history, tradition and desires in determining and legitimizing values are revealed in other situations. The sea and the land, as well as seasons, play a significant role in the productive cycles of most commodities; their significance is recognized in the manner in which these commodity auctions are organized. There tend, for example, to be fairly clear spatial-temporal boundaries between competing auction firms. The proprietors of most exchange auctions tend to be aware of other auctions dealing in similar commodities, but show remarkably little interest in them. Each seems to feel that it has its own clientele and special niche, and provided they run their own operation correctly there is no need to worry about the others. Competing firms work established geographical areas and attempt to schedule their sales at different times. Here, loyalty to one's own place serves to buffer competition and depress values.

As a tobacco warehouse owner said:

The farmer can get pretty much the same price for his tobacco wherever he takes it. We try not to get in each other's way, however. Each of us has our own areas where we have been handling the tobacco for years. As long as I have their bottle ready when they bring in their load, and as long as I talk to them correctly, the ones who have been coming in here for the last twenty years will keep coming in. I'm not about to try to steal anyone else's customers, but if a farmer gets fed up with the guy he or his daddy has been doing business with these last twenty years and wants to bring his stuff in here, he is more than welcome.

The situation in dealer-dominated auctions is somewhat different. The spatial-temporal boundaries of most exchange auctions are based largely on the geographical locations their goods come from. Such a natural basis does not exist in dealer-dominated auctions. Moreover, dealer auctions tend to draw the same buyers. (The need for boundaries in commodity auctions is primarily not to compete over sellers, which is accomplished by each exchange soliciting primarily the producers-sellers in their geographical area.) In dealer auctions, consequently, spatial boundaries serve no purpose and can even be dysfunctional if they make it difficult for dealers to get to all the auctions they want to attend. The solution is to separate auctions temporally. Professional periodicals carry advertisements and dates of upcoming sales, with the more-established auction firms tending to hold their auctions at regular times and places. This scheduling is essential in maintaining consistency of values across auctions, because it allows a sufficient number of the same buyers to be present at different auctions.

Scheduling can become difficult, however, for the major auction houses that run auctions on an almost daily basis, as do Sotheby's and Christie's, or must hold sales for specific overlapping periods of time, as occurs in the seasonal sales of thoroughbreds. The less communal character of these auctions also serves to increase the flow of competitive juices of the auction houses themselves. To some extent such competition is probably unavoidable, since each of these houses claims to be dealing with the most select of select items and there can only be so many such items. Like the buyer who simply *must* own a particular item, it often appears as if these auction houses simply *must* have particular consignments. Both Sotheby's and Christie's, for example, will give up part or even all of the seller's commission to acquire a particularly desired consignment. Keeneland and Fasig-Tipton, for their part, will go out of their way to ensure a particularly attractive dispersal sale. Often it could be argued that such actions are only good business: You have to get what your customers want. At times, however, it appears that the auction house is mimicking some of its own best clients and is on an ego trip of its own. Such competition between firms may force firms to inflate the estimates they give potential consignors, which, in turn, may force the auction firms to set their reserves high, which can and does influence the values determined in the auction.

What is fascinating about such competition, however, is that it tends to avoid direct spatial-temporal confrontation. Each competing house will attempt to consign the most attractive items, but they will seldom attempt to sell against each other. Keeneland and Fasig-Tipton sales will occur on alternating days within the same week but not at the same time. Similarly, moving to the second-level art and antique auction houses of New York, Doyle's main sale begins Wednesday morning and Manhattan Gallery's Thursday morning, which leaves Saturday for Tepper's and Lubin's (they're very close to each other). Given the number of auctions that Sotheby's and Christie's run—up to six a week—it is impossible for them not to overlap. Seldom, however, will they schedule major sales of similar-type items for the same time.

The exceptions prove the importance of such scheduling. When the Matchmaker organization challenged the thoroughbred establishment, particularly Keeneland, a few years ago by organizing an auction of stallion seasons and shares, Keeneland made a move toward direct confrontation by allowing their auction to overlap with the Matchmaker auction. Matchmaker had scheduled their first few sales as dinner auctions to follow the last day of the various Keeneland Select sales in November, January, and July. In response to the views of the dominant stallion syndicates, Keeneland had refrained from expanding this aspect of its business, auctioning only a modest number of stallion shares in some of its sales. In November 1986, however, Keeneland not only elected to sponsor a major stallion share and season auction but at the last moment arranged things so that a conflict occurred between the end of its sale and the beginning of the Matchmaker sale. There is still a good deal of disagreement over whether this was planned or accidental. What is relevant is that the general response, even from people negatively disposed toward Match-maker, was that it was not the right thing to do. It cheapened the auction process and indirectly threatened the legitimacy of the values determined. The practice has not been repeated.

Auctions not only demonstrate that values are grounded in complex social contexts, but they also make clear many of the subtleties of these contexts. We have already seen how specific locations and settings are used in different auctions to convey specific meanings. But auctions also reveal that specific locations entail different rights of empowerment, which play no role whatso-ever in the neoclassical model, where the power of participants is limited solely by their economic resources. In most exchange auctions, in contrast, just being allowed to participate is the most important right, which means that the right to be there is often the most defended right. There are obviously other rights and powers that people have by virtue of their resources or their social status, but the simple right of being there tends to be the most important. As a consequence, just getting into most exchange auctions is a major accomplishment. Whether it is the New Bedford Fish Exchange, a Florida tobacco warehouse, or the Chicago Com-modity Exchange, strangers pushing their nose into their business are not wanted. On the other hand, once allowed in, a visitor becomes one of the "boys" and tends to have more freedom than in other types of auctions.

It took the author some time, for example, to get into the New England Fish Exchange. Once in, however, I was allowed to roam about quite freely. I was able to go in and out of the back office, read and collect reports dealing with daily transactions, ask questions, and follow buyers into the back areas where the fish was unloaded and weighed. I was also allowed to videotape the auction. When a member of the exchange who had not met me saw me there one morning with my camera, he yelled out, "Hey, who the hell is this guy? What is he doing here?" When another member responded, "Don't worry, he's Ok," not only did he not question the fact that I was videotaping everything, he made sure that no one got in the way of the filming.

Proprietary attitudes toward place in dealer and country auc-tions, be they automobile, liquidation, country, or local produce auctions, are quite different. Place is perceived more as neutral territory for buyers, sellers, and others to congregate. In part this is due to the fact that many of these auctions do not have a permanent location. This indifference was reflected in the way people responded to my videoing of these auctions; more often than not, I was simply ignored. On occasion I was asked what network I worked for or why I was filming, but there was no sense of private turf on the part of buyers or sellers.[14] The only time that I was treated in a hostile manner was when tape-recording a small, nearly exclusively dealer jewelry auction held in the Waldorf-Astoria. A woman dealer, seeing that I was recording what was happening, started to yell at me. The issue wasn't one of turf, however, but her fear that the IRS might obtain the tapes.

The situation in sales auctions, especially the up-market sales, has elements of both exchange and dealer auctions. The regulars clearly see the auction as their place. On the other hand, they are generally as eager to welcome outsiders as they assume outsiders are to be invited. This attitude is reinforced by the fact that most major auction houses film their own auctions, coupled with the fact that there are always numerous reporters with video and still cameras present. Many participants not only expect to be filmed but seek it out.

PLACE and time modulate auctions in yet other ways. Keeneland wouldn't be Keeneland if it were anywhere but in Lexington, Kentucky. It is not just that so many consignors have their farms in the area. There is also a sense of place that is part of these auctions; it is not accidental that Fasig-Tipton, despite the fact that its premier auction is held in Saratoga, New York, recently moved its headquarters from New York to Lexington. In an even more focused case, the New England Fish Exchange has been carrying on a long-standing holding action against the Boston Port Authority, which has been attempting to move the auction into a nearby building. The exchange members insist that it just wouldn't be the same. As one member said, "This is where the auction has been held as long as I can remember. It's carved in stone right in the front of the building. Why should we move?"

In both of the cases just described, the sense of place is also tied to a particular history. This particular mix characterizes not only established auctions, but many one-time-only auctions, particularly estate auctions. When John Connally was recently forced to auction off most of his belongings to satisfy creditors, his wife was heard to comment, "There's a story behind almost every one of the 1,100 items you see here. It's more than giving away a physical item. It's giving away a part of what we are."[15] For most of the people attending the auction, one of the things that John Connally was and is is a famous Texan whose political career is remembered. Place and history served as the context within which the 1,100 items were judged.

Auctions occur within a rich interpretive and normative social context, which not only constrains what can occur but also makes possible what does occur. Moreover, it is a context that is constantly being reproduced and modified through the auction process. This is the lesson that auctions teach. They do not support a model of human behavior in which individual rational actors seek to maximize their own interests. Rather they support a vision of human behavior that is inherently social and interpretive, subject to a wide variety of external constraints, yet open to the creative input of individual actors. Nowhere are these factors more vividly documented than in the auctions that are not allowed to occur—the bankruptcy auctions, particularly farm foreclosures, which the community prevents.

These communities don't ignore such auctions. They attend in great numbers. Once there, however, they either refuse to bid or ensure through organized cooperative bidding that all bids are kept so low that it becomes counterproductive for the bank to carry on. Often, many in attendance are themselves in financial distress and could benefit from the bargains that such auctions offer. In preventing such auctions, these communities are actually continuing to function in the auction spirit. They are deciding to whom the goods belong—the original owner. They are also making judgments over value; namely, that in this particular case, financial value is of secondary importance. Nothing is more in keeping with the social dynamics of auctions than for an auction crowd to chant, "No auction, no auction!"

THERE is something somewhat ironic about the fact that auctions, which embody this communal character and are affected by so many exterior, nonrational, and contextual factors, should have become the paradigm of the rational, individual-choice model of behavior.[16] Real auctions as described here present a very different view of human behavior than does the neoclassical model—a view so different that it is not enough to modify the "rational choice" model by introducing such notions as "bounded rationality" or augmenting the model with additional variables. It isn't even sufficient to attempt to locate auctions within existing institutional structures. What is required is a radical reformulation of what constitutes "auctions" and a rethinking of the broad economic, political, social, and moral implications of this new model for our understanding of social behavior in general.

Appendix

Methodological Note

Tнis project began with only a marginal concern for the theoretical status of auctions. I was initially concerned with examining how existing social practices and meanings influence the action and knowledge of individual social actors, and how such actions and knowledge form and transform social practices and meanings—what Anthony Giddens refers to as the process of structuration.[1] I was particularly interested in continuing my analysis of the ways in which interests and practices of different sorts—economic, libidinal, political, and ideological—affect the ways in which knowledge and practice are mutually determined.[2] I selected auctions as an area of study because of the fairly unique way they (1) combine routinized practices with high degrees of both behavioral and definitional flexibility, and (2) take place in a variety of areas dealing with a variety of items and a variety of persons.

Though I was initially interested in auctions as a means to other ends, as my research proceeded, I became more and more aware of the importance of auctions as a theoretical paradigm. This compelled me to confront the question of the theoretical status of auctions per se. I gradually realized more fully that the auction model was not only the dominant model in economics but was also widely used in anthropology, political science, psychology, and sociology. I was particularly impressed by Lester Thurow's argument in *Dangerous Currents* (1983) that the core problem for economic theory is its dependence on the price-auction model of human behavior. As a sociologist, I found myself agreeing with Thurow's characterization of human behavior. Based on my firsthand knowledge of auctions, however, I found myself strongly disagreeing with his, or rather the microeconomic, characterization of auctions.

Admittedly, I encountered some economists who recognized the social component of auctions. Ralph Cassady, Jr. (*Auctions and Auctioneering*), clearly appreciated the importance of social factors. He did not, however, analyze these factors in any detail. Auctions remained for him primarily a means for matching individual expectations rather than a means for generating such expectations. The only other economists who seemed to have taken the social aspects of auctions seriously have been some marketing economists, particularly those interested in commodities. Nearly all of this work, however, precedes World War II. None of these people, however, attempted to document the social dynamics of auctions. For them, an auction remained, theoretically, an abstract analytical model and, practically, a sequence of bids.

Economic transactions in general, of course, have been studied by sociologists and anthropologists, who have evidenced clear interest in the social character of such transactions. To note just a few examples, from Simmel's (1900) analysis of the social nature of money through ethnographic studies by Malinowski, Mauss, Geertz, Cancian, and Plattner to recent collections by Appadurai and Zukin and Dimaggio, the social and political nature of economic exchanges has been documented.[3] These studies, however, have tended to focus on specific cultural systems of exchange in which private treaty transactions dominate, or on the more formal fixed-price systems of industrialized economies.

While clearly revealing the extent to which processes of exchange (a) create values, (b) are constrained by different levels of knowledge, (c) produce and reproduce communities, and (d) reflect political and social interests as well as economic interests, these works do not focus on auctions. It was specifically the distinctive ways in which auctions encompass these social processes, as compared to fixed-price and private treaty transactions, that was my concern.

Through a library search, I found three unpublished ethnographic Ph.D. theses that focused specifically on auctions: *The Structure of the Tobacco Auction: A Sociological Analysis*, by Roger G. Branch, University of Georgia, 1970; *On the Block: An Ethnography of Auctions* by Robert E. Clark, University of Montana, 1973; and *The Market Report: A Folklife Ethnography of a Texas Livestock Auction* by George Albert Boeck, Jr., University of Pennsylvania,

1983. Another unpublished thesis, *Power in the Auction Setting* by
Susan Gray, CUNY, 1976, though based on participant observation, is much more focused in its concern and significantly less
rich ethnographically.[4]

The number of published and unpublished anthropological
and sociological articles are also limited in number. Clark published
an article with Halford entitled "Going . . . going . . . gone:
preliminary observations on 'deals' at auctions."[5] Turner and
Stewart analyzed role conflict among auctioneers created by their
need to convince sellers they were getting a high price and buyers
that they were getting a low price.[6] Olmsted has presented materials on gun auctions and J. N. Gray presents a rich ethnographic
account of lamb auctions across the Scottish-English border.[7]
Though limited in number, these works serve to emphasize the
highly social character of actual auctions. There also exists what
could be called an "anecdotal" and a how-to auction literature,
which serves this same function.

While all of these materials proved useful in my attempt to
understand the wide range of auctions I was discovering, I knew
from the very beginning that I would have to rely primarily on
my own fieldwork. I also knew from previous experience that
efforts to study independently minded people of comparatively
high social status, especially when they are engaged in professional
or otherwise "closed" activities, would not always be successful.[8]
I knew that I would not only have to attempt to obtain sponsorship
wherever possible, but that I would have to know a good deal
about each type of auction before I attempted to interview anyone
in detail. I also knew that much of my time would be spent simply
becoming sufficiently familiar to informants in order to reassure
them that my objectives were not hostile. In short, I knew that I
would have to plan to engage in ongoing participant observation
for a number of years. It would be necessary not only to attend
a wide range of auctions and to engage participants in dialogue,
but also to follow the day-to-day activities of these auctions and
to keep abreast of their internal publications.[9]

As originally planned, the study was to have three stages.
Stage 1 was to consist of entry into various auction settings, utilizing
participant observation, coupled with a number of unstructured
interviews. Stage 2 was to be a continuation of stage 1, but with
greater emphasis on increasing the number of auction settings
visited, coupled more formally with semi-structured interviews

and the collection of secondary materials (catalogs, rules, and other written materials). Stage 3 would include lengthier explicit critiques of my findings with specific informants, coupled with whatever formal survey materials were deemed appropriate. I initially intended to study at least five different types of auctions and to make entry into minimally four sites of each type.

In actuality, my research proceeded much as planned. The major changes that occurred resulted from theoretical adjustments. Initially, for example, most auctions were categorized by the items being auctioned. Only later did the distinctions among commodities, collectibles, and art emerge. These distinctions later become further modified by the exchange-market, dealer-dominated–communal, and sales distinction. The more deeply involved I became in a given type of auction, the more important became those key informants who could probe with me into the underlying dynamics of what was happening. The more I attempted to understand each type, the more I found myself dependent on the reflections of knowledgeable participants rather than on the ongoing practices themselves.

I began my research with a strong interest in the definitional aspect of auctions. As a sociologist, I was also sensitive to both the communal/social and the legitimacy issues developed in the text. Initially, I was much less aware of the central role of ambiguity and uncertainty. It was literally years before the issue of allocation, as distinct from pricing, emerged. As noted above, it was also some time before the relevancy of the neoclassical microeconomic model became apparent. While I was aware early in the study that very different types of goods were auctioned, it took some time before I was able to connect these differences to the different type of social relationships.

On the more routine level, I attempted, nearly from the beginning of my more formal research, to collect data on a number of specific points:

1. the reasons offered to explain why a particular auction was used in the specific context as opposed to other pricing and exchange methods;
2. the comparative price structures expected and received from auction sales versus other forms of sales;
3. attitudes and practices regarding the inherent value of items auctioned as compared to items exchanged in other ways;

4. the comparative price stability of items auctioned as compared to goods exchanged by other means;
5. the legitimating function of auction transactions and factors related to this function;
6. the social contexts out of which the needs to legitimate
   emerge (family-friends frictions, estate sale, legal fiduciary
   responsibilities, or foreclosure);
7. the existence and significance of various subgroups and
   their influence on auction practices as well as techniques
   used to control such groups;
8. the manipulation of "auction markets"—that is, the exclu-
   sion of specific participants and goods;
9. auctions as means for controlling "social distance";
10. significance of noneconomic and semieconomic factors
    such as prestige (ego), visibility, excitement, in determining
    participation and price;
11. auctions as mechanisms of allocation rather than as price
    determinants;
12. relationship of auctions to, including transformation from
    and into, flea markets, bazaars, or fix-priced systems; and
13. price stability in terms of different types of ambiguity.

As part of these inquiries I was also interested in the broader
related and overlapping issue of the similarities and differences
between fine art, collectibles, and commodity auctions and the
relationship between auctions, private treaty sales, and fixed-price
sales. At a more concrete level, I was interested in the use of
such practices as reserve bids, previews, acceptance of split bids,
priority bids, timing between bids, and the range of private preauction agreements entered into by participants.

In search of this information, over a period of seven years I
visited approximately eighty separate auctions, more than half
of them repeatedly. In some cases, such as the major thoroughbred
auctions, I made multiple visits with each visit entailing five to
ten days of continuous auctions. These visits were augmented
by formal and informal interviews with dealers, collectors, other
buyers and sellers, observers, auctioneers, spotters, and auction
house personnel. Most of these interviews were held outside the
auction setting since these people were usually too busy during
the auction.

In nearly all cases, it was necessary to establish some sort of
"casual" preliminary contact with these people, often at an earlier

auction, and often on more than one occasion, as a precondition for a successful interview. Such preliminary contacts and observations make possible a degree of probing and reality testing which is impossible in an initial meeting. As in my stock market study, I discovered that it was necessary to be perceived as an "insider" at the start of such interviews if I hoped to get an "inside" account. It was also necessary in most cases to keep such interviews informal and to allow the informant to lead. To compensate for this informality, I arranged in nearly all cases to tape the interview and then restructure the questions later. If I found that I had missed something important, I generally recontacted the informant, preferably in person but sometimes by telephone, and asked the specific questions needed. In addition to interviewing informants, I also spent a considerable amount of time monitoring various publications associated with the different types of auctions, since I was more interested in the collective view than in individual views.

Although I visited a wide range of auctions, I clearly was not able to become an "insider" of all of them. This was particularly the case in regard to a number of futures auctions and various international spot-market auctions. Given the particular dynamics of these market dominated auctions, which are described in detail in chapter 7, I elected not to pursue these auctions in great depth since they were more tangential to the "social construction of value" theme I was interested in developing. Fortunately, secondary materials on these auctions, and a few key informants, proved sufficient for my needs.

Large portions of the data collected were recorded on audio tapes. Where possible, interviews were directly recorded as were large segments of different auctions. These recordings were augmented by my commentaries, generally entered shortly after the events occurred. In the beginning of the fourth year of this research, I also began to record on videotape a number of auctions. I was able to obtain a record of a session of each major type.[10] These materials were transcribed and coded according to fairly standard qualitative and ethnographic methods.

I note all of these factors on the one hand to provide a more detailed record of the types of materials used in constructing the account presented in the text proper. On the other hand, I review this process to underscore the extent to which this research itself reflects the same processes reported in the text. Social science is engaged in a process very similar to that of auctions, namely, the social construction of meanings. As with auctions there is a reality to explain, a communal context in which to do so, and a range of practices that can be used in doing so. The reality, however, is not the reality of positivism or nomothetic empiricism. It is independent of both given individuals and collectivities, but as a meaningful reality it is imbued with symbolic forms that have human origins. These meanings, in turn, are accessible to individual actors, but only insofar as these actors are themselves part of the communities from which these forms emerge.

It is when we turn to the practices of social scientific research, however, that the practical implications of this philosophy of the social sciences emerge. To understand the underlying structures of human behavior, it is necessary to solicit the collaboration of those being studied. It makes no sense to treat them as objects. Rather they must be enticed into participating in the reflexive process through which the relevant social factors, be they ideas or practices, can become articulated. Trained social scientists normally possess specific reflexive capacities that most lay persons may not have. Those engaged in a particular practice generally understand nuances of their practices that an outsider is likely to miss, though under normal conditions such nuances may go unnoticed even by those who are affected by them. It is only in the collaborative effort, therefore, that a fuller picture becomes possible.

I emphasize a "fuller" rather than a "full" picture. The picture is never full, because the picture is never completed. Accounts and practices are in the continual process of being reproduced and modified. All we can aspire to is a reasonably good sketch of the highlights of human behavior at any given moment. I hope and trust that I have been able to do this in the case of auctions. Insofar as I have been successful I am most grateful to all those persons, only some of whom I have been able to mention in the preface and text proper, who have collaborated with me. The whole process has left me more fascinated and intrigued by auctions then I was when I first began this research. There are many aspects of which I have so far only scraped the surface.[11] Few things would give me greater pleasure than if this study served to induce others to join me in this effort.

Notes

CHAPTER 1. *Auctions Everywhere*

1. For discussions of ancient Roman auctions, see Marcus Antonius Aurelius, *Meditations* 17.4 and 21.9.

2. See, for example, *Barron's,* December 1, 1986, p. 93, and *Fortune,* October 12, 1987, pp. 79–92.

3. Rather than a switch to auctions, much of the growth in these auction markets is due to growth in specific economies, where the auction format has traditionally been dominant. The growth of auctions, however, is uncontestable.

4. For an in-depth essay on this sale, including a historical account of the painting and extended commentary on Sotheby's, see Calvin Tomkins in *The New Yorker,* April 4, 1988, pp. 37–67.

5. The assumption of individual preference sets is a basic assumption of nearly all economic auction models.

6. The broad implications of this study for conventional economic theory are discussed in more detail in the last chapter.

7. It is the norm that on a given day, a particular type of fish will be sold at the same price, though the catch of a particular ship may bring slightly more or less than the others if the captain has a particularly good or bad reputation. The key, of course, is to get the catch from one of the preferred boats at the same price others are paying for less-desired fish. Discounts may also be given to buyers who take the entire catch of a ship, particularly if it is a large one.

8. The time limit has since been dropped to four minutes.

9. Paperback rights may be auctioned after a book has been published or in advance of publication. The decision on timing is determined by what is seen to be most advantageous. For a known author an early auction may prove most lucrative. On the other hand, for an unknown author, but one for whom there are expectations of good reviews, a later auction may be preferred.

10. Such "floor bids" will be discussed later in more detail. Basically, however, a floor bid is a beginning bid obtained from a particular bidder to insure a minimum bid. In return for starting things off at a reasonable level, this bidder, who then stays out of the bidding, is given the option of winning if willing to top the last bid by 10 percent.

11. The Matchmaker organization, which will be discussed in greater detail later, is a fairly new enterprise that concentrates on the auctioning of shares (part ownership) and seasons (breeding rights) in stallions.

12. In most auctions, the auctioneer does his or her own announcing. That is, he or she introduces the item to be auctioned with a brief description before beginning the auction proper. In the United States, it is common at most thoroughbred and standardbred auctions, especially the more select (that is, expensive) ones, to have both an announcer and an auctioneer.

13. The rules commonly run between four and six pages and cover such things as disputes, payments, rights of return, and rights of the auction house.

14. At nearly all horse auctions, horses are assigned numbers in accordance with the order in which they are to be auctioned. These numbers are carried on the animals' rear hips and are hence called hip numbers. During a sale the horses themselves are often referred to as hips, as in, "Let's bring Hips Two-fifteen through Two-twenty up to the waiting area" or, "We are going to bring Hip Two-twelve back into the ring since there seems to be some problem with the credit of the winning bidder." In the case of yearlings, which are generally not named until after the auction by their new owners, such hip numbers are the only "names" they have.

15. Strictly speaking, the so-called pedigree of the horse for sale is not a real pedigree but rather a selected list of blood relations that have been successful. A half-brother that has won stake races will be listed, but not one that never won a race.

16. The more select sales of yearlings normally only run for two or three days at a time, for usually no more than eight hours each

day. The evening sessions at Saratoga are even shorter. The September sales in Lexington, however, run for over twelve hours, for close to two weeks, with scarcely any breaks.

17. At one time burley tobacco was auctioned on sticks. Now it comes in bales of approximately one hundred pounds that are grouped into stacks or baskets of seven bales, making the four-by-four-by-three pile described above.

18. A few congregations still auction off "honors" at weekly Sabbath services. The big auctions for most of these synagogues, however, tend to be those held on the High Holidays and the festive holiday of Purim. All such auctions, however, are much rarer than they were even twenty years ago.

19. These various forms are commonly recognized by most auction professionals and labeled as such. They are not, however, generally recognized by economists as formal categories, although they have been formally described by Ralph Cassady in his *Auctions and Auctioneering*, pp. 11–14. The price in fixed-price systems may vary, but they are set by sellers rather than negotiated directly with buyers. There is no one-to-one fit between the fixed-price, private treaty, auction-classifying system and the more familiar economic distinctions between competitive and noncompetitive, monopolistic, and oligopolistic transactions.

20. In actuality, such values and communities must also be reproduced in fixed-price and private exchange transactions, but in these situations it is governed to a greater extent by routinization.

21. Private treaty transactions can and do also occur in situations in which buyer and seller maintain different evaluative criteria, provided the seller's criteria generate a lower price than do the buyer's. There generally tends to be little bargaining in such situations, since both buyer and seller think that they are getting a bargain.

22. Cassady, *Auctions and Auctioneering*, p. 32.

23. Ibid., pp. 63–66.

CHAPTER 2. *For How Much and To Whom?*

1. The fact that this process normally does work, coupled with the fact that the applicable prices, and so on, are part of a broader, social consensus, underscores the fact that most economic behavior, like most social behavior, tends to be governed by social rules, which are grounded in patterns of behavioral practices, rather than the products of individual rational, maximizing calculations.

2. For a fascinating discussion of the emergence of the concept of artistic genius and its economic ramifications, see Gerald Reitlinger's *The Economics of Taste,* vol. 1 (London: Barrie and Jenkins, 1961).

3. In economic theory supply reflects costs, but the concepts are here being used as analytically distinct to underscore the distinct social factors related to each.

4. This relates to the fact to be discussed in more detail later, that many collectors do not want to buy one-of-a-kind items because there often is no way to determine their value.

5. Tobacco auctions are also one of the few kinds of commodity auctions that have been studied by a sociologist: Roger G. Branch, *The Structure of the Tobacco Auction: A Sociological Analysis* (Ph.D. diss., University of Georgia, 1970). Except for some minor changes, this remains a quite accurate ethnographic description of various aspects of tobacco auctions. George Albert Boeck's *The Market Report: A Folklife Ethnography of a Texas Livestock Auction* (Ph.D. diss., University of Pennsylvania, 1983) and Robert Edward Clark's *On the Block: An Ethnography of Auctions* (Ph.D. diss., University of Montana, 1973) are the other two ethnographic studies of auctions of which I am aware. The findings of both works are consistent with the general thesis of this book.

6. Although it is normally possible to distinguish these factors from one another, it should be noted that they often merge. Changes in expert opinion may both cause and be a result of changes in public tastes, as both may be both cause and effect of changing markets; changes in categorization, in turn, may be both cause and effect of market manipulation or of changes due to natural causes. Genius, for its part, is often perceived as governed by fortune, as fortune is often seen as governed by genius.

7. In a piece by Mark Singer in *The New Yorker* (November 30, 1987), pp. 44–97, focused on W. Graham Arader III, a strong case is presented to support the view that Arader was successful in doing just this in a number of different print markets. Some of the implications of such actions are discussed in more detail in chapter 6.

8. For an anthropological discussion of this aspect of economic behavior see Arjun Appadurai, ed., *The Social Life of Things: Commodities in Cultural Perspective* (New York: Cambridge University Press, 1986).

9. These same pressures are less commonly used against sellers who engage in similar flights of self-expression. Such situations tend to be limited to consignors of very expensive livestock who attempt to overprice their goods either by setting their reserves very high or running the bids up themselves in the auction. There is often a

sound commercial objective behind such demonstrations, namely the desire to give one's products an extra splash of glamour. At times, however, consignors have appeared instead to be on ego trips. If, as is likely, bankruptcy results, there is usually little sympathy for such trippers, in dramatic contrast to the type of sympathy that a less-flamboyant player could expect to receive if he or she failed.

10. For a discussion of the social embeddedness of objects see Mark Granovetter, "Economic Action and Social Structure: A Theory of Embeddedness," *American Journal of Sociology* (November, 1985) 91:481–510.

11. The setting of tobacco prices is dependent in part on the existence of government support prices, which set floors for different grades. Tobacco companies know they must bid more, but providing it still pays farmers to plant tobacco even if they can only get a few pennies above support level, they need not offer much more. When supplies are down, the companies pretty much decide among themselves how high they will go that year. The extent to which the companies actually collude with each other is unclear. Some warehousemen have grave suspicions. Given that the companies have access to pretty much the same information, it could just as easily be argued that they come to similar prices independently.

12. It could be argued here that such a single price is exactly what is expected from the neoclassical competitive-price model, in which the price is the equilibrium point for supply and demand. In actuality, this is seldom the case. The single price is not the result of the hidden hand of the market at work, but rather of the fairly open hand of group consensus.

    This is most clearly true in the New England (Boston) Fish Exchange, where most catches of the same species of fish will be sold for the same price on a given day. The situation is slightly different in New Bedford, where catches are sold by boat. Generally speaking, however, buyers know what they are paying for each species, though the official bid may be quite different. Someone can buy a boat by bidding very high for a small allotment of one species rather than increasing his bid on the major catch in the boat by a penny or two. The situation may also prove to be different in New York, where an effort is being made to distinguish between different grades of the same species through a display Dutch auction.

13. The risk of bidding too high in any auction is known as the winner's curse. It has been shown that in auctions where value is unknown, but there is a probability of high value, the high bidder tends to overbid. This has been documented in various oil lease auctions.

14. She clearly had a specific university in mind. As a knowledgeable collector or agent, she knew who the possible competing buyers were likely to be.

CHAPTER 3.   *Creating and Maintaining Auction Communities*

1. The view being presented here—that social interactions normally entail a normative structure of some sort—is basically that developed by Emile Durkheim in his classic, *The Division of Labor in Society* (New York: Free Press, 1956). Durkheim argues that social contracts are only possible within societies; they cannot and do not generate societies.

2. Though accepted as given, these, like all expectations, are reproduced through social practices. For those interested in the subtleties of this issue see Anthony Giddens, *The Constitution of Society* (Berkeley and Los Angeles: University of California Press, 1984); and Roy Bhaskar, *The Possibility of Naturalism* (Brighton, England: Harvester, 1979).

3. Ibid.

4. I am referring here to the actual auctions of these commodities, not the auction of futures in these commodities. In commodity futures auctions, as with stocks and bonds, it is also true that only members of the exchange can actually participate in the auction but, as with stocks and bonds, others can participate through a broker.

5. If a buyer is willing to take the entire catch of a given species from a particular boat, especially if it is a large catch, he may be able to get the lot for a few pennies less than the split lots of other boats are sold for. Nine out of ten times, however, a given species will go for a single price.

6. The fact that the entire catch of boat is bought by one buyer and then sold off by this buyer to others makes the New Bedford system a mix of public and closed auction coupled with numerous private treaty arrangements. It is not uncommon, in fact, for buyers, claiming that the catch is not what they thought it would be, to attempt to renegotiate with sellers on price after the auction. This has caused a good deal of bad feeling among fishermen.

7. This situation may change dramatically with the planned introduction of a Dutch-clock display auction in New York.

8. An exception are futures auctions, where the term *market* normally does refer to the auction.

9. It may be the case that various economic models are able to simulate the behavioral consequences of some of these processes, but the assumption of individual decision making is simply not con-

firmed by the empirical evidence bearing on the decision-making process.

10. There are exceptions. In the case of copper and other minerals controlled by a few major producers, it is the producers who tend to be in control. Auctions, however, are not the primary means of selling these minerals. There are futures auctions and spot auctions, but the bulk of such goods are sold through a system in which the producing companies set the price.

11. The implicit strategy built into most commodity-exchange auctions is technically called a maximin or a minimax strategy. The objective is to minimize major losses at the cost of minimizing major gains in contrast to a maximax strategy that seeks to maximize gains even at the risk of maximizing losses. It is an inherently risk-averse strategy; it does not treat the probabilities of all losses and gains equally but overweighs large losses. A risk-neutral player would happily risk one thousand dollars to make one dollar if the probabilities were five thousand to one that he would win. A risk-averse player would prefer to risk ten dollars to make a hundred even if the odds were against him twenty to one. For a more detailed discussion of such game strategies, see James T. Tedeschi, Barry R. Schlenker, and Thomas V. Bonoma, *Conflict, Power and Games* (Chicago: Aldine Publishing Company, 1973); John von Neuman and Oskar Morgenstern, *Theory of Games and Economic Behavior* (New York: John Wiley & Sons, 1944); Thomas C. Schelling, *The Strategy of Conflict* (Cambridge: Harvard University Press, 1960); P. Milgrom, and R. J. Weber, "A Theory of Auctions and Competitive Bidding," *Econometrica* 50 (September 1982): 1089–1122; J. G. Riley and W. F. Samuelson, "Optimal Auctions," *American Economic Review* 71 (June 1981): 381–92; Eric S. Maskin, and John Riley, "Optimal Auctions with Risk Averse Buyers," *Econometrica* 52 (November, 1984): 1473–518; and Eric S. Maskin and John Riley, "Auction Theory with Private Values," *American Economic Review* 75 (May 1985): 150–55.

12. In point of fact, market professionals are also caught up in the worldviews of other professionals as I attempted to document in my book *The Mind of the Market*. In the stock market as in most fixed-price situations, however, individuals tend to be more passively constrained by the governing normative order than do participants in auctions, in which the normative-definitional order is constantly being regenerated.

13. The feeling of belonging often gives rise to the sense of an in-group. Such in-group identity, in turn, can acquire other qualities, including ethnic associations. On more than one occasion I have heard members of a particular auction community referred to in

ethnic terms as well as auction subgroups refer to other subgroups or outsiders in the same way. "The Jews, you know are bigger in standardbreds than in thoroughbreds." "The Portuguese are bigger in New Bedford and the Italians in Boston" (referring to fish auctions). "The WASPs still control that market."

14. *Lexington-Herald Leader,* July 21, 1986 (First Security National Bank and Trust Co. advertisement).

15. A typical page will give three generations of sires and dams with successful relatives highlighted in bold type, with numbers and types of victories and money earned. It will also note if the horse is eligible for specific races and purses.

16. It is possible for such a person to bid at one of these auctions. The rules are, however, that a winning bidder sign for the horse immediately, with the acceptance then sent directly to the back office. If the bidder has no credit standing, he or she will be called to the office immediately, at which time the sales company must be satisfied or the horse will be reauctioned.

17. In the Northeast, the two main weeklies are *Antiques and the Arts Weekly* published by the Bee Publishing Company of Newtown, Connecticut, and the *Maine Antique Digest.* Nearly all the major auction houses also send out monthly if not weekly announcements of upcoming auctions.

18. The effort to keep one's bid private is not limited to such auctions. This technique is used quite often by the top bidders in horse auctions. In these cases, however, the purpose of such secrecy more often than not is to keep the sellers ignorant of the buyer rather than other potential buyers. This relates to other issues to which we will return.

19. In a round-robin knockout, a free rider can earn a full share on a piece reauctioned without taking any risks by putting in a very low bid. Such a low bid in an English knockout will only earn a small amount.

20. For a more detailed discussion of the system see William Vickrey's "Counterspeculation, Auctions and Competitive Sealed Tenders," *Journal of Finance* 16 (1961):8–37.

21. This theme is well developed in the documentary film produced and directed by Robert Aibel, Ben Levin, Chris Musello, and Jay Ruby entitled *A Country Auction; The Paul V. Leitzel Estate Sale* (University Park, PA: PCR:Films and Video in the Behavioral Sciences, The Pennsylvania State University, 1984).

22. It is worth noting here that idiosyncratic bids are common at nearly all open auctions. An item catches the particular fancy of this or that person for any of a hundred different reasons. In most cases, however, such bids, as with "low" bids, do not prove to be the winning ones.

23. The neoclassical microeconomic auction model may not adequately account for what seems to happen at most auctions, but in ascribing self-interest to individual actors, it does provide an understandable basis for the actions of these individuals.

24. The distinction between bestowing meaning—signification—and legitimation is a subtle but important one commonly ignored. For an excellent theoretical discussion of this issue see Giddens, *The Constitution of Society,* chapter 1.

CHAPTER 4. *The Search for a Fair Price*

1. Such a relationship is consistent with Durkheim's classical analysis of the relationship between social solidarity and moral order. In homogeneous, simple societies, social solidarity is evident to all and the moral order assumed; in modern complex, more diffuse societies, the moral order must be explicitly promulgated.

2. The typical set of rules found at these auctions will take up a single mimeographed page and emphasize that there are no guarantees or warranties. Most of the page will then be used to spell out the charges and commissions for different-price cars, storage charges, as well as the types of payments acceptable—normally only cash or certified check.

3. There are occasions, of course, such as John Lennon's Rolls-Royce mentioned earlier, or the 250 GTO Ferrari racing car confiscated from an accused drug dealer and auctioned in November 1987 for $1,600,000, when the auction price, due to the uniqueness of the automobile and the attending hype, may be in excess of either the fixed price or expected private treaty price. There is also less concern with the legitimacy of the values so generated, since they apply to little if anything else. In auctioning most used automobiles, the legitimacy of the process tends to take precedence over maximizing return.

4. If the meaning system of the family proves inadequate, the members will rely on the meaning system of the encompassing society, which normally means the experts of this society.

5. I should note that this conversation occurred sometime in 1983, when the art auction market was less volatile.

6. The one exception was a very unusual and rare piece of sculpture whose value could really not be determined.

7. This technique is used quite often in charity auctions. Friends will often pressure one of their group to bid up on an item they know he or she is interested in by bidding against him or her to the level they think is appropriate. This is often done in good spirit, with the intended winner telling them when he or she isn't about to go any higher.

8. A cribber is a horse that chews on wood, which some believe can produce breathing problems. Many horsemen think it means nothing, however.

9. Those instances where auctioneers are guilty of questionable practices are usually cases where the auctioneer is selling his or her own goods.

10. Two dealers may both be willing to overpay for an item if each believes that there is a buyer for the item who is willing to pay whatever is asked.

11. If the bidding has been going up by a hundred dollars a bid—two hundred, three hundred, four hundred, for example—and then someone offers four hundred and fifty, the four-hundred-and-fifty bid would be a split bid.

12. In some auctions the rules stipulate minimum increments. Select thoroughbred auctions, for example, have an "upset," that is, starting, price of $1,000. If a horse doesn't bring that quite quickly, it will be passed over. The minimum increment up to $25,000 is then $100, and $500 after $25,000. At select standardbred auctions the upset price is the same, but the minimum up to $25,000 is $500 and $1,000 over that. In practice the normal increments are much larger and only come down to these limits when someone offers a split bid. The size of increments in most other auctions is at the discretion of the auctioneer, who can, by the rules, ignore any bid he or she chooses.

13. In England, the sequence is more likely to be 2,000, 2,200, 2,500, 2,800, 3,000; for some reason, the 2, 5, 8, 10 sequence is used extensively in England, while in the United States increments tend to be consistent.

14. At most select auctions, a thousand dollars is set as the minimum increment. In practice most increments are considerably higher.

15. The issue of fairness does not normally arise in more traditional commodity auctions, since there tend not to be any winners and losers, and where consequently the acceptance of split bids is really a nonissue. Legitimacy per se, however, tends to be of secondary

importance in such auctions, given that community tends to overshadow the question of legitimacy.

16. In this particular case, a junior person was actually running the
auction. The car was expected to sell for around two hundred
thousand dollars. When the bid passed two hundred thousand, the
young auctioneer looked around for some help and was told to
keep the increment at ten thousand dollars—which, following orders, he did all the way up to the final bid. My guess is that a more
experienced auctioneer would have increased the increment at
the half-million and million-dollar levels, with perhaps negative results.

17. Most charity auctions are built around a core group of organizers
who are generally the big spenders, with a looser group of friends
and acquaintances appended.

18. In sealed bid bond auctions two systems are commonly used. One
is to pay out at the rates bid until all bonds are placed. If one
hundred million dollars worth of bonds are offered and the highest
bid is 8.5 percent for five million, 8.45 for five million, 8.4 for
twenty million, 8.35 for thirty million, 8.3 for twenty-five million,
8.2 for forty-five million, 8.15 for thirty-five million, and 8.1 for
fifty million, those bidding 8.3 percent or higher would get their
full allotment at the rate bid since their total request is for 8.5 million
with those bidding 8.2 percent receiving one-third of what they
had asked for at the 8.2 rate, since the request at 8.2 is for 45
million and only 15 million are left. Everyone else would get nothing.
The second system would allocate the bonds to the same bidders
but at the single rate of 8.3375, which is the average rate of the
winning bids. In both cases, when government bond are auctioned,
a sizable portion of the offering will be offered to the public after
the auction at this average rate regardless of the rate paid to those
actually participating in the auction.

19. Ten years ago, most country and art and antique auctions charged
the seller a 20 percent commission with discounts for very desirable
lots. Today the practice, brought in by Christie's from England, of
charging sellers and buyers each a 10 percent commission is becoming
the norm. In many cases in which very valuable estates are concerned,
the seller's commission may be forfeited.

20. See Elizabeth Hoffman and Mathew L. Spitzer, "Entitlements, Rights,
and Fairness: An Experimental Examination of Subjects' Concepts
of Distributive Justice," *Journal of Legal Studies* 14 (June 1985): 259–
297.

21. Racing, especially track racing—as compared to turf and jumping—
takes a tremendous toll on a horse. Any aberration in anatomy is

likely to create problems and lead to a breakdown of one sort or another.

CHAPTER 5. *The Show*

1. *As You Like It,* act II; sc. 7, lines 139–140. The view that life can be seen as a performance pervades Shakespeare's work. For a fascinating discussion of this see Erving Goffman, *Frame Analysis* (New York: Harper & Row, 1974).

2. See in particular Goffman's *Presentation of Self in Everyday Life* (Garden City, N.Y.: Anchor Books, 1959) and *Frame Analysis,* and Harré's *Social Being* (Totowa, N.J.: Rowman and Littlefield, 1981).

3. Economists make similar claims for the explanatory capacity of auctions, but their claims are based on the assumption that auctions embody and reflect the rational, self-interested, individualistic model of human beings celebrated in neoclassical economic theory. The fact that auctions lend themselves so well to a dramaturgical model, coupled with the many incongruities of the two paradigms, seriously challenges this economic model.

4. The physical situation at the new display auction in New York is considerably nicer. The auction room is more like a brand-new version of Luther's auction room described below. This is consistent with the attempt to make this auction a more retail operation than are the Boston and New Bedford auctions.

5. The use of a clock also serves to depersonalize the auction, which—given the interpersonal tensions that can arise and the desire to put a business-as-usual face on the auction—is an additional benefit.

6. The order of sale, however, is not always open to change. Contention among consignors, for example, has led to a practice whereby horses are sold in an alphabetical order, starting with a letter selected randomly; yearlings are sold according to their dam's name, dams by their own name, and mixed groups by consignor's name. Standardbreds are also sold alphabetically, but named yearlings are sold by their own names, which allows for some juggling, especially if an entire sale is by a single farm.

7. His use of the expression *two bits* did not refer, of course, to money, but rather to his views.

8. See particularly Goffman, *Presentation of Self,* pp. 77–105.

9. By marginal I mean auctions where many of the goods are owned by the auctioneer at a known cost, and where consequently there is little real concern for establishing a fair price.

10. During some performances, such as a magic show, members of the audience may be included in the show. When this happens, however, they are made part of the process of creating the magician's "reality."

11. During a performance, members of the audience may react with oohs and aahs, laughter or screams, but the actors are meant to continue their performances as if they did not hear them, though they are allowed to wait sometimes for the audience reaction to subside.

CHAPTER 6. *Bargains and Bonanzas*

1. This is most apt to happen at auctions where the goods are not inspected before the auction, as in most fish auctions. It can also happen, however, when there is a prior inspection.

2. The proposed display auction for New York and the two-year-old display auction in Portland, Maine, are intended to deal with some of these problems and to reverse the balance of power between buyers and sellers somewhat. If my analysis is correct, however, part of the problem is structural and not amenable to the sorts of corrections being considered.

3. I am specifically speaking here of perhaps the most common situations where the relevant government agency does not possess its own experts capable of determining a proper price for a job and where there are time pressures to move forward with a project as soon as possible.

4. Here again we see how different auctions respond differently to the same basic type of behavior. In the open auction of the New England Fish Exchange, no one thinks anything about a number of buyers starting to yell at another buyer who has put in a bid that they think is unreasonable. Similar action—be it in person, by telephone, or by mail—in the case of a government sealed-bid auction is an indictable offense, as it is in many nonexchange auctions.

5. This is most clearly the case with Kentucky breeders, but there are geographic concentrations in the Pennsylvania, New York, and New Jersey areas, especially for standardbreds, and California and Florida.

6. Although reserves are used in nearly all art, antique, and collectible auctions, they tend to be used very sparingly in your everyday bread-and-butter auction. In contrast, in recent years, nearly every item sold at Sotheby's and Christie's has been sold subject to a reserve.

7. I deliberately call them fixed-price—private treaty stores because in most cases items are marked, but it is normally possible to negotiate the price.

8. It is specifically this sense of surprise that Larry McMurtry plays up—I would say overplays—in his novel *Cadillac Jack*.

9. For more detailed figures see *The Blood-Horse*, January 31, 1987.

10. The expression *taking a bid "off the wall"* is used to describe situations where an auctioneer appears to be taking a bid from someone in the room when there really is no such bid. This is different from bidding against a reserve, where there often is no attempt to make believe that there is a live person making the bid, though the two practices may appear very similar to someone unfamiliar with auctions.

11. The commission in nearly all antique-type auctions is 20 percent; 10 percent from the seller and an extra 10 percent added on for the buyer. The five-thousand-dollar table is actually sold for fifty-five hundred, with the owner getting forty-five hundred. In past years, the full commission of 20 percent was taken out of the final price, which, in effect, meant that the seller paid the full commission.

12. In most horse auctions the standard commission is 5 percent paid by the seller. When a horse does not meet its reserve, or when there is a buy-back, the commission is commonly reduced to 2.5 or 3 percent.

13. An interesting account of this affair is contained in a story about Christie's by John Taylor in *Manhattan, inc.* (April 1986): pp. 104–113.

14. The extent to which regulars are expected to understand a good deal is reflected in the differences between ongoing auctions and new auctions. Where the New England Fish Exchange functions with a single page of rules, it was necessary for the Port Authority of New York and New Jersey to produce a document of over twenty pages in order to spell out all the details of their proposed auction. Similarly, many local American real estate auctions function with a simple set of rules, but Allsop & Co. thought it necessary to print four pages of rules and conditions in their catalog when they initiated their auction.

15. A "Dutch" auction, it will be recalled, is one in which the initial bid is set high and then let fall until a bidder enters a bid at that level.

16. Attributed to Elaine Markson in Robert A. Carter, "Auctions Now," *Publishers Weekly* (October 17, 1986): pp. 20–25.

17. There are still some publishers who will not participate in an agent auction. Similarly, there are still a number of stallion syndicate managers who maintain a less-than-friendly relationship to Matchmaker's

even though a number of their shares may have traded through a Matchmaker auction.

CHAPTER 7. *What Auctions Tell Us about Values*

1. See for example, William Vickrey, "Counterspeculation, Auctions and Competitive Sealed Tenders," *Journal of Finance,* 16 (1961): 8–37; P. Milgrom and R. J. Weber, "A Theory of Auctions and Competitive Bidding," *Econometrica,* 50 (September 1982): 1089–122; Eric Maskin and John Riley, "Optimal Auctions with Risk Averse Buyers," *Econometrica* 52 (November 1984): 1473–1518, and "Auction Theory with Private Values," *American Economic Review* 75 (May 1985): 150–155; James Cox, Vernon Smith, and James Walker, "Experimental Development of Sealed-Bid Auction Theory: Calibrating Controls for Risk Aversion," *American Economic Review* 75 (May 1985): 160–165. Admittedly, there are economists who are more sensitive to the social character of auctions. Ralph Cassady, Jr., who is the author of *Auctions and Auctioneering* and is mentioned in the text, is clearly aware of the importance of social factors. It remains, however, implicit in his observations dealing with the need to maintain "confidence" in whatever methods are used (*Auctions and Auctioneering,* p. 260), as well as his comments highlighting cross-cultural differences. He does not, however, develop the connection between the need for "confidence" and cultural differences with the more general social process of maintaining a shared normative order. For him, auctions remain primarily a means for matching individual expectations rather than a means for generating such expectations.

2. It may be argued that the economic analysis of the process of "signaling" serves to incorporate these social factors. Though it provides a very valuable contribution to economic theory, it doesn't. Signaling deals with ways of judging changing conditions, but it is still individual economic actors who do the judging. Others might suggest that institutional economists such as Oliver Williamson successfully incorporate the necessary social factors. While a useful corrective to conventional economic reasoning, such works remain caught within the neoclassical economic model. Neither orientation is capable of doing justice to the cooperative, definitional character of auctions.

3. For what I consider to be the strongest argument in favor of such a realist position on philosophical grounds, see Roy Bhaskar, *The Possibility of Naturalism* (Brighton, England: Harvester, 1979). For a less detailed but more accessible argument see Peter Manicas, *The History and Philosophy of the Social Sciences,* part 3 (Oxford, England, and New York: Basil Blackwell, 1987), pp. 241–293.

4. The study of "abnormal" cases is commonly the best way to understand the normal as evidenced in the history of science. I owe special thanks to Everett Hughes for first making this fact clear to me when I was a graduate student.

5. A double auction is one in which different prices are being offered simultaneously by both buyers and sellers.

6. This ranking is consistent with George Herbert Mead's theory of mind, or reflexive consciousness, which sees human consciousness as inherently social and grounded in social interaction. Accordingly, ideas and meanings should never be posited in opposition to behavior. They emerge from and are grounded in behaviors. Human behavior, in turn, is itself commonly constrained and formed by meanings and expectations.

7. An additional difficulty in relying on the "market" in these situations is the fact that between, and often contemporaneous with, such auctions, there are likely to be private treaty and even fixed-price transactions in different secondary markets, further confusing matters.

8. The Dow Jones averages are indexes based on various sets of stocks intended to reflect general market conditions. There exist today a number of other indexes, including the more broadly based New York Stock Exchange Index, but the Dow Jones Industrial Index, known simply as the "Dow," remains the most widely discussed.

9. Stock futures, like other commodity futures, are agreements to deliver certain goods, in this case a specific set of stocks, on a given date at a set price. They were first traded in the latter half of 1982. As in other future contracts, stock futures set the amount and the date and allow the price to fluctuate. In the case of cattle, chocolate, and so on, the items may actually be accepted at the end date. Stock futures, however, are settled for the cash equivalencies of the set of stocks represented by the future contract. It is important to note that such contracts are really little more than promises between two persons. Moreover, since the future price is set in a manner that is acceptable to both parties at the time, the "promise" has no inherent value. They are consequently not actually sold or bought; all that is required is that both parties set aside what amounts to good-faith money, which may be very small in comparison to the value of the goods being promised. On the other hand, both parties are liable for all changes in price that might occur.

   Options, in contrast, are rights to buy (calls) or sell (puts) particular stocks at particular prices for a period of time. To acquire such a right, the option buyer pays a premium to the person who is willing to sell to him or accept from him the stock at the set price for the period of time. The option buyer, however, has no liability. He can execute his option if a market advance or decline makes it worth doing so, or he can simply let it expire. Options on individual stocks have been traded for some time. Only since 1983, however, has it been possible to buy options on a set of stocks that are reflective of the market as a whole.

10. As useful as concrete auctions may be supporting such a view, in and of themselves they do not provide a general theory of human behavior capable of rivaling the "rational maximizing individual" conception that underlies the neoclassical auction model. Defenders of the neoclassical model, consequently, may respond by simply asserting that while concrete auctions do not exemplify their auction model, their model remains the best model of human behavior in general. In actuality, this is not so. Rival theories do exist.

More specifically, I would argue that the social behaviorism of George Herbert Mead, the multidimensional vision of Max Weber, Giddens's theory of structuration, and Bhaskar's transcendental realism provide in combination a fully articulated theoretical alternative. There is also the rich body of empirical work produced by Erving Goffman, which (though less explicitly theoretical) supports this view.

It is clearly beyond the scope of this work to present here an overview of these theoretical works. Many of the major points, which have been incorporated in the text, however, are worth noting: the multilevel nature of social reality; the emergent character of meanings and values; the social nature of meanings; the "duality of social structures" (that is, that social structures are both the results and the medium of social behavior); the contextual character of social behavior; the intentionality of human behavior; the distinction between tacit practical knowledge and discursive knowledge; the political aspect of both behavior and social structures; and the essentially reproductive quality of social practices.

For Mead, I would recommend the first part of his *Mind, Self and Society,* which tends to be overlooked, and his *Philosophy of the Act.* Weber's *Theory of Social and Economic Organization* is probably the best single source book on his views, though a careful reading of *The Protestant Ethic and the Spirit of Capitalism* conveys most of his key insights in a more easily digested form. For Bhaskar, his *A Realist's Theory of Science* and *The Possibility of Realism.* For Giddens, his *New Rules of Sociological Method* and *The Constitution of Society.* I would also recommend Harré and Secord, *The Explanation of Social Behavior* and Manicas, *A History and Philosophy of the Social Sciences.*

11. Perhaps the most outspoken proponents of this view are Gary Becker and others in the Chicago school.

12. Lester C. Thurow, *Dangerous Currents* (New York: Random House, 1983).

13. To summarize Giddens's position quite briefly, he argues that human behavior has an interpretive component; social actors are knowledgeable actors. Much of this knowledge, however, is tacit; actors could not easily discuss it. In addition, this knowledge is quite complex. It not only serves to endow situations with meaning—signification—but to legitimize situations. All of this, moreover, occurs within relationships that have their own dominance structures.

14. The proprietors, of course, do exert some sense of ownership, but I have had very little trouble in getting permission to film a wide variety of such auctions. I do, of course, ask for permission first.

15. Reported in *The New York Times,* January 24, 1987.

16. A number of economists have pointed out the limitations of the neoclassical microeconomic model of human behavior. In addition to Thurow's *Dangerous Currents,* see Albert O. Hirschman, "Against Parsimony," *Economics and Philosophy* 1 (1985): 7–21; Amartya K. Sen, "Rational Fools: A Critique of the Behavioral Foundations of Economic Theory," *Philosophy and Public Affairs* 6 (1977): 317–344; H. A. Simon, *Models of Man* (New York: John Wiley, 1957); *Human Problem Solving* (Englewood Cliffs, N.J.: Prentice-Hall, 1972); Oliver E. Williamson, *Markets and Hierarchies: Analysis and Antitrust Implications* (New York: Free Press, 1975); and *The Economic Institutions of Capitalism* (New York: Free Press, 1985). The difficulty with all of these critiques is that the authors still seem committed to modifying and correcting the model rather than abandoning the methodological individualism that is its fatal flaw.

APPENDIX   *Methodological Note*

1. Giddens is highly productive. For an excellent comprehensive formulation of his theoretical overview see Anthony Giddens, *The Constitution of Society* (Berkeley and Los Angeles: University of California Press, 1984).

2. Charles W. Smith, *A Critique of Sociological Reasoning* (Oxford: Basil Blackwell Publishers, 1979); *The Mind of the Market* (Totowa, N.J.: Rowman and Littlefield, 1981; paperback, 1983, Harper Colophon); and "On the Sociology of Mind," *Explaining Human Behavior,* ed. Paul F. Secord (Los Angeles: Sage Publications, 1982).

3. Georg Simmel, *Philosophie des Geldes* (Leipzig: Duncker und Humblot, 1900; 6th ed. Berlin, 1958); Bronislaw Malinowski, *Argonauts of the Western Pacific* (New York: E. P. Dutton and Co., 1922); Marcel

Mauss, *The Gift* (New York: Norton, 1976); Clifford Geertz, *Peddlers and Princes* (Chicago: University of Chicago Press, 1963); Clifford Geertz and H. Geertz and L. Rosen, *Meaning and Order in Moroccan Society* (Cambridge: Cambridge University Press, 1979); Stuart Mark Plattner, *Peddlers, Pigs and Profit: Itinerant Trading in Southeast Mexico* (Ann Arbor, MI: University Microfilms, Inc., 1969); Arjun Appadurai, ed. *The Social Life of Things: Commodities in Cultural Perspective* (New York: Cambridge University Press, 1986); and Sharon Zukin and Paul Dimaggio, "Special Issue on Economy and Society," *Theory and Society* 15 (1986).

4. Branch's study provides an overview of the tobacco auction business with primary emphasis upon the flue-cured tobacco part of the business. He focuses primarily on the various ways the auction house balances the needs and interests of both the sellers and buyers of tobacco. Clark's work is also rich ethnographically. He is primarily interested in control and maintenance of order, and the ways auctioneers try to establish trust and the impression of "good deals." Boeck's work stresses the folk-life aspects of livestock auctions and is primarily descriptive; it does, however, conscientiously underscore the community—gemeinschaft—quality of the livestock auction. Gray examines the ways in which auctioneers maintain or lose control through their manipulation of various intangible resources; her analysis is limited primarily to a number of vocal auction sequences.

5. Robert E. Clark and Larry J. Halford, "Going. . . . going. . . . gone: preliminary observations on 'deals' at auctions," *Urban Life* 7 (1978): 285–307.

6. Ronny E. Turner and Kenneth Stewart, "The Negotiation of Role Conflict: A Study of Sales Behavior at the Auction," *Rocky Mountain Social Science Journal* 11 (1974): 85–96.

7. A. D. Olmsted, "What Will You Give Me?: Buying and Selling at Public Auction," Paper presented at the *Qualitative Research Conference* (May 13–16, 1986, University of Waterloo); J. N. Gray, "Lamb Auctions on the Border," *European Journal of Sociology* 25(1) (1984): 59–82.

8. My research on the stock market (Smith, 1981) confronted very similar difficulties.

9. My stock market research utilized similar methods—that is, participant observation coupled with both unstructured and later semistructured taped interviews with key informants generated through a snowball technique from previous informants.

10. In most cases, it was necessary to make the recording myself. This necessitated in most cases a good deal of prior negotiation. In some

cases, it was unnecessary to make such recording because acceptable recordings already existed, often as part of an exchange public relations package.

11. One issue of particular interest touched on in this study but not examined in great detail is how different types of auctions lend themselves to different decision-making processes. The difference between psychological, social, and market-dominated decisions is noted and related to sales, communal, and exchange auctions, but a thorough analysis of the dynamics of each decision-making process is yet to be done.

Selected Bibliography

Abt, Vicki, James F. Smith, and Eugene Martin Christiansen. *The Business of Risk* (Lawrence: University Press of Kansas, 1985).

Aibel, Robert, Ben Levin, Chris Musello, and Jay Ruby. *A Country Auction: The Paul V. Leitzel Estate Sale* (University Park, PA: PCR: Films and Video in the Behavioral Sciences; The Pennsylvania State University, 1984).

Appadurai, Arjun, ed. *The Social Life of Things: Commodities in Cultural Perspective* (New York: Cambridge University Press, 1986).

Auerbach, Sylvia. *An Insider's Guide to Auctions* (Reading, Mass.: Addison-Wesley, 1981).

Baudrillard, J. *For a Critique of the Political Economy of Sign* (St. Louis, Mo.: Telos Press, 1981).

Bazerman, Max, and William Samuelson. "The Winner's Curse: An Empirical Investigation," in *Aspiration Levels in Bargaining and Economic Decision Making*, Reinhard Teitz, ed. (Berlin: Springer-Verlag, 1983), pp. 186–200.

Becker, Gary. *The Economic Approach to Human Behavior* (Chicago: Chicago University Press, 1976).

Benn, S. I., and G. W. Mortimore. *Rationality and Social Sciences* (London: Routledge and Kegan Paul Ltd., 1976).

Berger, Peter L., and Thomas Luckmann. *The Social Construction of Reality* (Garden City, N.Y.: Doubleday, 1966).

213

Bhaskar, Roy. *A Realist Theory of Science* (Atlantic Highlands, New Jersey: Humanities Press, 1975–78); *The Possibility of Naturalism* (Brighton, England: Harvester, 1979).

Boeck, George Albert, Jr. *The Market Report: A Folklife Ethnography of A Texas Livestock Auction* (Ann Arbor, Michigan: University Microfilm International, 1983).

Branch, Roger G. *The Structure of the Tobacco Auction: A Sociological Analysis,* University of Georgia: Ph.D. dissertation, 1970.

Brough, James. *Auction!* (Indianapolis and New York: Bobbs-Merrill, 1963).

Carter, Robert A. "Auctions Now," *Publishers Weekly,* October 17, 1986, pp. 20–25.

Cassady, Ralph, Jr. *Auctions and Auctioneering* (Berkeley and Los Angeles: University of California Press, 1967).

Clark, Fred E. *Readings in Marketing* (New York: Macmillan, 1924).

Clark, Robert E. *On the Block: An Ethnography of Auctions,* University of Montana: Ph.D. dissertation, 1973.

Clark, Robert E. and Larry J. Halford. "Going . . . going . . . gone: preliminary observations on 'deals' at auctions." *Urban Life* 7 (1978): 285–307.

Cox, James C., Vernon L. Smith, and James M. Walker. "Experimental Development of Sealed-Bid Auction Theory; Calibrating Controls for Risk Aversion," *American Economic Review* 75 (May 1985): pp. 160–165.

Durkheim, Emile. *The Division of Labor in Society* (New York: Free Press, 1956).

Engelbrecht-Wiggans, Richard, Martin Shubik, and Robert M. Stark, eds. *Auctions, Bidding and Contracting: Uses and Theory* (New York: New York University Press, 1983).

Feinstein, Jonathan S., Michael K. Block, and Frederick C. Nold. "Asymmetric Information and Collusive Behavior in Auction Markets," *American Economic Review* 75 (June 1985): pp. 441–460.

Garfinkle, Harold. *Studies in Ethnomethodology* (Englewood Cliffs, N.J.: Prentice-Hall, 1967).

Geertz, Clifford. *Peddlers and Princes* (Chicago: University of Chicago Press, 1963).

Geertz, Clifford, H. Geertz, and L. Rosen. *Meaning and Order in Moroccan Society* (Cambridge: Cambridge University Press, 1979).

Giddens, Anthony. *New Rules of Sociological Method* (New York: Basic Books, 1976); *Central Problems in Social Theory* (Berkeley and Los Angeles: University of California Press, 1979); *A Contemporary Critique of Historical*

Materialism (Berkeley and Los Angeles: University of California Press, 1981); *The Constitution of Society* (Berkeley and Los Angeles: University of California Press, 1984).

Goffman, Erving. *Presentation of Self in Everyday Life* (Garden City, N.Y.: Anchor Books, 1959); *Frame Analysis* (New York: Harper and Row, 1974).

Granovetter, Mark. "Economic Action and Social Structure: A Theory of Embeddedness," *American Journal of Sociology* (November 1985).

Gray, J. N. "Lamb Auctions on the Border," *European Journal of Sociology* 25: pp. 59–82.

Gray, Susan. *Power in the Auction Setting*, C.U.N.Y.: Ph.D. dissertation, 1976.

Habermas, Jurgen. *Knowledge and Human Interests* (Boston: Beacon Press, 1971); *Communication and the Evolution of Society* (Boston: Beacon Press, 1979).

Hamilton, Charles. *Auction Madness* (New York: Everest House, 1981).

Hansen, R. G. "Empirical Testing of Auction Theory," *American Economic Review* 75 (May 1985): pp. 156–159.

Harré, Rom. *Social Being* (Totowa, N.J.: Rowman and Littlefield, 1981).

Harré, Rom and Paul Secord. *The Explanation of Social Behavior* (Oxford: Basil Blackwell Publishers, 1972).

Hermann, Frank. *Sotheby's: Portrait of an Auction House* (New York and London: W. W. Norton and Company, 1981).

Hildesley, C. Hugh. *Sotheby's Guide to Buying and Selling at Auction* (New York and London: W. W. Norton and Company, 1984).

Hirschman, Albert O. "Against Parsimony," *Economics and Philosophy* 1 (April 1985): pp. 7–21.

Hoffman, Elizabeth and Mathew L. Spitzer. "Entitlements, Rights, and Fairness: An Experimental Examination of Subjects' Concepts of Distributive Justice," *Journal of Legal Studies* 14 (June 1985): pp. 259–297.

Holtzclaw, Henry F. *The Principles of Marketing* (New York: Thomas Y. Crowell, 1935).

Insight, "Art for Profit," Special Issue (March 31, 1986).

Ketchum, William C., Jr. *Auction! The Guide to Bidding, Buying, Bargaining, Selling, Exhibiting, and Making a Profit* (New York: Sterling Publishing Company, 1980).

Learmount, Brian. *A History of the Auction* (Great Britain: Barnard & Learmount, 1985).

Levi-Strauss, Claude. *Structural Anthropology*, trans. Claire Jacobson and Brooke Grundfest Schoepf (New York, London: Basic Books, 1963).

Malinowski, B. *Argonauts of the Western Pacific* (New York: E. P. Dutton and Co., 1922).

Manicas, Peter T. *A History and Philosophy of the Social Sciences* (Oxford and New York: Basil Blackwell Publishers, 1987).

March, James G. and Herbert A. Simons. *Organizations* (New York: John Wiley and Sons, Inc., 1958).

Maskin, Eric S. and John Riley, "Optimal Auctions with Risk Averse Buyers," *Econometrica* 52 (November 1984): pp. 1473–518; "Auction Theory with Private Values," *American Economic Review* 75 (May 1985): pp. 150–155.

Mauss, Marcel. *The Gift* (New York: Norton, 1976).

McAfee, R. Preston and John McMillan. "Auctions and Bidding," *The Journal of Economic Literature* XXV (June 1987).

Mead, George Herbert. *Mind, Self and Society*, ed. Charles W. Morris (Chicago: University of Chicago Press, 1934); *The Philosophy of the Act*, ed. Charles W. Morris (Chicago: University of Chicago Press, 1938).

Milgrom, P. and R. J. Weber. "A Theory of Auctions and Competitive Bidding," *Econometrica* 50 (September 1982): pp. 1089–1122.

Olmsted, A. D. "What Will You Give Me?: Buying and Selling at Public Auction," Paper presented at the *Qualitative Research Conference*, May 13–16, 1986: University of Waterloo.

Plattner, Stuart Mark. *Peddlers, Pigs and Profit: Itinerant Trading in Southeast Mexico* (Ann Arbor, MI: University Microfilms, Inc., 1969).

Plott, Charles. "Industrial Organization Theory and Experimental Economics," *Journal of Economic Literature*, 20 (December 1982): pp. 1485–527.

Reitlinger, Gerald. *The Economics of Taste*, Vol. 1 (London: Barrie and Jenkins, 1961); *The Economics of Taste*, Vol. 2 (London: Barrie and Jenkins, 1963); *The Economics of Taste*, Vol. 3 (London: Barrie and Jenkins, 1970).

Riley, J. G. and W. F. Samuelson. "Optimal Auctions," *American Economic Review* 71 (June 1981): pp. 381–92.

Schelling, Thomas C. *The Strategy of Conflict* (Cambridge, MA: Harvard University Press, 1960).

Schutz, Alfred. *Collected Papers*, Vol. 3 (The Hague: Martinus Nijhoff, 1962).

Schutz, Alfred and Thomas Luckmann. *The Structure of the Life-World* (Evanston, IL: Northwestern University Press, 1973).

Sen, Amartya K. "Rational Fools: A Critique of the Behavioral Foundations of Economic Theory," *Philosophy and Public Affairs* 6 (Summer 1977): pp. 317–44.

Simmel, Georg. *Philosophie des Geldes* (Leipzig: Duncker und Humblot, 1900; 6th ed. Berlin, 1958).

Simon, H. A. *Models of Man* (New York: John Wiley, 1957); *Human Problem Solving* (Englewood Cliffs, N.J.: Prentice-Hall, 1972).

Singer, Mark. "Profiles: Wall Power," *The New Yorker* (November 30, 1987): pp. 44–97.

Smith, Charles W. *A Critique of Sociological Reasoning: An Essay in Philosophical Sociology* (Oxford: Basil Blackwell Publishers, 1979); *The Mind of the Market* (Totowa, N.J.: Rowman and Littlefield, 1981; paperback, Harper Colophon, 1983); "On the Sociology of Mind," in *Explaining Human Behavior*, ed. Paul F. Secord (Los Angeles: Sage Publications, 1982); "A Case Study of Structuration: The Pure Bred Beef Business," *The Journal for the Theory of Social Behavior* 13 (1983); "The Social Structure and Meaning of Auctions," Paper presented at A.S.A. Annual Meeting, 1984, San Antonio, TX; "Auction Drama: Its Importance and Meaning," Paper presented at the *Qualitative Research Conference: Interactionist Research:* University of Windsor, Windsor, Ontario; May, 1988.

Smith, John George. *Organized Produce Markets* (London: Longmans, Green and Co., 1922).

Smith, Vernon L. "Experimental Studies of Discrimination Versus Competition in Sealed-Bid Auction Markets," *Journal of Business* 40 (January 1967): pp. 56–84; "Microeconomic Systems as an Experimental Science," *American Economic Review* 72 (December 1982): pp. 923–55; "Experimental Methods in the Political Economy of Exchange," *Science* 234 (October 10, 1986): pp. 167–73.

Taylor, John. "Hard Knocks," *Manhattan, inc.* (April 1986): pp. 104–13.

Tedeschi, James T., Barry R. Schlenker, and Thomas V. Bonoma. *Conflict, Power and Games* (Chicago: Aldine Publishing Company, 1973).

Thurow, Lester C. *Dangerous Currents* (New York: Random House, 1983).

Tomkins, Calvin. "A Reporter at Large: Irises," *The New Yorker* (April 4, 1988): pp. 37–67.

Turner, Ronny E. and Kenneth Stewart. "The Negotiation of Role Conflict: A Study of Sales Behavior at the Auction," *Rocky Mountain Social Science Journal* 11 (1974): pp. 85–96.

Vickrey, William. "Counterspeculation, Auctions and Competitive Sealed Tenders," *Journal of Finance,* 16 (1961): pp. 8–37.

Von Neuman, John and Oskar Morgenstern. *Theory of Games and Economic Behavior* (New York: John Wiley and Sons, 1944).

Wagenvoord, James. *Cashing in on the Auction Boom* (New York: Rawson, Wade Publishers, Inc., 1980).

Weber, Max. *The Theory of Social and Economic Organization,* trans. by Talcott Parsons (New York: Oxford University Press, 1947); *The Protestant Ethic and the Spirit of Capitalism* (New York: Charles Scribner and Sons, 1958).

Williamson, Oliver E. *Markets and Hierarchies: Analysis and Antitrust Implications* (New York: Free Press, 1975); *The Economic Institutions of Capitalism* (New York: Free Press, 1985).

Zorber, Merton. *Principles of Marketing* (Boston: Allyn and Bacon, 1971).

Zukin, Sharon, and Paul Dimaggio. Special Issue on Economy and Society, *Theory and Society* 15 (1986).

Index